T0293615

Praise for *Stop. Think. Invest.*

A balanced combination of intuitive storytelling and rigorous academic research makes worthwhile reading for both professional and serious nonprofessional investors. All investors will benefit from Mike Bailey's coaching tips and revelations about behavioral missteps on their journey to investing success.

—Bob Browne, CFA, retired Chief Investment Officer, Northern Trust

Mike Bailey has pushed the field of behavioral finance in exactly the direction it needed: practical application in pursuit of better investment results. *Stop. Think. Invest.* is a compelling read for anyone wanting to be a smarter investor.

—Brian Portnoy, PhD, CFA, founder, Shaping Wealth,
author of *The Geometry of Wealth*

Stop. Think. Invest. helps reduce the emotional cost of investing by coupling years of professional stock picking with behavioral finance theory from Nobel laureates. Stop. Think. Read this book.

—Michael P. Krensavage, founder, Krensavage Asset Management

Coupling decades-old but still-relevant investment theory with modern day insights in an era of Reddit and Robinhood, Mike Bailey weaves personal stories and lessons learned from two decades in the bulge bracket and white shoe healthcare and investment world. This one will make you Stop and Think before you Invest. Mike breaks down complex theory into simple actionable advice, whether you have been in the business for a lifetime or are just starting out.

—Ipsita G. Smolinski, MBA and MPH, founder and Managing
Director of Capitol Street, and Healthcare Finance and Economics
Faculty, Johns Hopkins Carey School of Business

Stop. Think. Invest. is a must-read for serious equity investors. Mike Bailey's insights cogently bridge investing with psychology. The durable concepts he shares, apt examples, and key takeaways are delivered to the reader with Mike's distinctive talents for critical thinking and characteristically upbeat messaging. A marvelous read—enjoy this book and the returns it will bring you!

—JOSEPH F. HEALY, CFA, Managing Director and Senior Equity
    Strategies Manager, Beacon Investment Advisory Services

This is a great read for all investment analysts, portfolio managers, and anyone who is interested in investing. Fantastic and practical behavioral tips are well written from a seasoned investment professional who has had decades of experience following various industries and leading investment teams.

—XUYING CHANG, CFA, Senior Equity Analyst, Adams Funds

STOP.
THINK.
INVEST.

A Behavioral Finance Framework for Optimizing Investment Portfolios

MICHAEL BAILEY

New York   Chicago   San Francisco   Athens   London   Madrid
Mexico City   Milan   New Delhi   Singapore   Sydney   Toronto

1 2 3 4 5 6 7 8 9   LCR   26 25 24 23 22 21

ISBN   978-1-264-26838-2
MHID   1-264-26838-6

e-ISBN   978-1-264-26839-9
e-MHID   1-264-26839-4

This publication is designed to provide accurate and authoritative information in regard to the subject matter covered. It is sold with the understanding that neither the author nor the publisher is engaged in rendering legal, accounting, securities trading, or other professional services. If legal advice or other expert assistance is required, the services of a competent professional person should be sought.
>   —*From a Declaration of Principles Jointly Adopted by a Committee of the American Bar Association and a Committee of Publishers and Associations*

Library of Congress Cataloging-in-Publication Data

Names: Bailey, Michael (Chartered financial analyst), author.
Title: Stop, think, invest : a behavioral finance framework for optimizing investment portfolios / Michael Bailey.
Description: New York : McGraw Hill, [2021] | Includes bibliographical references and index.
Identifiers: LCCN 2021034895 (print) | LCCN 2021034896 (ebook) | ISBN 9781264268382 (hardback) | ISBN 9781264268399 (ebook)
Subjects: LCSH: Investment analysis. | Portfolio management.
Classification: LCC HG4529 .B347 2021 (print) | LCC HG4529 (ebook) | DDC 332.6—dc23
LC record available at https://lccn.loc.gov/2021034895
LC ebook record available at https://lccn.loc.gov/2021034896

McGraw Hill books are available at special quantity discounts to use as premiums and sales promotions or for use in corporate training programs. To contact a representative, please visit the Contact Us pages at www.mhprofessional.com.

Disclosure: This book reflects the author's opinions for educational purposes and is not intended as investment advice related to any securities mentioned. Additionally, the book does not necessarily represent the thoughts or opinions of the author's current employer or any other organizations.

To my wife, Maria, and our children,
Andrew, Tessa, Matthew, Gigi, and Joseph

Contents

	Preface	vii
	Introduction	xxiii
	Acknowledgments	xxxiii
1	Explore a Brand New Idea or Theme	1
2	Begin Initial Research	29
3	Complete the Research Process	39
4	Craft an Investment Thesis	67
5	Decide on Timing and Sizing of Trade	85
6	Make Initial Purchase	105
7	Analyze Early Results and Stock Movement	111
8	Consider a Follow-on Trade	125
9	Execute a Follow-on Trade	147
10	Review Long-Term Investment Thesis	157
11	Evaluate a Complete Sale	171
12	Sell and Focus on Continuous Improvement	185
	Epilogue	207
	Notes	211
	Index	225

Preface

I n the teen comedy *Better Off Dead*, Johnny, an aggressive newspaper delivery boy, felt that his customer, the Myers family, shortchanged him. Throughout the 80s cult classic, Johnny desperately chased members of the Myers family around town on his dirt bike, demanding repeatedly to be paid two dollars! In the real world, emotional stock pickers desperately try to beat the market and chase returns, hoping repeatedly to be paid back for every penny of their investment.

GE: An Emotional Roller Coaster for Investors

Investors in General Electric (GE) may have borrowed a page from *Better Off Dead* as emotions clouded their judgment of the company's future prospects. In December 2015, GE's former CEO Jeff Immelt lit up the imaginations of investors with promises of jet engines, healthcare technology, and gas-fired power plants driving surging growth in the years ahead. Investors cheered, expecting GE's profits to soar from roughly $1.20 per share in 2015 to Immelt's audacious goal of $2.00 per share in 2018. Unfortunately, the initial ecstasy turned to agony and frustration as investors clung to the hope of $2.00 in future earnings despite a crumbling business and a stock price that was nose-diving from the low thirties to the teens. How could this happen?

After almost two years of telling investors everything was fine, GE finally fessed up in November 2017 and cut the $2.00 per share target nearly in half as business fundamentals collapsed, especially in its fossil fuel–based power segment. When all was said and done, GE actually earned an eye-watering 65 cents per share in 2018, and the GE share price fell into the single digits (Figure P-1). The reality was a far cry from the CEO's initial enthusiasm about exciting long-term growth that could support GE's stock price.

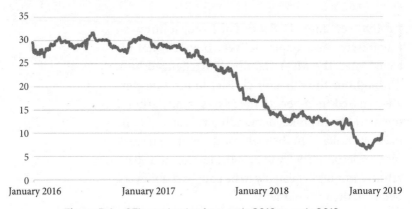

Figure P-1   GE's stock price from early 2016 to early 2019

The rise and fall of GE in the decade after the great financial crisis of 2008–2009 was a rude awakening for many long-term shareholders. But why did investors ignore the warning signs at GE? Perhaps investors fell into a sense of complacency after years of getting comfortable with a trusted blue chip stock that kept going up and paying attractive dividends.

GE's board felt that Jeff Immelt and his immediate successor were "better off fired" amid the dismal company performance and stock price. Was this a simple story of bad luck in a competitive industry, or can we see examples of emotional decision making that can help us avoid the next GE in our portfolio?

Many GE investors in the late 2010s drowned in a sea of bias and emotion. GE was a household name with a charismatic CEO, which may have fueled a sense of overconfidence that biased investors into believing the company's story, creating a collective blindness to risk and uncertainty.

By trusting GE's management, many investors implicitly said, "I know GE, so I don't need to do extra work to figure out the risk." Making matters worse, the company's $2.00 earnings guidance may have propped up the stock and investor sentiment. Finally, investors anchored to GE's $30 stock price and were unwilling to sell, cheered on by Wall Street analysts who also clung to buy ratings as the stock tumbled down a slippery slope.[1]

For GE, the self-destruction of an American icon had a string of behavioral warning signs that seem obvious in retrospect. However, many investors were unable to fully grasp the stock's potential risk when its price was still in the $30s in 2016.

So what can professional investors learn from the chaos at GE? One approach would be to look for some of the warning signs that GE exhibited within our current stock holdings and as we research new investments. Going a step further, we can break up the entire investment process and look for potential GEs every step of the way. This is the goal of this book.

Lowering the Emotional Cost of Investing

Owning GE stock during the late 2010s may have felt like an emotional roller coaster, but why does money make us so emotional? Does making or losing money trigger an emotional response that makes us feel like winners or losers? When we mix money and emotions, we create a potent cocktail that can cloud or bias our ability to process facts and information as we make decisions.

Emotions may lead us to make bad financial decisions, which have a real cost for professional investors, such as underperforming the market, losing clients, or failing to reach our long-term investment goals. Employees at GE who held big chunks of their retirement savings in GE stock may have experienced a severe emotional cost by holding the shares even as the business became a slow-moving train wreck. This book provides a framework so that investors can make better financial decisions and lower the emotional cost of investing.

So where do investors begin as they try to make better financial decisions? Fortunately, there is a body of academic work that gives investors the tools to lower the emotional cost of investing. Unfortunately, the first step toward making better investment decisions may be an uncomfortable one.

Professional and individual investors need to realize that they have to keep cool and actively push back against emotions and biases that seem to come naturally. When markets are falling and emotions are rising, as my colleague Michael Mussio likes to say, "Stay frosty!" In other words:

- Stop what you're doing.

- Think hard about your next move.

- Then invest.

At the core, this is the idea behind *Stop. Think. Invest.*

Now let's turn to some of the experts who created the ideas and concepts supporting a better way to invest. Daniel Kahneman, a psychologist and Nobel laureate who helped create a field of study called *behavioral economics*, says that in an altered, emotional state we "believe our impressions and act on our desires."[2]

Real-world practitioners support Kahneman's views, as seen in the example of Howard Marks, a successful investor who uses behavioral economics at his firm, Oaktree Capital. Marks believes that "one of the biggest mistakes an investor can make is ignoring or denying his or her biases."[3] Uh-oh.

Are professional investors missing out by ignoring a sea of bias and emotions that could lead to bad decisions? Fortunately, we can lean on insights from intelligent people across different fields who have been trying to answer this question for decades.

Benjamin Graham, the original value investor, supported the idea of behavioral economics when he recommended unpopular and less expensive stocks over fashionable or high-valuation investments.[4] Famed economist John Maynard Keynes, whose ideas may have helped the United States emerge from the Great Depression, also tried to save individuals from making bad economic decisions.

Animal Spirits

The market can stay irrational longer than you can stay solvent.

—John Maynard Keynes

Keynes realized that individual investors can make irrational decisions and that at a macro level these decisions can move markets in financially painful ways. If a thundering herd of bad decisions creates wild moves in markets, perhaps individual investors are acting on more primal emotions rather than using human logic and intellect.

Keynes coined the term *animal spirits*, referring to gut feelings, emotions, or whimsical changes in consumer and investor attitudes that can play an important role in investment decisions.[5] Robert Shiller, another behavioral economist and Nobel Prize winner, refers to animal spirits as "a sense of optimism and ready energy to be entrepreneurial and take risks."[6] Turn on a business news channel sometime and you'll hear plenty of chatter about animal spirits when markets become choppy and investors careen from agony to ecstasy or vice versa.

But is *animal spirits* just a catchy term used to sell cable airtime, or is there something to it? If animal spirits go to extremes, investors should take notice, following Keynes's earlier quote. Shiller also notes that "[h]igh animal spirits in the stock market are often associated with the disparagement of traditional authority and expert opinion."[7] When we get excited, we often go with our gut rather than seeking external resources as we make decisions.

Is there a "disconnect between dreams and expertise" in the stock market, as Shiller proposes?[8] If this is true, perhaps we should focus a bit more on how changes in attitudes can change our financial well-being. If emotions or feelings influence a lifetime of financial decisions, we can end up with a much lower quality of life than we intended.

However, investors can fight back against these visceral feelings and emotional urges to simply *trust your gut*. We can make better decisions if we look for warning signs that tell us that we are about to make a big mistake. Perhaps we can lean on the expertise of Nobel Prize winners to prevent our dreams from becoming financial disappointments.

Another behavioral economist and Nobel laureate, Richard Thaler, has a great sense of humor and plenty of good advice for financial decision makers. Thaler had a cameo role alongside pop star Selena Gomez in the 2015 movie *The Big Short* in which he explains in plain English the mental shortcuts and biases that fueled the housing bubble.

In the movie, Thaler refers to the *hot hand fallacy*, in which sports fans overestimate the chances that a basketball player on a hot streak will hit the next shot. Many investors during the housing bubble felt that home prices were on a hot streak and that the next move would be up. Does this seem logical? Thaler knocks that idea down like a house of cards in *The Big Short* by suggesting that we rarely act logically. The rise and fall of asset prices during the housing bubble suggest that plenty of humans glossed over logic as they made investment decisions.

Speaking of asset bubbles, history suggests that these major imbalances occur every few years. And perhaps paying closer attention to our biases and emotions can help us avoid falling into a major financial calamity like the housing bubble. Thaler may provide some assistance here because when he takes time away from his Hollywood career, he advises people to pay very close attention to decisions that are difficult, rare, and risky.[9] Assets bubbles check all three of these boxes, suggesting that investors should be on high alert when stocks or other commodities start *melting up*.

Aside from asset bubbles, my sense is that financial professionals, who look at stocks on a daily basis, could benefit from Thaler's warning signs. In my experience, every stock is a different situation, suggesting that full-time investing can have difficult, rare, and risky moments. When professional investors sell a stock that they've owned for years, they are making a difficult and risky decision on a stock that they've rarely traded.

While this book takes a systematic approach to handling these types of investment decisions, Thaler's basic recommendation is that you need to slow down, pay attention, and be reflective. Investors can make better decisions in areas where they have "experience, good information, and prompt feedback."[10]

I wish that it was this easy. Unfortunately, on the long-term investment journey, we can encounter lots of emotional twists and turns before reaching a final destination. Here's one way to look at it. Investing requires us to make difficult decisions, but emotions and biases can lead us to bad decisions. Fortunately, smart Nobel laureates have created tools to help people make better economic choices. However, this solution has its own problem for investors. How do you know which concept to use at what time, because there are so many?

This book compiles a comprehensive list of these tools as a guide for making better financial decisions throughout the ups and downs of our investing experience. Think of this book as an instruction manual for a toolbox that contains more than 100 different hammers, drills, saws, and screwdrivers. In this case, however, rather than building a house, we're trying to build long-term investment performance.

In a way, reading this book is like working with a trainer or coach to help nudge us in the right direction as we make financial decisions. We don't have to *unlearn* or *unfreeze*[11] the way we've always invested. In contrast, we can add some new tools to help put a few more points on the board as we try to improve performance and avoid costly mistakes.

This book breaks down the investment process into foundational building blocks and takes a behavioral coaching approach. The book's framework helps investors identify emotions and biases while also creating strategies for improving performance for each step of the investment process. The term *behavioral coaching* has a fairly loose definition across the fields of sports (training athletes), business (managing employees), and psychology.[12] However, for this book, I use the term to refer to a process of applying concepts from economics and psychology to *nudge* people into making better decisions.[13]

By taking a step-by-step approach to researching, buying, trading, and selling stocks, we can turn to our *virtual* trainer each step of the way. Just as a real trainer will recommend a specific exercise for building your biceps, this book offers specific behavioral coaching tips for each step in the investment process. Perhaps if we use a behavioral coaching framework and think about money in a different way, we can reduce emotional volatility and feel more secure about our future.

100 Steps to Better Investment Decisions

In 2015, a former employer encouraged me to read Daniel Kahneman's *Thinking, Fast and Slow* and be prepared to discuss it at an internal conference. *Thinking, Fast and Slow* gives the origin story of behavioral economics and describes dozens of situations where emotions and feelings cloud our financial decisions.[14]

I left my employer before the conference, but I decided to read the book anyway, and in fact, I read it twice. As a professional investor, I kept saying to myself, "Wow, these are great tools! I should try to use these to help improve my stock picking process." Before I knew it, I had taken dozens of notes. But what was the best way to use the Kahneman toolbox to pick better stocks?

At first, I summarized the *Thinking, Fast and Slow* tools and pinned the summary to my wall, but sadly, that turned into wallpaper. The ambitious planner in me turned into the lazy doer as I unsuccessfully tried to change my investment process. I also tried to incorporate some of the tools during weekly investment meetings, but this felt like a disorganized and haphazard approach.

During this trial-and-error process, I came across another treasure trove of behavioral economics tools in Richard Thaler's books, *Nudge* and *Misbehaving*. As I was collecting behavioral investing tips, my interest and excitement took off in 2017, when Richard Thaler won the Nobel Prize for Economics. Susan Fulton, who cofounded my firm, met Richard Thaler during a class, and she highly recommended incorporating Thaler's ideas into the investment process. With this renewed energy, I gathered scores of other ideas from Thaler as my newly expanded toolbox approached 100 tips for better investment decisions.

Thaler's behavioral research spans fields from finance to politics to sports. In football, Thaler found that many NFL owners overpay for a first-round draft pick, even when data suggest that the top draft pick is expensive. Thaler's work suggests that owners can get more bang for their buck by paying less for a later draft pick. In describing a pattern of overconfidence and overpaying for draft picks, Thaler says, "the stupidity continues."[15] In contrast to what NFL owners often do with draft picks, the point of this book is to use behavioral finance concepts and data to stop, think, and make better investment decisions.

While most of the concepts in this book come from Nobel Prize–winning economists, I've also incorporated a few behavioral coaching tips that I've picked up during my ~20-year investment career that come from experience or from authors other than Kahneman and Thaler. As these tips began to accumulate, I wasn't sure how best to translate this raw material into a finished product that would help me or anybody else make better financial decisions.

I googled around to see if anyone else had organized this long list of behavioral economics themes[16] into a guide for investors, but nothing really fit the bill. Most of the research I found in the area went deep into a short list of widely known behavioral finance tools, but what about the other 80 or 90 concepts?

I started to feel sorry for the forgotten tools in the Kahneman and Thaler toolbox, so I decided to create some kind of guidebook or instruction manual that includes all the ideas in an easy-to-use format for investors. But where to begin?

After some deep thinking, two light bulbs popped in my head. First, I needed to organize the 100 Kahneman and Thaler concepts into a user-friendly format so that investors could quickly find the right behavioral coaching tip at the right time. And second, I needed to apply each of the theoretical tools to the real world of investing.

By way of background, most of the Kahneman and Thaler ideas cover a broad range of economic decisions, such as buying a house, taking a job, or shopping at a grocery store. The field of behavioral economics tries to identify recurring flaws in our decision-making processes, such as *recency bias* (only focusing on recent events rather than all events). Once we identify these flaws, Kahneman and Thaler give us recommendations for leaping over these pitfalls and getting to better decisions.

Before getting deeper into the world of behavioral finance, I need to give credit to Amos Tversky, the third giant in the field who worked closely with Daniel Kahneman. Tversky probably would have shared a Nobel Prize with Kahneman had he lived a few years longer.[17] In 1974, Tversky and Kahneman began establishing a behavioral approach to economics and finance that says that a variety of biases, such as overconfidence, loss aversion, and anchoring, limit individuals from making totally rational choices.[18] In this book, every time I refer to Daniel Kahneman, I implicitly also refer to Tversky's extensive contribution to the field.

As I learned more about these innovators in the field of behavioral finance, I began to see challenges and opportunities. On the one hand, these Nobel laureates revolutionized the understanding of our brain's shortcomings. Additionally, Kahneman and Thaler identified ways that we can overcome some of these problems, thereby improving decision making and our investment process and results. On the other hand, how could I take the broad body of knowledge from these experts and apply it to a specific part of the economy: the investment world?

My solution was to take about a hundred of the Kahneman and Thaler recommendations and divide them into 12 smaller groups that correspond with each step in the investment process. Why 12 groups? In keeping with a goal of full disclosure, I used my judgment in allocating these 100 behavioral coaching tips across the 12 parts of the stock-picking process.

As my colleague Zach Weiss once told me, the decision to break up the 100 bias warning signs into 12 smaller parts is itself a shortcut or form of bias! Yes, even people writing about the dangers of behavioral bias can make mistakes that they tell others to avoid.

To be sure, there are many behavioral theories that could help several parts of the investment process. For example, in Chapter 1, we talk about confidence bias, where confident speakers or experts can have an outsized influence on investment decisions. Using my taxonomy, we look at defeating confidence bias early in the investment process because investors may be starting from scratch and highly influenced by new information from outside experts.

However, you could justly argue that investors should be cautious of overly confident people and sources across the entire investment process. This means keeping an eye out for confidence bias throughout the initial research screening process, during heated debates with investment committees, and even while watching a TV commentator discussing a stock that's way up or way down after you've bought it.

Another way to think about organizing the 100 tools is a knowledge framework called *Bloom's taxonomy*, which follows the progression of basic knowledge as it transforms into applications, evaluation, and creation of new ideas. In a similar way, the 100 tools in this book start out with basic stock research, advancing to an investment thesis, and finally reaching a pinnacle for judging a buy or a sell. The book's table of contents is a good starting point for visualizing which behavioral coaching tip we need during each step of the investment process.

Now that I've described the fairly messy process of allocating the 100 behavioral coaching tips, I next try to bring some order to the chaos by providing real-world examples that connect theory to practice. Because many of the Kahneman and Thaler tools can seem a bit abstract, this book gives clear examples of how investors can apply these broader economic theories to financial analysis and portfolio management. This book is the final product of these efforts, and I hope that investors, financial advisors, and savers will benefit from a new way of looking at the body of work that Kahneman and Thaler created.

In the spirit of transparency, this book starts with a premise that Nobel Prize winners in behavioral economics can help our investment process and potentially improve our returns by lowering the emotional cost of investing. Research suggests that behavioral mistakes can cost portfolios nearly 1.5 percent in annual performance (as described later), and over time, this can erode long-term savings. Additionally, we discuss in Chapter 1 the idea of the *behavioral edge* as a way of attempting to outperform the broader market.

As the behavioral finance field evolves, we may start to see more hard data supporting the idea that Thaler and Kahneman's concepts can help us improve performance, but in the meantime, my experience suggests that investors continue to make costly emotional mistakes. My bottom line is that any help in identifying and correcting these mistakes should benefit performance.

Can Computers Save Us from Our Emotions?

According to Kahneman, "we trust our intuitions even when they're wrong."[19] If we simply rely on our own intuition for investment and retirement planning, a lot could go wrong. So what's the best way to apply the wisdom of Nobel laureates to day-to-day financial decisions?

The good news is that many of these tools are commonsense and easy to understand. The bad news is that the human brain is probably—make that *definitely*—unable to remember or process these 100 behavioral coaching tools when we need them most. This brings up an interesting point. Maybe human brains have no business trying to pick stocks or save for retirement on our own because we're unable to multitask the way computers can.

Should we turn our financial futures over to robo-advisors or low-cost passive investment vehicles as a way to avoid the perils of emotional investing? As a professional investor, I'm biased to say, "Of course not," because my livelihood stems from a fundamental stock-picking process.

However, investors fall across a diverse spectrum, including those in the early part of their asset-gathering phase. Many of these investors and savers can do well with simple automated investment tools that can reduce the emotional cost of investing. Still, as many of us "blossom" into more complex families with diverse assets (e.g., stocks, bonds, funds, real estate, etc.) and liabilities (e.g., mortgages, college tuition, weddings, healthcare, etc.), the human touch becomes increasingly important.

In fact, I would argue that we can get ourselves into more trouble by trusting computers to plan our retirement because we have more complex financial lives. This is because we as humans need to tell the computers what to do. A robo-advisor might recommend rebalancing (or buying stocks) when markets are crashing, but will we pull the trigger and tell the computer to buy? The field of behavioral economics would say probably not. Exhibit A is Thaler's recommendation to be very careful when making financial decisions that are rare, risky, complex, and have limited opportunity for feedback.[20] If we buy high or sell low, even using low-cost investment tools, we can get ourselves into financial quicksand. If this is the case, then most investors should benefit from a greater awareness of how emotions and feelings influence our financial decisions.

Have Fun and Get Better . . . at Investing

As a father of five kids, I've had the pleasure of coaching several youth sports programs, and I've generally encouraged most of my players to "have fun and get better." By keeping it simple, I've hopefully led some of the kids to focus more on foundational skills, having a good time, and enjoying the process of developing rather than obsessing about the scoreboard.

So what do youth sports have to do with investing? In a sense, both activities rely on practice and decision making. Practice is a definite for sports, and I have high conviction that repetition and experience are crucial for investing. Malcolm Gladwell's book, *Outliers*, suggests that if you want to get serious, you need to put in 10,000 hours to get really good at something.[21] If you are a professional investor working 40+ hours a week, it might take you five years to accumulate 10,000 hours of experience. And during those five years, what kind of decisions are you making? Are you getting better, worse, or perhaps stagnating?

Often we make bad decisions, either in sports or in investing, because we are in a rush or we take shortcuts rather than taking the time to weigh the pros and cons of a decision. You might argue that decision making is totally different in sports relative to investing because athletes have to make split-second decisions on the field or on the court that determine wins and losses. However, in some ways, busy financial professionals are constantly making decisions during the workday that determine gains and losses in volatile capital markets.

Most of this book focuses on getting better at making investment decisions, but what about having fun? One way to make stock picking fun is to imagine that you are solving puzzles every day. Just as crossword puzzles give you clues, capital markets give investors clues about long-term economic trends and short-term financial dynamics.

By lowering the emotional cost of investing, this book can hopefully help you get better but also allow some time for fun as you solve challenging investment puzzles. Having fun and getting better at investing can be a *learning-by-doing* process that can become more important as you make bigger and bigger financial decisions over time.

Who Should Read This Book?

This is essentially a self-help book for anyone who wants to get better at investing and have a little fun along the way as you learn about the intersection of money, emotions, biases, and psychology. It reinforces the importance of continual practice, creating a framework for better investment decisions and laying out a road map for when and how to practice these decision-making tools. It is for investors of all types, but particularly those who are busy and end up taking shortcuts that lead to mistakes (guilty as charged!).

Stanford professor Carol Dweck established the idea of a *growth mindset*, a "belief that your basic qualities are things you can cultivate through your efforts, your strategies, and help from others."[22] With a growth mindset, the process of learning from mistakes can lead to more satisfying outcomes over time. In contrast, a *fixed mindset* "creates an urgency to prove yourself over and over,"[23] potentially leading decision makers to look back on failures with regret.

If your stock goes down, do you feel bad and have regret? Or do you try to figure out what went wrong so that your next stock can do better? This book should help readers avoid the fixed mindset of regret over losses by taking a growth mindset approach of trial and error and making better investment decisions.

Going back to the youth sports analogy, I've generally encouraged my kids to learn from mistakes and do better in the next game rather than get depressed over a tough loss. In sports and investing, the idea that you win some and you lose some can help to redirect you away from the heat of the moment toward longer-term goals.

Nobel laureates also can help us learn from mistakes in decision making. Daniel Kahneman talks about two ways of making decisions, using either fast *System 1* or slow *System 2* thinking.[24] System 1 thinking involves easy, automatic decisions that require little effort and lack a sense of control. Given the choice, most people would rather use less effort to accomplish the same goal.

In contrast, System 2 thinking requires paying attention to effortful mental activities and concentrating on choices that are available. In the stock-picking world, System 1 thinking might lead to a quick and easy decision, whereas a System 2 approach would focus, reflect, gather data, compare choices, and agonize over a final decision.

Fast System 1 thinking works just fine for everyday decisions, such as what to order for lunch. However, we get into deep trouble when we use our lazy System 1 thinking for big, life-altering decisions such as college selection, home buying, and retirement savings. This book tells our busy, distracted System 1 selves to stop, switch to slow System 2 thinking, and then invest. This is the core message behind *Stop. Think. Invest.*

Richard Thaler takes a slightly different approach to defining two types of decision makers. The first group, called *humans*, makes up a large part of society. Humans make automatic decisions, and their human emotions can lead to mistakes.

Thaler calls a much smaller group of people *econs*, dismal scientists who rationally and thoughtfully reflect on the best possible decisions. In comparing the two groups, Thaler suggests that humans are like Homer Simpson, whereas econs are like Mr. Spock from *Star Trek*.[25] Many humans make the same mistakes over and over, suggesting that they fail to look at the results. As a way out of this vicious cycle, we can follow Thaler's idea that "[o]ur understanding of human behavior can be improved by appreciating how people systematically go wrong."[26]

The goal of this book is to identify moments in the investment process when we as *humans* are doing System 1 thinking. At the same time, this book also provides tools to encourage System 2 thinking that *econs* might use to make big financial decisions. Investing is a challenging business, and perfect decision making is nearly impossible, but if we can flag systematic errors that we make again and again, we can increase our odds of success.

In theory, anyone making a major or trivial financial decision might learn a few tips from this book, and at a minimum, these tips can make us feel better about saving and spending money. Although this book could take a much broader approach to all the pieces in the financial services food chain (as discussed in the economic web of bias commentary in the Introduction, which follows), I've decided to keep the focus on investing for future financial security.

While the book tries broadly to help investors make better decisions, I limit the scope of this book to a traditional stock-picking process of buying low and selling high, which looks at business fundamentals and stock prices. I generally avoid commenting on exotic or highly specialized types of investing, such as (1) technical analysis, which uses lots of stock charts and price movement, (2) quantitative analysis, which relies on massive computing power, and (3) hedge fund approaches, which can increase risk and return by borrowing money (leverage) and by betting that stocks go down (shorting).

Traditional stock picking makes qualitative judgments on companies, with a focus on products, management teams, and competition, leaving plenty of room for human error. Behavioral finance tools can help us minimize these errors when picking stocks. While the book focuses primarily on individual equities, many of the themes apply to other asset classes, such as bonds, preferred stock, and stock baskets (exchange-traded funds [ETFs] and mutual funds).

In trying to help investors, advisors, and savers make better decisions, this book draws bright lines between the three groups. However, in reality, many readers will belong to more than one group, as seen in Figure P-2. Imagine being a saver who also acts as an advisor when try-

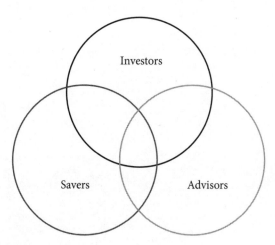

Figure P-2 Overlapping roles of investors, advisors, and savers

ing to teach your kids how to save. Or what about a financial advisor who also has to save for her own retirement?

Additionally, many professional stock pickers also advise clients on asset allocation or tax strategies, blurring the lines between the three groups. This book focuses primarily on professional investors, but many of the tools can also help advisors and savers.

How can professional investors, financial advisors, and individual savers benefit from behavioral coaching? Some experts argue that the incremental benefit from professional stock picking over going it alone by passively buying a market basket of stocks may be declining[27] and the emotional cost of investing may play a role here.

Moving from professionals to advisors, some experts believe that financial advisors can use behavioral coaching to improve long-term performance for clients.[28] For financial advisory firms in particular, the behavioral coaching tips in this book may provide helpful suggestions for both investment professionals and advisors.

Finally, many of the tools in this book are essentially self-help tips for individual savers. Individuals can use these behavioral coaching tips themselves or partner with advisors and professional stock pickers to work toward long-term goals. With that, let's begin our journey into the process of researching, buying, and selling stocks that starts with a simple premise. Stop what you're doing as a way to reduce some of the emotional noise. Think deeply about your options. And then invest.

Introduction

We are about to take the plunge into the investment process as we navigate the troubled waters of behavioral shortcuts and emotions that can eat into performance. But before we get our feet wet, let's take a step back and set out a broader framework that can prepare our investment process for success.

First, we start out with a high-level view of the many sources of bias that can impact our research, analyses, and stock trading. It's important to know who is trying to influence our investment decisions within a broader *economic web of bias*. Then we turn to a step-by-step approach to the *investment life cycle*, which can help investors figure out which behavioral concept to use along the journey of researching, buying, and managing stock portfolios.

Finally, I'll walk you through an investment style I've used in my career that emphasizes the idea of the *behavioral edge* as a way of investing. There are many ways to invest, and I respect other investment styles. However, for the purposes of this book, I feel that readers may better understand my approach to the 100 behavioral coaching themes if they also have a sense of my general investment approach.

Information, Money, and the Economic Web of Bias

> *The world is in a constant conspiracy against the brave. It's the age-old struggle: the roar of the crowd on the one side, and the voice of your conscience on the other.*
> —GENERAL DOUGLAS MACARTHUR

MacArthur's quote reminds us that we may often feel alone as the tide of public opinion crashes over us. Should we go with the flow or push back and listen to our conscience if we disagree with the crowd? For professional investors, this decision can be the difference between beating the market and facing up to embarrassing and painful losses if we buy at the top or sell at the bottom.

Many investors go with the roar of the crowd because it's a shortcut. But are investors the only people who take shortcuts or have a biased approach to decision making? Probably not. Taking a holistic approach, we can apply behavioral economics across the broader investment life cycle to see where bias is creeping in. We can visualize these interlocking sources of bias in Figure I-1, which I define as an *economic web of bias* that spreads across the economy and society, making rational investment decisions more difficult.

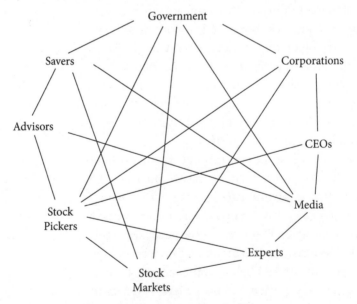

Figure I-1 The economic web of bias: the financial services "food chain" and sources of bias

As we think about which decision makers influence this web of bias, we can start with political leaders and regulators, such as central bankers. These elected and appointed officials influence interest rates, economic growth, regulations, trade barriers, deficits, the national debt, and currency movements. While many politicians and bureaucrats can be altruistic public servants, others may have conflicts of interest and focus more on job security or reelection, making biased decisions that impact millions of people in the private sector.

Another important link in this web of bias is the interconnected free market, made up of customers, competitors, and suppliers and led by executive decision makers, such as CEOs and CFOs. These corporate leaders can act irrationally, for example, if short-term incentives lead to decisions that are good for the CEO now but bad for broader stakeholders longer term. Each of these public- and private-sector groups can make emotional decisions that affect other parts of the system.

The next strand in this web comes from the message and the messenger as investors learn about economic activities. Additional complexity in the web of bias, in my experience, stems from the way the media and experts report on the government and free markets.

Decision makers often get their financial news from journalists who strive for high ethical standards and improving information efficiency by uncovering new facts. However, the media also have a profit motive, which may influence or bias their reporting. What's more, industry experts and stock analysts also may introduce biased information into the marketplace. If an expert makes a dramatic comment on a stock during a live television interview, do you think there are any emotions that might be clouding his or her analysis?

Moving from the real world to the financial world, the broader investment marketplace can exhibit a herd mentality when it places bets on the future actions of companies and corporate managers. Some would argue about the wisdom of crowds, but in contrast, a torrent of human emotions courses through the blood of liquid financial markets, potentially creating bias, bad decisions, and extreme reactions to modest events. Within this broader financial world, each individual must make his or her own buy, hold, and sell decisions. As I discuss in great detail later, there are plenty of ways for emotions and feelings to get the best of individual investors.

In a professional setting, an investor may work with an advisor or client service specialist who has different emotions and goals than the stock picker. Trying to reduce volatility in a client's portfolio, for example, may lead an advisor to the lowest common denominator of exceedingly low-risk and low-reward securities.

As this book lays out the 100 behavioral coaching themes, I try to separate the concepts into two general groups: internal biases and external biases. Looking introspectively, people are born with all too human instincts that generally lead to shortcuts and automatic choices. This book tries to warn us when these internal biases could pose a problem.

In contrast, we also can make bad financial decisions by the way we interpret external factors, and I refer to these potential red flags as *external biases*. In essence, this idea of an economic web of bias creates an environment where decision makers can make choices that are interconnected with other decision makers who also have biases.

The Investment Life Cycle

Can investors learn anything from country music? In one song, singer Dierks Bentley struggles because he knows that he has a strong *feeling* for Becky, but when something bad happens, he refers to the song's title and asks himself, "What was I thinkin'?" Feelings can get in the way of clear thinking, especially when it comes to money and investing. Emotional cycles of fear and greed, along with exhilaration and anxiety, can lead to boom/bust phases in markets and individual securities.

Understanding our own emotions and feelings as well as the behavioral biases of others across the economic web of bias can help us avoid these investment mistakes. However, the trick is to know which emotions to watch out for at what time.

As mentioned in the Preface, I've separated the 100+ Nobel laureate investment tips into 12 categories that correspond to the broad phases of many investment life cycles. In a way, you can think about this as a life-cycle clock, where a brand new idea starts at 1 o'clock and the final sale of that idea takes place at 12 noon. Here are the 12 parts of the investment life cycle, which correspond to this book's 12 chapters:

1. Explore a brand new idea or theme

2. Begin initial research

3. Complete the research process

4. Craft an investment thesis

5. Decide on timing and sizing of trade

6. Make initial purchase

7. Analyze early results and stock movement

8. Consider a follow-on trade

9. Execute a follow-on trade

10. Review long-term investment thesis

11. Evaluate a complete sale

12. Sell and focus on continuous improvement

Before going deeper into how investors can use behavioral coaching tips during this life cycle, let's spend a minute on how I structured the 12 parts. If you ask most professional investors, they would never refer to their day job as having 12 distinct segments. However, if you asked them to break down all the mental activities of the soup-to-nuts investment process, pros would probably agree that these 12 steps are basically a good match.

Professional investing has a few ground rules, such as a common accounting language, widely used valuation techniques, and a centralized trading and pricing system. Beyond this framework, however, you're basically on your own in terms of picking stocks and investing. With this in mind, let's take a look at 12 common steps in the investment process and look for ways to avoid behavioral mistakes.

Within each hour of the investment life cycle, we will discuss the theory behind each concept and then apply the concept to an investment process and give a real-world example with a stock. For instance, in Chapter 1, we discuss *recency* bias, in which people focus on recent events rather than all events as they make decisions. We then say that recent events may lead investors to focus on certain themes that are in the news or "hot" stocks.

After a major cyber security breach, for example, investors may pile into tech companies such as Palo Alto Networks (PANW) that sell products aimed at preventing such threats. If many investors have the same recency bias and buy these types of cyber security companies at the same time, investors may end up buying a good company but at a bad (high) price. Hopefully this combination of theory and practice will help investors make better decisions.

As you read through this book, you'll notice that some chapters, such as Chapters 1, 3, 5, 8, and 12, are much longer (including some two-part chapters). This is because I argue that certain parts of the investment life cycle are much more prone to emotional influence and could benefit from more behavioral coaching. Alternatively, Chapters 2, 6, 7, and 9 are shorter because these parts of the investment process may have less room for emotional error, in my opinion.

Investment Style

I developed my investment style in the early 2000s when I worked as an equity research analyst following big healthcare companies, such as Pfizer (PFE), Abbott Labs (ABT), Baxter International (BAX), and Johnson & Johnson (JNJ). However, as a twentysomething starting an exciting career with big Wall Street investment banks,[1] my ego hit a wall in 2004 when a manager told me that my investment style was nearly worthless.

During an early meeting with an assistant department head (the person in charge of hiring and firing), the manager told me that she believed that it was impossible to add value for large-cap US companies. Her message was essentially, "the large caps have been picked over, and if you think you have a special angle on one of these stocks, you're wrong!"

While this was a bit of a depressing way to start a new job, I forged ahead anyway and tried to develop an investment style even if the chips were stacked against me. In general, I've come to learn that there are many ways to invest and add value. Looking back on that moment in 2004, I would argue that investors in Abbott, Baxter, and Johnson & Johnson have enjoyed meaningful shareholder returns over the years despite full transparency of information on the companies.[2]

Now let's turn to the 12 parts of the investment life cycle and overlay this framework with some background on my investment style because there are many different ways to approach the stock-picking process. If I were to put my investment style on a bumper sticker, it would read, "Secular change—Beat and raise."

There's a lot packed into these five short words, but essentially my investment style starts by looking for companies that are transforming over a multiyear period, or what I call *secular change*. These meaningful changes can include spinning off a division, making a large acquisition, bringing on new management, restructuring operations, or kicking off a new product cycle.

These companies have an opportunity to outperform because many investors may struggle to fully grasp the multiyear transformation. Once I've identified these companies, I try to winnow the group down further to those that have the potential to exceed investor expectations during this period of meaningful change.

The concept of *time arbitrage* comes into play here. Arbitrage is a fancy way of saying buy low, sell high, and ideally, I look for opportunities to do this over several years as a business is undergoing significant changes—hopefully for the better. As a patient investor working on behalf of clients who have a long-term investment horizon, I have the liberty of looking through short-term issues that may grab the attention of day traders and hedge funds, which are under pressure to beat the market on a monthly or quarterly basis.

One way to think about time arbitrage is having the freedom or flexibility to avoid getting whipsawed by short-term emotional gyrations as stocks move between fear and greed. Investors with a mandate to generate short-term performance over months or quarters that beats a benchmark, such as the Standard and Poor's (S&P) 500 Index, have a strong incentive to buy low and sell high within a brief window of time.

In Figure I-2, short-term investors need to buy near point A, for example, and sell near point B to generate a profit. If these short-term investors get either side of this equation wrong, they may underperform the market. In contrast, a long-term investor can put the emotional volatility aside and take advantage of overreactions from the short-term crowd. When short-term investors decide they've made their money and sell at point B, the selling pressure may push the stock down and allow a better entry point for a long-term investor (point C). Time arbitrage allows long-term investors the flexibility to buy at points A, B, or C and still generate attractive returns over several years before selling at point D.

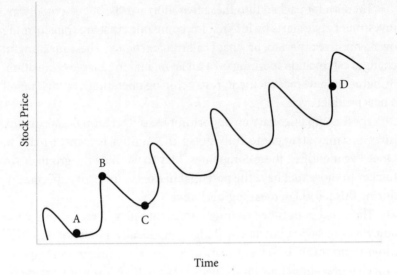

Figure I-2 Time arbitrage and stock picking

Short-term investors may underappreciate the long-term potential upside of companies in the early stages of a complex transformation. As companies exceed investor expectations, we see a pattern of *beating* estimates and *raising* guidance. Because stocks generally chase fundamentals such as profits, as companies beat and raise, stock prices can see a valuation improvement.[3] This is the opportunity I'm trying to capture.

Behavioral Edge

I use the concept of time arbitrage to give my clients a *behavioral edge* in the market. Why is this important? Some investors believe that a behavioral edge is the only realistic way to attempt market outperformance, especially when compared with the alternatives.

Famed investor Bill Miller believes that there are only three ways to get an edge in investing: informational, analytical, and behavioral.[4] I generally agree with Miller's approach, which says that finding an informational edge is becoming tougher every day as technology drives more information into the public sphere in real time.

The CFA Institute teaches that investors can cobble together little nuggets of nonmaterial, nonpublic information to create a mosaic that tells you whether to buy or sell a stock. The opposite side of this *mosaic theory*[5] is true inside information, which could lead to profiting from stocks and also jail time! Howard Marks says that everyone has access to the same information about the present and "the same ignorance regarding the future."[6]

If all investors have access to the same information, perhaps we can do a better job of analyzing those data as a way of finding attractive stocks. This may be true for some stock pickers, especially experts such as investors with advanced degrees in medicine, engineering, or other hard sciences. An oncologist may judge the success or failure of a cancer drug company differently than a generalist investor. For the rest of us, finding an analytical edge may be a tough path to follow.

If Miller's three sources of edge are correct, that leaves understanding investor behavior as the best way to find companies and stocks that can perform well and perhaps beat the market. The 12 sections outlined in *Stop. Think. Invest.* should help us navigate the economic web of bias and potentially improve our behavioral edge as we aim to meet or exceed market performance.

Before diving into Chapter 1 and the early stages of the investment research process, I want to warn readers that this book leans heavily on behavioral coaching as a way of identifying and overcoming emotions and biases that can torpedo performance. Speaking of coaching, if we compare managing a portfolio to managing a sports team, we can get a good sense of how to avoid bad decisions that stem from emotional ups and downs.

Continuing the finance and sports analogy, Richard Thaler's comments suggest that both professional investors and big-league coaches can become highly skilled after years of experience. However, both stock pickers and team managers need nudges to avoid biases that can lead to bad decisions.

As discussed in the Preface, coaches often get caught up in the excitement of the NFL draft and the drama of the fourth-down play, leading them to make irrational decisions.[7] In a similar way, I hope that the first section of this book can nudge investors toward better decisions, especially when emotions are high and the crowd is cheering (or booing!). With this pep talk in mind, let's start to tackle some of the emotional obstacles that can limit our potential investment successes.

Acknowledgments

To my wife, Maria, for showing me how to Stop, Think, and Love! To my kids, Andrew, for giving me hope; Tessa, my vice president; Matthew, my ninja warrior; Gigi, my beautiful ballerina; and Jojo, who's ready for action! Thank you to my father, Jon, my mother, Leona, brother, Chris, and my in-laws, Bo and Abita, for your support over the years.

Great thanks to my colleagues at FBB Capital Partners: Susan, Mike, Stein, Zach, Alex, John, Bridget, Sandy, Maggi, Jaime, Toni, Katy, Jane, Jackie, Samantha, and Sheleen. A big thank you to my former colleagues, especially Bryan Watts for his guidance, also Joe Healy, Amanda Agati, Xuying Chang, and Mike Krensavage. Thanks to Stephen Isaacs, Judith Newlin, and Scott Sewell at McGraw Hill and the Gregory FCA team, Sandy, Marissa, and Kara, for keeping the project going!

Thank you to Fr. Dan Leary, my angel investor, to Laurance Alvarado and Jan-Hein Cremers for helping to bring the book full Circle. To scholars and educators Michael Moynihan, Mike Ortiz, and Matthew Meehan for bringing the book to new Heights! Also, thanks to Jonathan Cummings, Nathan George, Greg Smith, Tom Spence, Thor Olavsrud, Brian Portnoy, Erik Olson, Bill Bell, Colin Camerer, and Bob Browne for your insights. Finally, thanks to Rich Moss, Josue Zelaya, and Brian Burke for your support.

Explore a Brand New Idea or Theme

INTERNAL BIASES

It's not hard to be happy if you're a collector and don't run out of money.
—CHARLIE MUNGER[1]

C harlie Munger, a quirky and pithy sidekick for Berkshire Hathaway's Warren Buffett, compares investing to collecting things, in that both can be fun, especially if you don't run out of money! Munger's comment supports the notion of having fun and getting better at investing.

But just as in collecting artwork, or coins, or baseball cards, emotions can lead you to bad decisions, even in the window-shopping phase. We are about to start our journey of collecting the next stock in our portfolio. Let's have fun and try to get better as we go.

Choice Architecture
and Libertarian Paternalism

Our first stop in the investment life cycle is like standing at the top of a mountain and surveying the land below. What looks interesting? Where do we want to go next? Similarly, many investors start out their journey with a clean slate as they look for a new stock or a broader set of themes and trends that can direct them to an investment idea.

As we begin our journey toward better investment decisions, it may be helpful to think about how professional investors add value to a firm through stock selection. Ideally, professional stock pickers earn their keep by meeting or beating a preset benchmark, such as the Standard & Poor's (S&P) 500 Index. However, beating the market usually requires taking more concentrated bets on a smaller number of stocks. You can't beat the market if you are the market.

With this in mind, Richard Thaler's book, *Nudge*,[2] talks about a type of person called a *choice architect*, which is generally a skilled professional who helps people or groups make better decisions. Why do we need big shots telling us how to make decisions if traditional economic theory suggests that *more* choices are better for most consumers? Thaler makes a strong case that sometimes *less* is more. For investors trying to beat the market, a choice of fewer stocks is usually the way to get more performance.[3]

Thaler's best example of limiting choices, in a way that helps decision makers, could be retirement savings plans such as 401(k)s. Economic theory might tell you that rational savers will sock away the optimal amount of retirement savings they will need through their monthly paychecks. However, because most workers fail to save enough, Thaler says that choice architects can create a system where the default option is a small amount of monthly salary automatically going to savings. Workers can always opt out of the automatic savings, but they have to make an active choice to change rather than going with the flow and passively adding to their savings.

In this case, employers are acting as choice architects who set up a default option as the best choice, in their opinion. Thaler goes further and describes choice architects as an example of *libertarian paternalism*. Decision makers can respect free markets (libertarian) but also influence choices (paternalism) in a way that makes choosers better off, as judged by themselves.

So what does all of this have to do with stock picking? Using Thaler's framework, investors need to be choice architects who narrow down a universe of stocks to a smaller group of securities that have a reasonable chance of beating the market. Some professional investors or analysts winnow a large number of stocks down to a shorter list that they present to a committee. Such an investor is libertarian in looking at all stocks in the market but also paternalistic in recommending his or her favorites to the committee.

I view choice architecture as a way to fight back against an internal bias of indecision. Behavioral scientists call this the *paradox of choice*, where people say that they like having more choices, but "having too many options can end up making it impossible to make a decision at all."[4]

This paradox of choice might make us feel more comfortable if we keep all our options open. In the investment world, this translates into owning the market. However, as described earlier, if you own the market, it's impossible to beat the market. Choice architecture and libertarian paternalism remind us that it's okay to make choices and limit our options as we work toward achieving our investment goals.

My experience with Palo Alto Networks (ticker "PANW"), a cyber security company, provides a good example of how choice architecture can help achieve an investment goal. I selected Palo Alto Networks through a combination of bottom-up stock picking and a review of top-down themes.

In 2016, I decided to take an open-minded (libertarian) approach to looking at longer-term investment themes, such as cloud computing, self-driving cars, and cyber security. I then took a paternalistic turn and settled on internet security, especially because the frequency and severity of hacking seemed to be on the rise. Another round of paternalism in the form of company-specific research led me to select Palo Alto Networks. In the end, choice architecture led me to recommend cyber security as a theme and Palo Alto Networks as a way to own this theme.

BEHAVIORAL COACHING TIP

When working with a group, be a good choice architect and develop a short list of investment ideas that nudge the team toward its investment goals. Be libertarian and open-minded but also be paternalistic and recommend high-conviction themes and stocks, backed up with data and analysis.

Multitasking and System 1 Thinking

Is there any overlap between cyber security and behavioral finance? While investing in Palo Alto Networks and also taking cyber security training at work, I learned about the dangers of multitasking, a shortcut that can bring down a network and a portfolio.

During a cyber security review, I watched a video warning employees that criminals prevent us from thinking critically because they rev up emotions such as fear, greed, and curiosity. Under the hackers' spell, our distraction lets the bad guys steal personal or business data.[5] For investors, distraction can lead to bad decisions and lost performance.

As we think about the early parts of the investment research process, investors who are multitasking may lose focus and go down the wrong path as we sort through new stocks to buy. Sometimes corporate training can add value in surprising ways!

Let's go a little deeper on multitasking. In the last section, we talked about an internal bias to keep all investment options open as we look for new stock ideas. Similarly, multitasking is another human tendency that can have a bad influence on the initial part of the investment process. Research suggests that only approximately 2 percent of people can multitask successfully,[6] but for the rest of us, according to a neuroscientist at Massachusetts Institute of Technology, "when people say they can [multitask], they're deluding themselves."[7]

Multitasking while investing may have some similarities to other complex activities. Public speakers often have to multitask as they think and interact with the audience. A clergyman once told me that trying to focus while speaking to a congregation was difficult because there are so many distractions, such as background noise, shuffling feet, and crying babies. In some cases, the clergyman said that he felt like he had 40 squirrels running around in his head as he tried to address the audience! The initial part of the investment process might feel a bit like this.

In the early stages of looking for a new investment idea or theme, most investors jump around to sample different news topics or research reports. There is a tension here because on the one hand, you need to be open-minded and flexible as new ideas cross your desk or in-box. On the other hand, you have to pay attention and judge what you are learning as you start to narrow down to a shorter list of ideas. There is a fine line between surveying a variety of investment themes from 30,000 feet and lazy multitasking.

Daniel Kahneman suggests that you can only multitask while System 1 thinking.[8] Red flags should go off here. Multitasking is fine if you are waiting in line at Starbucks and checking your smartphone. However, if you are looking for new investment ideas that will support a client's future retirement, I highly recommend that you use System 2 thinking and focus on the task at hand!

Kahneman's work suggests that when humans multitask, it's essentially impossible to do any kind of reflective System 2 thinking. Imagine driving your car in busy rush-hour traffic. This is a complex task requiring mental effort, even for experienced drivers. While making a left turn at a crowded intersection, Kahneman suggests that performing a System 2 task, such as multiplying 17 times 24, is impossible.[9]

Accidents happen when drivers multitask and use lazy System 1 thinking to drive, talk to friends, change the music, or check the navigation system. Similarly, accidents can happen to your portfolio if you start the investment process while casually multitasking as you research new ideas.

When I began my search for new technology investment themes in 2016, I took a deliberate approach to looking at each long-term trend. I felt, for example, that self-driving cars could become a meaningful investment theme, but I had concerns with the investment time horizon. As I did more digging, I felt that this opportunity might be a better fit for my clients as the self-driving car technology matured. Additionally, I looked at cloud computing as a long-term investment theme but came away thinking that our existing holdings of Microsoft and Google (Alphabet) already took advantage of this technology trend.

In contrast, I viewed cyber security as a here and now problem that was driving immediate demand for new cyber defense technology and an area where we had little investment exposure. I also felt that cyber security would continue to be a threat for years to come, likely driving growth for companies that could limit the damage of hackers. Rather than multitasking, I focused on each macro theme and made careful judgments as to which long-term trend would be the best fit for a new investment idea.

If you casually *browse* for new investment ideas, you may fall into a trap of multitasking, distraction, and bad choices. Put on your System 2 thinking cap as you dig for gold in terms of new potential investments.

Familiarity Bias

Don't buy what's on the front page of the Wall Street Journal.
Buy what's on the back page.
— BOB BROWNE, RETIRED CHIEF INVESTMENT OFFICER,
NORTHERN TRUST[10]

We've just talked about the importance of paying attention when you are browsing for new stock ideas and themes because multitasking can get you in trouble. Now let's go a bit deeper into another internal bias that might unconsciously push us toward the familiar and away from the unfamiliar at the beginning of the research process. Investors often favor household names and shy away from stocks (or companies) with names that sound strange to us, such as stocks based outside our home country. We can miss out on meaningful opportunities if we fail to acknowledge this *familiarity bias.*

I came across a personal example of this when I was advising my sons' elementary school stock market club. One of my sons, Andrew, was browsing for some hot stocks with a friend, and they googled the stock ticker "WINS." Andrew figured that this stock would help his team win the stock picking contest. The company, Wins Finance Holdings, is actually a highly volatile microcap Chinese lender, and although the stock went up for a few days, it later blew up. Andrew learned a lesson about the dangers of going with a stock based on a familiar name, and professional investors can, too.

Why do we go with the familiar? Kahneman goes primal here and suggests that organisms facing a dangerous environment survive by taking a cautious and fearful approach to the unknown.[11] Whoa. So, does this mean that investors should fear for their lives when presented with a new stock? This is a bit extreme, but in a dramatic example, imagine that you could only pick one stock to last you to retirement. Would you go with something familiar, like Procter & Gamble, or something untested, like Zoom Video (which was great in 2020) or Valeant Pharmaceuticals (which blew up in 2015)? In this example, most investors might stick with a familiar choice.

Kahneman backs up the idea of familiarity with data from a Swiss study of stock initial public offerings (IPOs). IPOs with strange-sounding names, such as Ypsomed and Geberit, did worse than stocks with more familiar connotations, such as Comet, Swissfirst, and Emmi.[12] Perhaps investors had a slight bias toward a business that sounded like something they previously experienced.

Kahneman suggests that a repeated experience can lead to a feeling of comfort or cognitive ease, and when our relaxed System 1 thinking kicks in, we choose what feels familiar. One way this plays out for investors is the *home-country bias*. If you live in Canada and hear the word *Canada* all the time, do you think you would own more stocks based in Canada or Japan? Both countries have large, profitable corporations, but real-world data suggest that most investors go with the familiar.

If you put every stock in the world into a bucket, about 55 percent[13] of the total market value would be US stocks. In other words, perfect diversification would require every investor on the planet (including Americans) to have 55 percent of their portfolio in the US market. However, data suggest that the average American portfolio has about 75 percent in US stocks, with the remaining 25 percent from other countries.[14]

In fact, these data may be underrepresenting a home-country bias among individuals because the 75:25 ratio includes big institutions, such as pension funds and endowments, which may have mandates to invest more globally. In my experience, most individual Americans have probably 90 percent or more of their equity holdings in US-based companies. Perhaps American investors struggle with the unfamiliar currency, political, and economic risks of buying foreign stocks and choose to go local.

The familiarity bias also extends within countries because investors in different regions often buy more of what they know. For example, investors living in the tech-heavy West Coast region own 10 percent more tech stocks than the national average. Similarly, investors living closer to Wall Street in the Northeast own 9 percent more financial services stocks than the national average.[15] Some of these imbalances may reflect illiquid investments, such as company stock held in a retirement plan. Overall, different regions and countries appear to show a familiarity bias, which may impact their investment outcomes.

Familiarity bias may have had an impact on me as I looked at stocks in the cyber security sector. As described earlier, I generally favored Palo Alto Networks because I wanted a midsized company that was small enough to generate rapid growth but big enough to have profits and some barriers to entry. Most of the cyber security companies at the time were based in the United States, so the home-country bias was less of an issue.

Within the United States, there were few companies that fit my description of a midsized cyber security company, but perhaps the familiarity bias steered me away from similar companies that had stranger-sounding names, such as FireEye and Fortinet. Subconsciously, going with a company that's named after a widely known high-tech hub (Palo Alto, California) may have given me more comfort than a company whose name was a mash-up of two unrelated words.

BEHAVIORAL COACHING TIP

Be open-minded when initially browsing for new stocks or investment themes, especially those with unusual names or ticker symbols or those based outside your home country.

Taking the Outside View

There are also unknown unknowns—the ones we don't know we don't know.

—DONALD H. RUMSFELD

In the last section, we reviewed an internal bias that can steer us toward the familiar and away from the unfamiliar. Internal bias can continue to have a bad influence on the early part of our investment efforts as we explore the difference between the *inside view* and the *outside view*.

If most humans use quick and dirty System 1 thinking, which generally means going with your gut rather than doing the heavy lifting of System 2 thinking to reach a decision, we may think we've got all the answers inside our head, but in fact there are many unknowns that require exploring an outside view. To be fair, taking the inside view is an efficient way to accomplish small goals, such as ordering from a menu or getting from A to B. However, more important decisions are another story because laziness can trigger the inside view, and "brash qualities [such as] egotism and hostility" also can lead us to say it's *my way or the highway.*[16] Putting aside simple decisions, such as restaurant choices and basic navigation, the inside view can cause trouble for more consequential choices like selecting securities.

Kahneman writes that we should take an outside view when making important decisions, especially when we think all we need is the inside view.[17] Similarly, Howard Marks points to *intellectual humility* as a way to be open-minded, humble, and willing to be proven wrong as we appreciate "other people's intellectual strengths." Marks suggests that those with intellectual humility realize that their knowledge is provisional, incomplete, and subject to revision as new data emerge.[18]

How can we channel this humility and an outside view during the early stages of investment research? Kahneman believes that we can go beyond educated guessing (going with your gut) by researching three factors: (1) the changing market, (2) the competition, and (3) the unknown unknowns.[19] Understanding these three factors forces us to go way beyond an inside view and out of our comfort zone.

Let's use an example to see how we can apply an outside view to the initial stages of the investment process. When I was looking for a cyber security stock, I focused on Palo Alto Networks because I wanted a company that was neither a risky startup (perhaps like FireEye or Fortinet) nor a big, mature, slow-growth company (like Cisco or Checkpoint). Palo Alto Networks seemed to fit the bill because it was in a sweet spot: big enough to be profitable but small enough to be nimble.

However, picking Palo Alto Networks because it seemed to fit the bill is an example of taking the inside view. Our inside view created a desire for a midsized cyber security stock, and Palo Alto Networks appeared to be a good fit. However, what would an outsider say? When looking at the competition, perhaps the most attractive way to own the space was actually through a brash startup. Or perhaps the changing market of cyber security customers and vendors was so risky and dynamic that a big, established player was the best way to go.

In my experience, unknown unknowns are the trickiest part of taking the outside view. Essentially, you have to pick up the phone or go to a meeting and ask, "What questions should I be asking?" This can be bit tricky and awkward at times, but I've found most experts to be pretty approachable if you show true curiosity about a theme, industry, technology, or company.

During my research process, I attended a cyber security conference and learned that the market was moving away from hardware and toward cloud computing software. Perhaps the best decision was to own a company that's gaining a share in cloud-based security software. Getting a handle on the competition, changing markets, and unknown unknowns helps us avoid an internal bias of thinking that the inside view is the best, or only, way to pick stocks.

> **BEHAVIORAL COACHING TIP**
>
> Avoid getting sucked into the inside view when looking for new stocks or investment themes. Take an outside view by researching markets, competition, and unknown unknowns, ideally by interacting directly with experts.

Availability Bias

Analysts also tend to predict the past.

—DANIEL KAHNEMAN[20]

Another way of thinking about the inside view is that we make decisions based on our own experiences rather than seeking knowledge and insights from the experiences of others. But how do our experiences create this inside view? What experiences, memories, sights, and sounds are available when we go with our gut and make a decision? During the investment research process, we need to be careful if we only use information that's easily available rather than doing the hard work of digging up new information outside our comfort zone.

Kahneman's quote at the beginning of this section suggests that investment analysts look around at what's available when making predictions. The past is readily available and makes an easy way to forecast that the future will be similar to the past.

The *availability bias* goes deeper into why we often take the inside view during the decision-making process. Kahneman describes availability bias as a recent or dramatic event, a vivid image, or a personal experience that makes us judge a category to be large.[21] Essentially, humans can take a vivid memory and blow it out of proportion as they think about what the memory implies.

A recent car accident might make us think that all cars are more dangerous than they really are. An emotional image of a famine in Africa might make us think that all emerging markets are struggling to provide for basic human needs. A bad customer-service experience with a department store might lead us to think that all department stores have terrible management. If we make quick and easy investment decisions based on personal experience, we generally turn to what's readily available rather than taking an outside view.

Most of these examples leave emotional traces of pain, risk, and disappointment in our memory banks, likely leading us to avoid these categories in the future. However, the availability bias also can work in the opposite way if we have favorable memories or experiences.

Kahneman connects these ideas to investing by suggesting that "when things have been getting worse for a while, you become pessimistic, and when things have been getting better for a while, you become optimistic, and it's those feelings that really control the investment."[22] In other words, the available emotions (optimism or pessimism) can create a bias for our next move.

Going back to our example stock for this chapter, Palo Alto Networks, we can see how the availability bias can impact investor behavior. Major security breaches at companies like Yahoo, Marriott, and Equifax have created vivid memories that it may be impossible to stop hackers. However, the attention-grabbing headlines about security failures also frequently drive a spike in demand for cyber security stocks because investors judge the category of hacking to be larger than it truly is.

If the availability bias drives a temporary spike in the stock prices of these companies, it would be wise to let these memories fade a bit before considering a long-term investment. Luckily for me, as I researched the cyber security industry, there was a temporary lull in major hacking activity, making me less susceptible to availability bias.

BEHAVIORAL COACHING TIP

In the early stages of the investment research process, seek out new sources of information and fight the urge to fall back on recent vivid events or personal experiences that can create an availability bias.

Risk Aversion

*Think of all the people you know who have tried to take one
extra step and have fallen off a cliff.*

—CHARLIE MUNGER[23]

Most of the internal biases we've discussed are fairly straightforward
and perhaps what you might expect if we asked you the differences
between making easy versus difficult choices. Easy choices are more of
a gut check that relies on internal knowledge that's available. You might
even be multitasking when making an easy choice. However, now we
are going deep into an internal bias that affects how we think about risk.
For investors, the way we handle risk can be the difference between
meeting our objectives and suffering major financial disappointments.

Although risk permeates all parts of the investment life cycle, this
section focuses on how risk affects the early part of the investment
research process because this is where a stock picker might casually
disregard a potential winner by saying, "Nah, it's too risky." Behavioral
coaching can help us get a better handle on the level of risk we're willing to take relative to the potential reward as we're narrowing down our
investment choices.

So what is risk, and why are most humans (and investors) averse to
it? Simply stated, *risk* is the probability that something bad will happen.
A risky activity might be jumping out of an airplane or riding a motor-
cycle without a helmet. For investors, risk can be the chance that a stock
goes down (absolute risk) or fails to exceed a benchmark (relative risk).
Another way to define investment risk is a stock's volatility or choppiness as measured by standard deviation.

Let's go a little deeper. Most humans feel more pain from a loss
than they feel pleasure from a gain. Think about it. Do you feel the same
winning $10 or losing $10? For most of us, we feel twice as bad about
the loss compared with a similar gain. In other words, we are generally
indifferent between losing $5 and winning $10. This 2:1 ratio supports
the idea that people are risk averse.

Let's try another example. If you have a 50 percent chance of winning $100 and a 50 percent chance of losing $75, most people walk away
(remember the 2:1 risk aversion rule). However, the rational, reflective
System 2 thinker would realize that this is a pretty good bet and that the

odds are in your favor (50 percent × $100 gain + 50 percent × $75 loss = $12.50 expected gain).

Kahneman goes further and says that risk-averse decision makers choose a sure thing that has a lower expected value than a risky thing. In other words, we may choose something with a lower dollar value but a higher psychological value.[24] Finding $5 on the sidewalk might feel better than getting a $10 refund that requires a stressful phone call with customer service.

So how does risk aversion impact investing, especially the early part of the research process? If most investors are risk averse, preferring a sure thing over a risky thing, then investors should be more inclined to buy lower-risk stocks. We can quantify this if we look at risky parts of the market (such as financial services stocks) compared with seemingly safer companies, such as consumer staples.

One way of measuring demand for stocks is the *price-to-earnings ratio* (PE ratio). When investors pay a higher price for a given amount of earnings, they push up the PE ratio, and vice versa. Over the last 30 years, the more volatile financial services sector has traded at a PE ratio of 12. In contrast, investors may be sending a different message about defensive sectors such as beverages, food, and personal care products. These industries tend to be more stable than a commoditized sector such as financials because consumer staple products benefit from loyal customers, recurring sales, and high profitability.

With these differences in mind, consumer staple stocks have traded at a PE ratio of 15 over the past three decades. Essentially, investors are paying up for a sure thing, relative to a risky thing. Said differently, investors are paying a premium (PE ratio of 15 for staples) to avoid the uncertainty of financials (PE ratio of 12), suggesting greater demand for buying defensive stocks.

Another way of looking at risk aversion is through the lens of regret avoidance. At the front end of the research process, investors may be already thinking about the potential regret they will feel if they pick a risky stock and it bombs. In a way, investors pay a premium to avoid risk on the front end and reduce the odds of regret on the back end.

So what are some practical ways of avoiding bad decisions that suffer risk aversion bias? One approach is to separate new stock ideas into lower- and higher-risk categories. If you find yourself mostly look-ing at safe *sure things*, then you might be suffering from risk aversion bias, especially if your investment goal is meeting or exceeding a broad benchmark such as the S&P 500 Index.

A next step might be to look at valuation. Using PE ratios or other metrics to look at comparative valuation, you might find that many of the safe low-risk stocks are also relatively expensive. If you are mostly considering safe expensive stocks in the early part of the research process, you may want to diversify and look at a broader range of securities in terms of valuation and risk-return tradeoffs.

During my search for new investment ideas and themes, I had to fight the urge to go with a seemingly lower-risk trend such as cloud computing. To be fair, I also viewed a more exotic theme, such as self-driving cars, as having excess risk compared with my investment goals.

I settled on cyber security, which was perhaps somewhere in the middle of the risk spectrum. Going a step further, I also decided to do additional research on Palo Alto Networks, which I viewed as having a risk level somewhere in between the smaller startups and the more established and diversified cyber security companies.

BEHAVIORAL COACHING TIP

A sure thing often can be a bad investment, especially if everyone is thinking the same thing. Step back, evaluate your investment objectives, and get comfortable with taking on a reasonable amount of risk, especially if you feel that there is the potential for a meaningful upside over the long term.

Narrow Framing

So far, most of this chapter has focused on internal biases that can steer us in the wrong direction as we consider new investment ideas and themes. We just wrapped up a section on why risk aversion can push us toward seemingly safer investment choices that may underperform. Taking this a step further, one reason humans tend to be risk averse is the way we frame a decision. Because most people prefer to make easy, simple decisions using System 1 thinking, we generally prefer a narrow view of our choices, such as answering a yes or no question. However, problems arise when we use this narrow frame because we often default to the least-risky option.

Richard Thaler tackles the problem of narrow framing and risk aversion using an example of corporate managers evaluating risky projects. If the managers take a single-shot approach to a single project, they are more likely to be risk averse about the potential for failure. Think about it. If someone said, "Do you want this risky thing or not?," what would you say?

A better approach uses a broader frame of many projects (a shotgun approach), which allows managers to take on more risk, knowing that successes will likely offset failures. For stock pickers, Thaler's work suggests that we will be risk averse if we look at risky investments one at a time. However, we can optimize by looking at several investments at once.[25]

Imagine that you are at a restaurant serving Chinese food and you are thinking about trying something a little different, such as the chef's special. A System 1 thinker might use a narrow frame (the exotic chef's special or nothing), but then risk aversion kicks in, leading us to go hungry. Similarly, an investor looking at risky choices (one stock at a time) for a possible new purchase has a narrow frame for making a decision. Because all stocks (and frankly most securities other than Treasury bonds) carry some level of risk, narrowly framing our decision as yes or no on a particular stock may bias us toward risk aversion.

Going back to our case study for this chapter, imagine that you are making a thumbs-up or thumbs-down decision on Palo Alto Networks. When I started looking at the company in 2015 and early 2016, the company was just barely a large-cap stock (market value of ~$13 billion), it was pretty volatile, and many investors believed that the company's momentum had run out. A risk-averse investor might have punted by taking a narrow view and choosing between Palo Alto Networks and nothing.

BEHAVIORAL COACHING TIP

Avoid looking at risky investments one at a time. This narrow decision-making frame can lead to risk aversion and poor investment choices.

Broad Framing

Our final stop on a journey of better understanding internal biases in this chapter is the counterpoint to the theme we just reviewed. After discussing the pitfalls associated with narrow framing, you can probably imagine where this section is going! Yes, the other side of the narrow framing problem is the broad framing solution. If you expand your horizons using scenarios or comparative analyses, you can avoid the risk aversion that stems from looking at one binary risky situation at a time.

In the preceding section we suggested that narrow framing might trigger a risk-averse diner to turn down an unfamiliar chef's special at a Chinese restaurant. However, through broad framing, you can look at the whole menu and try a more familiar entree that seems less risky. In some ways, using a broad frame for stock picking can be like making a dinner selection at a restaurant with a thick menu, like the Cheesecake Factory!

We are now creating a healthy tension with our behavioral coaching recommendations if we combine the benefits of broad framing with the risks of multitasking (discussed earlier). One way to thread this needle during the early part of the investment process is to pick a small group of new themes or stocks and then do a comparative analysis or create scenarios.

If the problem with narrow framing is a potential for risk aversion, then perhaps broad framing can help us take on a different level of risk that may allow better performance. Kahneman generally recommends broad framing when you are looking at multiple decisions at the same time.[26] In other words, have several decisions on the table and then narrow them down as a way of avoiding risk aversion.

One way to zero in on a new stock idea while keeping a broad frame is to pick a low-risk company participating in a high-risk theme. In my case, I viewed self-driving cars as generally a high-risk theme, but there are diversified ways to get exposure to the trend, such as owning Intel, which acquired technology from a company called Mobileye that sells specialized microchips that may enable self-driving cars. Alternatively, you could consider a high-risk company in a low-risk theme, such as owning Netflix as a disruptor in the mature media and entertainment industry.

Another way to take a broad frame on new investment ideas is to gauge the risk of your existing portfolio. If the portfolio is chock full of stocks that differ greatly from your benchmark (such as high-growth, momentum, deep-value, microcap, or emerging-market stocks), you may want to lean more toward a lower-risk new idea. Alternatively, if you've got a fairly defensive group of stocks, you could shake things up with some higher-octane themes. This was generally the case for my portfolio as I considered Palo Alto Networks. While some investors may have been scared off by the company's risk profile, I took a look at my portfolio of mostly stable, blue-chip holdings and decided that I could add one or two higher-risk stocks in sectors such as cyber security.

BEHAVIORAL COACHING TIP

Broad framing using multiple scenarios is generally superior to narrow framing. Instead of looking at one stock at a time, take a comprehensive approach by comparing several stocks as you delve deeper into the research process.

EXTERNAL BIASES

The ability to mislead people is greatly underestimated.
—CHARLIE MUNGER[27]

We are now leaving behind the internal biases that can impact how investors begin to select stocks and themes. The next string of behavioral finance ideas shifts to external influences and brings back the idea of an economic web of bias. In the next few sections, we will see a waterfall effect in which bias impacts one person or group and that bias flows down to the investor.

Mental Accounting, Self-Control, and Dividends

The first external bias we'll discuss is another potential red flag with the combination of self-control, mental accounting, and dividend preferences. These ideas may seem a bit complex, but in essence, professional investors who manage money for clients should be aware of a potential bias toward dividend-paying stocks. This is because clients in retirement or in harvest mode (more selling than buying) often prefer inflows classified as income (dividends).

This form of cash flow allows clients in retirement to feel better about spending dividend income rather than spending the proceeds of assets such as stocks for day-to-day living expenses.[28] Investment researchers can respect a client's interest in dividend-paying stocks, but it's important to avoid letting that bias dominate the initial stock selection process.

There's more to unpack in these overlapping emotions and biases, so let's get started. The first internal bias here, *mental accounting*, is basically an irrational way of treating different pots of money (or other assets), perhaps similar to favoring one brand of bottled water over another (potentially a marketing bias here!).

In one example of mental accounting, a gambler takes $100 into a casino and wins $50, but then the gambler treats the $50 differently than the $100 she walked in with. Generally, gamblers will take greater risks with the newly won $50, calling it *house money*, when in fact the gambler should treat the entire $150 the same way.

Similarly, many investors treat dividend cash differently from the cash generated from stock sales when in the end it's all the same form of money. These investors may feel comfortable spending dividend cash like the gambler's house money.

The second bias that can have an impact on initial stock selection, in favor of dividend payers, is self-control. In a purely rational world, humans wouldn't need to worry about self-control because they would make perfect choices. However, our emotions and desires can cloud our rational thinking and, in the real world, we need self-control strategies.

A simple example might be removing a bowl of nuts or chips before dinner so that you avoid spoiling your appetite. The rational dinner guest knows when to stop eating appetizers so that he or she can enjoy a good meal. However, our automatic System 1 thinking sees a table with chips and salsa, and the next thing we know we're stuffed on junk food just as the main dish arrives.

We can see examples where people combine self-control and mental accounting in our daily lives. Kahneman brings up the idea that people "pay for self-control by simultaneously putting money in a savings account and maintaining debt on credit cards."[29] We are using self-control to avoid spending too much while also using mental accounting by putting money in two separate categories. Professional investors need to remain alert if these types of tendencies show up during the early research process.

Another example of these overlapping biases is when workers take too much money out of their paychecks as a way of creating an imaginary bonus when their tax refunds come back. System 2 thinking employees would take the right amount of payroll deductions each month so that they can earn a return on their cash rather than overpaying on taxes and giving the government a free loan paid back with zero interest later (the tax refund).

Similarly, rational investors who are living off their wealth calculate exactly how much money they need to spend, making the source of the money (excluding tax issues) less relevant. This System 2 approach is indifferent between selling a stock and spending dividend income. However, irrational fears of running out of cash might lead some investors to extremes such as favoring dividend stocks and living off dividend income rather than diversifying into non-dividend-paying stocks such as high-growth stocks.

With that, let's turn to our case study for this chapter for an example of avoiding the bias stemming from mental accounting, self-control, and dividends. For this part, we'll take a look at Fortive Corp (FTV), an industrial machinery company focusing on instruments, automation, sensing, and transportation technologies. Fortive spun out of parent company Danaher in 2016.

When I started looking at Fortive in 2015, I knew that the company was unlikely to pay a big dividend. There's generally a tradeoff between high growth and high dividends, and my sense was that Fortive had plenty of growth plans. Put simply, Fortive would rather use its cash to grow and do deals as opposed to giving it back to shareholders as dividends.

I expected Fortive's stock performance and small dividend to drive an attractive total return in a diversified portfolio that also included mature industrial stocks with higher dividends. This approach avoids mental accounting, such as artificially separating stocks (assets) from dividends (income), and also avoids a self-control bias, such as only buying big dividend payers.

Try to avoid the mental accounting that comes with dividends. A juicy dividend yield, which may attract clients and investors, can obscure a disappointing stock. Use some self-control and keep an open mind when evaluating stocks with and without dividends. It's better to pick a good stock without a dividend than a lousy stock with a dividend.

Confidence Bias

When somebody tells you that they have a strong hunch about a financial event, the safe thing to do is not to believe them.
—DANIEL KAHNEMAN[30]

At this point in the journey of identifying a new stock or theme, we've diagnosed several internal biases that can influence our choices, and we've looked at an external bias (end clients, advisors, or savers) in favor of dividend-paying stocks. Going back to the economic web of bias, we next turn to the influence of experts and the media on our stock picks. These external factors, combined with confidence bias, can lead us toward or away from a new stock or theme. Essentially, investors need to have their guard up when hearing experts telling convincing stories about stocks or themes that are new to the listener.

Confidence bias comes into play here because most experts we see or hear are probably more confident than the experts who are too modest for TV, radio, or broader media coverage. Kahneman suggests that low-confidence decision makers often crash and burn in front of a live audience.[31] If this is the case, then most of the experts we see in the media likely have higher confidence in delivering their message than other less confident speakers.

So what's wrong with listening to an entertaining, dramatic, and likely optimistic storyteller as we search for new stock ideas? Plenty. Kahneman argues that society values optimism at our own peril because we succumb to exciting but potentially misleading information rather than rewarding moderates speaking the truth.[32] When highly confident speakers tell an optimistic tale, we see competition among experts pushing the message to extremes, creating "powerful forces favoring a *collective blindness* to risk and uncertainty."[33] Essentially, confidence and optimism can lead several parts of the economic web of bias to become blind to risk, put on rose-colored glasses, and focus only on the upside.

I view collective blindness as a line of reasoning or a strong opinion coming from an external influence within the economic web of bias (in this case the media and experts). These external forces can have a hypnotic effect because those consuming the highly confident message lose the ability to counter its arguments. Kahneman seems to be warning investors to remain skeptical when consuming mass-market commentary from financial experts.

In addition to causing collective blindness, many experts and pundits actually have little experience picking stocks, suggesting further caution in believing their confident messages. If you turn on a business news TV channel, such as CNBC or Fox Business, you'll likely see guest speakers such as CEOs, market strategists, academics, politicians, and investment banking stock analysts (also known as *sell-side analysts*).[34] None of these experts invests professionally, but they all tell confident stories about industries, businesses, and stocks.

On occasion, you may see a speaker that actually owns a stock he or she is discussing (a so-called buy-side analyst or investor). While I'm more open to listening to a buy-side opinion,[35] I would also be careful because these investors may have an incentive to talk up their current stock holding. These experts also may have a confidence bias, suggesting that we generally see highly confident buy-side speakers in the media.

In my experience, investors should be most sensitive to confidence bias if they know little about the stock or theme. A passionate bull or bear argument can sound exciting when the subject is a new company that you are just learning about. In the case of Fortive, I was familiar with the parent company, Danaher, so as the spinoff date approached, I had some perspective as I listened to confident bulls and bears discuss Fortive. Perhaps the takeaway here is to do your own homework on a stock or theme before listening to persuasive and confident experts giving their opinions.

BEHAVIORAL COACHING TIP

When searching for new stock ideas and themes, avoid falling into the trap of believing confident experts in the mass media. Take the time to seek out less biased information sources and alternative viewpoints.

Anxiety without Accountability

The sky is falling!

—CHICKEN LITTLE

Doomsayers such as Chicken Little can often get your attention, especially when they are highly confident. A few years ago, I attended an investment conference organized by a large asset management firm, and I heard a compelling story from the firm's chief investment officer (CIO) about confidence bias and pessimists. When the CIO was in his thirties, he decided to visit a palm reader who surprisingly told him that he would be seriously ill by the time he was 50.

If the CIO heard some bad news from a trusted source, such as a doctor, he might have taken the prediction more seriously. However, in this case the CIO said the palm reader was trying to spread *anxiety without accountability* because he would never see this palm reader again. This story has a happy ending because the CIO is healthy and well into his 50s. The punchline here is that we should be skeptical of doomsayers.

Before moving on, let's spend a minute asking why we often pay attention to pessimists. A financial researcher named Laurence Siegel believes that as humans evolved, we were in constant fear of extinction, leading us to take small dangers seriously. If cavemen saw an animal, which might be a rabbit or a tiger, he would assume that it's a tiger. However, this pattern of overweighting small risks continues in the modern world, leading us to "worry more about some dangers than we need to, because they rarely or never occur anymore."[36]

Siegel sums up this theme by saying that apocalyptic thinking "has always been wrong as a forecast, and it will continue to be wrong." We seem to be hardwired to pay attention to doomsayers and extreme pessimists, but perhaps we should be suspicious when market forecasters go off the deep end.

Let's try to connect our goal of finding a new stock with the potential for alarmists to grab our attention. Up to this point in this book, we are going on the premise that finding new stocks is a good thing. But what if stock markets are unusually expensive, and we would be better off sitting in lower-risk securities such as cash or bonds? Some confident speakers might try to instill a fear factor that a bear market is right around the corner, potentially leading to risk aversion.

In the last section we discussed the pitfalls of believing confident financial pundits in the media. A special case of these confident speakers involves those with an overly cautious or bearish message. If bad news sells, then pessimistic financial forecasts are also likely to grab viewers' attention (and ratings).

Paul Samuelson, another Nobel Prize–winning economist, once joked that "the stock market has predicted nine of the past five recessions,"[37] making light of how some people may use anxiety without accountability. Bearish talking heads may point to every stock market downturn as a strong signal that a recession is right around the corner, even though these predictions are often wrong.

To be fair, we should be open-minded at the beginning of the investment process to the possibility that markets could decline and that more cash or bonds are a good idea. However, we are wading into dangerous territory here known as *market timing*, requiring a dispassionate, reasonable strategy for underweighting stocks now and also a plan for getting back into stocks later. And by the way, getting back into stocks in the future can be a gut-wrenching decision.

Market timing, where you sell stocks now and try to get back in at a lower price, requires two good decisions: getting out at a high price and getting back in at a lower price. In my experience as a buy-and-hold investor, it's tough enough to make one right decision and even harder to do it twice! Most often, investors get out of stocks, but then the market continues to rise. *Anchoring*, or fixating on a historical number, can lead to behavioral mistakes such as waiting too long to get back into the stock market.

At the end of the day, it's okay to listen to the arguments of confident bulls and bears who are recommending that we get into or out of the market. However, we have to do our own independent research and push back against these external biases.

In July 2016, a bearish analyst from Citigroup projected that Fortive would underperform its peers because of a highly concentrated portfolio of businesses, uncertain end markets, and up-front costs after the Danaher spinoff.[38] However, I brushed off this anxiety because my research on the stock came to the opposite conclusion—that Fortive might outperform its peers.

Be skeptical of doomsayers, especially those who make pessimistic forecasts without accountability. Stick with trusted sources as you begin to look for new stock ideas and themes.

Performance Obsession, Risk Aversion, and Overweighting Stocks

In the last section, we warned investors that bearish financial pundits might create a risk aversion to stocks. The solution is to understand what kind of external bias might be impacting you and take a balanced approach to your next move. Similarly, we can feel an external bias if the entire market declines and leaves us worried that stocks could fall further. The solution here is also to figure out where the external bias is coming from and then make an independent decision on your risk tolerance for buying stocks.

Richard Thaler discusses times when many stock market participants are glued to performance. If the crowd is obsessed with market movements and the most recent direction is down, that can lead many investors to become risk averse. If you believe this is the case, Thaler writes that you should take advantage of an arbitrage (buying low and selling high) by overweighting stocks.[39]

This situation may be infrequent, but if we can get a sense that external biases are making a majority of market traders risk averse, we can take the other side of the coin and be a bit more tactical with picking new stocks or themes. Another way to describe a short-term investment strategy in this case is to be a *contrarian market timer* by buying when others are selling.

Fortive might be a mixed example of these themes because, for me, markets were fairly stable as I considered buying the stock in mid-2016. A better example, however, might be another spinoff called Covidien, a medical device company separating from a conglomerate called Tyco in mid-2007 just as global markets were beginning to tremble ahead of the great recession.

Market volatility in 2007 may have led to a greater obsession with performance, and as markets declined that August, investor risk aversion may have kicked in. I decided to recommend that my firm buy

Covidien despite the market choppiness and comments from my team such as "Are you sure you want to buy this stock now?" Although the stock was volatile initially, I ended up with an attractive entry price.

BEHAVIORAL COACHING TIP

In the initial stages of the investment process, keep an eye on the overall market. If it appears that the crowd is glued to performance, and if markets are in a pullback or correction (suggesting risk aversion), you may want to act quickly and take advantage of the depressed market pricing.

Mental Accounting and Conglomerates

As we reach the end of the beginning of the investment process, my last recommendation is a bit of a special case for investors interested in large, diversified companies. So far in this chapter we've outlined steps to take (e.g., outside view, broad framing, and single tasking) and pitfalls to avoid (e.g., risk aversion, inside view, availability bias, and overly confident bulls and bears) for most stocks and investment themes. We've also discussed behavioral finance themes for subcategories such as dividend payers, foreign stocks, and companies with unfamiliar names. For the final theme in the chapter, we'll focus on cautionary themes for another subgroup of stocks—conglomerates.

We previously reviewed the risks of mental accounting, where investors treat their long-term assets (stocks) differently from their income-generating assets (dividends). A preference for income leads to favoring dividend-paying stocks. Using the same idea of mental accounting, we'll now turn the focus on corporate managers who may be miscategorizing or mislabeling different divisions of the same company, a bias that can lead to disappointing stock performance.

Thaler reminds us that mental accounting can lead to problems for large organizations. Big firms can become financially inefficient and run into trouble if "there is not enough money in an assigned budget to take care of some urgent need."[40] If mental accounting can be bad for conglomerates, this may be one factor supporting a pattern where both the parent company and the smaller spinoff tend to outperform.[41] A more focused business has fewer divisions (or accounts), so managers have less temptation to fall into a mental accounting trap.

Spinoffs are one example of my broader approach to picking stocks, involving secular change, which we discussed in the Introduction. In this case, buying spinoffs is one way of taking advantage of mental accounting biases among corporate managers and time arbitrage (or recency bias) within the financial markets.

Case Study: Fortive

Fortive provides an example of the initial successes that spinoffs can have if a larger corporate parent engages in mental accounting. In 2015, a diversified science and technology hardware company called Danaher decided to spin out an industrial business as Fortive. The remaining parts of Danaher would focus more on healthcare sectors, including diagnostics, life sciences, and dental.

Prior to the spin, the parent company was milking cash flows from the mature industrial segments to beef up its higher-growth healthcare divisions. Some conglomerates successfully manage mature and growth divisions, but Danaher may have realized a potential mental accounting risk. For Danaher, a breakup could allow each business to run more efficiently as a separate entity.

The behavioral finance theory that conglomerates should avoid mental accounting worked in practice for Fortive. The Danaher spinoff did a better job focusing on a smaller business and allocating capital more efficiently, driving the stock from a $50 spinoff price in mid-2015 to the mid-$80s in early 2019. Getting rid of the mental accounting risk also may have helped the slimmed-down parent company because its own stock went from $65 at the spin to more than $130 in early 2019.

Be careful selecting big conglomerates at the beginning of the research process. Diversified companies often misallocate resources because they may treat each division separately (mental accounting). However, this risk can become an opportunity for conglomerates considering a spinoff.

Summary

Internal Biases

During the early stages of research on new investment ideas or themes, be sensitive to these internal biases:

- Use choice architecture and libertarian paternalism to sift through the broader market of securities and narrow down to a few high-conviction ideas.

- Avoid the temptation to multitask while looking for new investment ideas or themes. Focus, reflect, and evaluate as you go.

- Be open-minded to new stocks and themes even if they have unfamiliar names or are based outside your home country.

- Stretch your knowledge base and take an outside view by researching markets, competition, and unknown unknowns.

- Avoid falling into a trap of going with your gut on picking investment ideas or themes. Information that's easily available in our memory banks (personal experience or dramatic images) may bias our stock selection, favoring our comfort zone (what we know).

- It's okay to consider risky investments, within reason. Many investors become risk averse when evaluating a new purchase of a high-growth unprofitable or untested company. Still, a small holding of a higher-risk-return stock can help portfolio diversification.

- Looking at risky securities one at a time can make choosers (investors) even more risk averse, potentially leading to poor investment decisions. Be cautious with this kind of narrow framing.

- Evaluate risky stocks or themes on a relative basis or through scenarios. This broad framing will allow you to take on more risk than a narrow frame.

External Biases

During the early stages of research on new investment ideas or themes, be sensitive to these external biases:

- If you are picking stocks for clients, and if clients are using dividends as a self-control shortcut for budgeting and spending, be careful to avoid a potential halo effect around dividend-paying stocks.

- Low-confidence speakers struggle to attract attention, but high-confidence speakers often find themselves with broad media distribution. Be cautious of these often bullish experts and pundits.

- High-confidence speakers also can be overly pessimistic and discourage you from investing. Be skeptical of doomsayers who have little accountability for their grim predictions.

- If the crowd becomes transfixed by stock performance, risk aversion can kick in when markets are down, potentially opening up an opportunity to overweight stocks.

- Use caution if selecting a big conglomerate because big conglomerates can disappoint investors if they treat each division differently (mental accounting). Spinoffs, in contrast, may offer more attractive opportunities.

2

Begin Initial Research

We've just finished a busy chapter kicking off the investment process and discussing behavioral traps to avoid. Fortunately, this chapter will be short and sweet by comparison because the second step of the investment life cycle is a bit simpler than the initial screening process. At this stage, investors narrow down to one stock or theme and commit to going deep. Because time is a precious resource, we can use behavioral finance tools to point our investment research in the right direction.

This chapter discusses two online brokers, TD Ameritrade and Charles Schwab, as examples of narrowing down the research process. Both companies started out as discount brokers but grew to have broader banking and wealth-management services. This chapter's case study focuses on the period when the companies competed as rivals, but in an interesting twist, Charles Schwab bought TD Ameritrade in 2020.

Inside Lag

At this point in the investment process, we've spent some time broadly reviewing macro trends and focusing on a few stocks or a theme. Timing is a critical issue to consider before committing to a stock or theme that you've identified. If we go back to the ideas of time arbitrage and secular change, both require us to generally get the timing right for an investment idea.

I view time arbitrage as taking the long view on a stock when others are oriented to the short term. If hedge funds dislike a stock because next quarter's results look bad, you might have a time arbitrage opportunity if you think the long-term results could turn around. Mixing this idea with secular change, a mediocre business today could be masking a higher-quality business that will emerge in a few years. However, timing is crucial for both of these themes to pay off.

Unfortunately, an *inside lag*, or recognition delay, may get in our way if we are using secular change and time arbitrage for stock selection. Essentially, an inside lag is the gap between a trend and our ability to recognize that trend. For example, if we learn about an exciting new theme in the energy industry, such as hydraulic fracturing (in the early 2010s), we have to be careful if we're late to the party and all the related energy stocks already reflect the best-case outcome from this new exploration and production technique.

In my experience, the inside lag played an important role as I looked at the online broker space starting in 2016. I identified several medium-term trends impacting e-brokers such as Charles Schwab and TD Ameritrade, including rising interest rates and the potential for lower corporate taxes. Higher interest rates generally help online brokers because their banking segments can earn higher deposits. Lower US corporate tax rates also provide a meaningful profit boost, especially for companies with mostly domestic operations.

I decided to invest in the online broker sector, but in full disclosure, I may have had an inside lag on identifying the changing interest-rate theme. By the time I decided that higher interest rates would benefit brokers such as Charles Schwab, I started to see flattening and then declining yields for longer-term bonds such as the 10-year US Treasury, a trend that generally works against banks and brokers. When you think that you have a longer-term trend figured out, take a reality check and ask yourself if the trend is closer to the beginning or the end.

Another way to think about the concept of inside lag is in the area of economic policy. Governments often struggle to identify exactly where the economy is within long-term trends such as inflation, unemployment, and asset bubbles. By the time politicians, central bankers, or regulators spot a trend, such as the internet or housing bubbles, there can be an inside lag, or a time delay in recognizing the trend. Essentially, the train has left the station before governments can really fully understand the pattern, trend, or imbalance.

The flip side of the inside lag is the *outside lag*, another behavioral problem for investors and policymakers. An inside lag slows our ability to identify a trend, and an outside lag limits our effectiveness as we try to act on the trend. If an investment theme has nine innings, like a baseball game, the inside lag might lead us to pick up on the theme in the third inning, and the outside lag might delay our stock purchase until the seventh inning. Timing can be everything in sports and investing.

BEHAVIORAL COACHING TIP

Before committing to serious research on a stock or theme, ask yourself if you are late to the party. Buying into the latter innings of an investment theme can make outperformance difficult or impossible.

What You See Is All There Is (WYSIATI)

The most grossly obvious facts can be ignored when they are unwelcome.

—GEORGE ORWELL

This stage of the investment process is all about making a go versus no go decision. The preceding section reminded us to ask if we're late to catching onto a trend. But what kind of information should we consume to figure out if we're late to the party? Before moving ahead, let's quickly recap a few concepts from Chapter 1 that can help us dig deeper and get good information on a stock or theme.

We reviewed the advantages of taking a less comfortable outside view for learning about a stock or theme compared with taking an easier inside view. We also warned investors of the dangers of availability bias, where a recent experience can cloud our judgment about a potential investment. Additionally, we discussed familiarity bias, where we tend to avoid foreign stocks and companies with unusual names.

What do all these behavioral coaching tips have in common? Generally, investors can get in trouble by focusing on existing evidence and ignoring absent evidence. Kahneman refers to this bias as *what you see is all there is*, or the tongue-twister *WYSIATI* for short.[1] Kahneman's point is that when we use lazy System 1 thinking, we try to make sense of the world with whatever information happens to be in front of us rather than digging for all the relevant data. With limited information (WYSIATI), System 1 thinking can put us on autopilot as we jump to conclusions.[2]

How can we incorporate the idea of WYSIATI into researching a new stock? The main point here is that limited knowledge can lead us to jump to the wrong conclusions, especially as other behavioral finance themes, such as the inside view, availability bias, and confirmation bias, start to bleed into our thinking.

If we take an inside view, we might get overconfident and feel little need to do more research. If we read a sensational news article about Tesla's controversial CEO Elon Musk, the availability bias might lead us to think that management is the only relevant factor to understanding the company and stock. Also, if we favor domestic companies with common names, we might feel little need to research foreign companies or those with unusual names.

Additionally, a limited amount of research might confirm our prior beliefs (confirmation bias), whereas additional research might challenge our previous thinking. Researcher Shahram Heshmat describes confirmation bias by saying that "once we have formed a view, we embrace information that confirms that view while ignoring, or rejecting information that casts doubt on it."[3] If we have an investment idea or hunch and we see evidence supporting our views, we may pat ourselves on the back and feel little need to do more research.

Technology also may be encouraging us to do less research and stick with the idea of WYSIATI. If we get some of our information from social media, we need to be aware that we may be seeing "curated" news. Who's doing the curating? It's usually algorithms that are trying to maximize click-through rates. Investment strategist Michael Arone suggests that these "articles that do nothing but reinforce a unidimensional point of view and take users to extremes to keep them clicking."[4] Arone warns that curated information from social media may have "serious pitfalls that often arise from confirmation bias and tunnel vision."[5]

In my experience, the idea of WYSIATI also impacted my initial research on e-brokers. I have worked with two online brokers, TD Ameritrade and Charles Schwab, as custodians for client assets, and this experience may have biased my views as I narrowed down my investment choices.

An analogy might be if the office decided to use Apple computers instead of PCs and your investment team was looking at large-cap tech stocks such as Microsoft, Intel, and Apple. If you spend all day using an Apple computer, you might feel that Apple is probably a good company and maybe even a good stock, leaving little desire to do more research on PC-centric technologies such as Microsoft or Intel.

Going back to the online brokers, I decided to do some extra digging and avoid the WYSIATI bias. As a larger company, Charles Schwab seemed to offer a higher level of service than TD Ameritrade at the time. The WYSIATI bias may have led me to think that a higher service level meant that Schwab was a better company and a better stock. However, after reading some third-party research and consulting outside sources, I came away initially thinking that TD Ameritrade offered slightly faster growth compared with Charles Schwab, along with a higher dividend yield.

BEHAVIORAL COACHING TIP

Get outside your comfort zone and look for a variety of opinions and sources as you narrow down your investment choices. Be careful when information that's easily available (WYSIATI) confirms a feeling you have.

Expert Predictions

Sometimes wrong; never in doubt.

—Atul Gawande[6]

In the last chapter, we talked about the allure of bullish optimists who have a confidence bias and bearish pessimists who pedal anxiety without accountability. Both groups can influence our initial research into different stocks or themes.

We also just finished a section that recommended seeking sources of outside information in narrowing down your stock picks, but now I'm going to warn against putting too much faith in these sources, especially if they claim to be experts. Yes, I want it both ways! Who said behavioral coaching would be easy?

Speaking of having it both ways, it's interesting that many experts tell us to avoid believing other experts. Atul Gawande's quote focuses on medical experts (surgeons) who can be confident, but wrong. Irish playwright and critic George Bernard Shaw said "All professions are conspiracies against the laity,"[7] while ancient Chinese philosopher Lao Tzu advised that "Those who have knowledge don't predict. Those who predict don't have knowledge."[8]

The investor Howard Marks asks how we separate experts who "offer well-sourced information from charlatans who offer little but misdirection?"[9] Most investment experts have some degree of confidence as they make bets in a fog of risk and uncertainty. However, Marks suggests that we need to find a middle ground because "confidence is indispensable in investing, but too much of it can be lethal."[10]

So what exactly are good expert predictions? Howard Marks suggests that in the investment world, experts often use a good framework of facts, extrapolation, and opinion to support their predictions.[11] However, use caution if an expert simply relies on intuition outside of his or her domain of expertise. Marks goes further and suggests that expertise and prediction are two different things. He recommends avoiding confusion between factual knowledge and superior insight. Even if an expert has good insight, predicting the future can be a stretch.[12]

Kahneman goes further and points to a study of 80,000 expert predictions where the results were a disaster. The experts were worse than a coin flip. In other words, if you asked experts a simple question, such as "Will the market go up or down?," they would be wrong more than half the time. Kahneman suggests that highly trained specialists who live off their expert predictions might as well be throwing darts at a dartboard.[13]

So now that we've beaten up all the experts, what's the next step? Once we've got a short list of stock ideas, we should take an outside view and seek out new sources of information to help us predict which stock has the best upside potential.

Kahneman suggests that if we must seek out expert opinions, consider someone off the beaten path. More flamboyant experts often make wild, overconfident predictions that overshadow their meek and humble colleagues toiling away in the darkness.[14] As I looked at the e-brokers, I made sure to identify a diverse pool of expert opinions on the industry as a way of avoiding a preference for the most dramatic comments and the most outspoken experts.

BEHAVIORAL COACHING TIP

Use caution when listening to expert predictions as you narrow down your list of stock ideas because these forecasts may be wrong more than half the time. Seek out multiple sources of experts, including those less widely known, and other factual data as you work toward committing to one stock or theme.

Halo Effect

At this point in the investment life cycle, we've done some digging for new stocks and themes, and we are narrowing down our final choices. We're making sure that our investment ideas have plenty of time to play out (avoiding the inside lag), and we're seeking out third-party information sources while avoiding putting all our faith into a particular expert's prediction.

A final step before we commit to a stock for further research is to be careful with the *halo effect*, in which our feelings about one aspect of a person or object influence our perception of the whole.[15] For investment researchers, our impression of one part of a company can make us feel differently about an unrelated part of the same company. The halo effect can push investors toward the extremes of loving or hating a company (or stock), so it's worth understanding what's driving this emotional roller coaster.

Before digging into how the halo effect can impact investors, let's go a little deeper. Kahneman refers to a related concept called the *affect heuristic*, a mental shortcut in which our likes and dislikes influence our choices, decisions, and beliefs.[16] If your emotional attitude makes you averse to something, you may believe that its risks outweigh the benefits.[17]

In my experience, this affect heuristic can morph into the halo effect for companies and stocks. If you like one part of a company, you might think the other parts have low risks and high benefits. For example, if investors fall in love with Amazon's cloud computing business, perhaps they will take a more favorable view of the company's e-commerce growth despite a lack of new information on the e-commerce segment.

As a former healthcare analyst, I've seen how the halo effect can create wild swings in investor sentiment. A classic example of the halo effect is in the pharmaceutical sector, where investors betting on new drug approvals have to weigh a new medicine's efficacy against any potential side effects.

Let's imagine that investors are betting on the outcome of a cancer drug trial, and the Wall Street consensus is an expectation that the new medicine halts cancer for at least 50 percent of patients but also causes nausea in 10 percent of patients. If the pivotal trial shows efficacy that's greater than 50 percent, investors will be thrilled and put a halo around the product, viewing the drug's side effects as an unfortunate but acceptable nuisance. Enthusiasm around the cancer drug also may lead investors to look more favorably on the company's other products.

Alternatively, if the cancer drug effectively treats fewer than half of patients, then investors may feel that the 10 percent nausea burden is overwhelming, leading shareholders to run for the exits. In this downside case, the halo effect also might lead investors to become more pessimistic about other drugs in the company's pipeline besides the disappointing cancer drug.

Going back to the online brokers, I've seen examples of the halo effect in my investment process. When I was deciding between the brokers, I initially favored TD Ameritrade's larger dividend yield relative to Charles Schwab. However, TD Ameritrade has more exposure to online stock-trading revenue than Charles Schwab. As a side note, Schwab earns more from bank deposits than TD Ameritrade.

As discussed earlier, I initially favored TD Ameritrade because of its growth prospects and its dividend. However, when a price war for online stock commissions broke out in 2017, a halo effect emerged. I suddenly became cautious on TD Ameritrade's exposure to commissions, and I also felt less enthused about the higher dividend. I later decided to sell TD Ameritrade and buy Schwab because I felt that the benefits of dividends (good for TD) were less compelling than the risks of a price war for online trades (bad for TD).

In the spirit of transparency, I probably learned a lesson about the halo effect from this experience. I hope that this confession can be a reminder to investors to be aware of these types of biases, especially in the early stages of the investment life cycle.

BEHAVIORAL COACHING TIP

Before committing to a stock for further research, it can be tempting to extrapolate good news about one part of a company to mean good news for other parts, making the company and stock potentially more attractive (and vice versa). Resist this halo-effect temptation by digging a bit deeper into each risk and growth driver in the company.

Summary

When narrowing down your investment choices:

- Make sure that your investment ideas have plenty of time to play out, avoiding the inside lag.

- Seek out third-party information sources rather than using readily available sources (WYSIATI) that can confirm a hunch or feeling (confirmation bias).

- Avoid putting too much faith into a particular expert's prediction because many of these are only as good as a coin flip.

- For larger companies, be careful when you get a good feeling about one part of the business, which can make you feel better about an unrelated part, also known as the *halo effect*.

Complete the
Research Process

Now it's time to get down to business as we get into the groove of looking at broader investment themes and narrow them down to a short list of stocks. At this point in the investment life cycle we are getting into a focused research process with one stock. As we enter this deep dive, a quick word of caution: there can be plenty of potential behavioral pitfalls to avoid.

I've organized the comprehensive research process into three sections focusing on getting started, evaluating management, and using data and analysis. Hopefully these three perspectives will allow you to go deep with investment research, minimize behavioral bias, and reach a good investment decision.

Caveat emptor.

Case Study: Covidien

Covidien (COV) was a hospital products company that started out as US Surgical and was later acquired by the conglomerate Tyco. Covidien then spun out as an independent business in 2007 and in 2015 sold itself to medical device maker Medtronic.

This section should help investors find the right mindset as they look to get under the hood at a company. Highlighted by the Latin phrase *caveat emptor*, the key takeaway here is to be aware that others are trying to influence your investment decision and to actively seek out diverse sources to offset these external influences. Because this book focuses on buy and hold investors, "buyer beware" is good advice. There are plenty of sellers out there who may be looking to exploit the weaknesses or biases of the purchaser.

We will first discuss some tools that can help reduce the bias in the initial part of the deep research process. Meaningful due diligence at the outset can help you prepare to better understand the potential behavioral flaws and biases of CEOs and other managers that can influence your investment decision.

Cognitive Ease

There's a sucker born every minute.
—Associated with P. T. Barnum

A fool and his money are soon parted.
—Old folk saying

In business, it seems that everyone is selling something. Failing to keep this in mind can lead us astray as we try to understand a business and predict how its stock will perform. As investors, we're on the buy side, and it's important to remember that there are plenty of sellers out there with different incentives.

Brokers have an incentive to stimulate trading. Some managers and investor relations professionals want new buyers who can boost stock value. Although these facts are widely known, some investors can fall into a comfortable trap that limits their ability to detect the influence of these outside sources. Kahneman refers to this trap as *cognitive ease*.[1]

Imagine that you are planning to buy a car. You're having a good day, the weather's nice, the dealership has free coffee and snacks, and you meet a friendly salesperson who somehow tells you exactly what you want to hear about a car's features and benefits. Will you be more or less likely to sign on the dotted line?

Now let's turn the tables. Imagine that you've been car shopping for several weeks and are sick and tired of the process. You're having a bad day, it's raining, you're on an empty stomach, and your salesperson is a bad fit. Are you more or less likely to buy what the salesperson is selling? Perhaps not.

In the first situation, you're likely in a state of cognitive ease, where being in a good mood makes you more susceptible to external influences. The quotes at the beginning of this section are likely focusing on a similar group of buyers who are easy prey for a hard sell. Kahneman writes that in a state of cognitive ease, you are less likely to be vigilant and suspicious.[2]

So what does all of this have to do with investment research? I would argue that investors can get excited about a new stock idea, and in that excitement, they can let their guard down and allow sellers to work their magic on them. In contrast, Kahneman recommends *cognitive strain* as a better approach when preparing for big decisions. We use cognitive strain when we identify a problem and raise our level of effort by calling on System 2 thinking.[3]

Being vigilant can help us to remain on the lookout for external influences. In addition, as we consume research or speak with people about a company or stock, suspicion can remind us that these sources may have bias. Borrowing a phrase from the security and defense lingo, *situational awareness* can be helpful during the early stages of investment research. Put your head on a swivel, and be aware of the outside influences that are trying to change your views of a company or stock.

My experience with researching Covidien is one example of how cognitive ease can impact the investment process. I started warming up to Covidien when I learned that Tyco was planning to sell off its medical device business, a theme that checked several boxes on my new idea checklist. First, I've generally favored healthcare spinoffs because they tend to outperform. Second, Covidien seemed poised for secular change following years of underinvestment as part of Tyco. Third, I favored Covidien's product line of medium value-add technology (rather than either high-tech or commodity-type products).

Because Covidien seemed to fit the profile of a good stock, I started to get excited, and I began the research process in a state of cognitive ease. When I met with company managers, they tended to confirm my favorable assumptions. However, I decided that I needed to push back against the cognitive ease and add some suspicion and vigilance. In the end, I did some extra digging and still came away thinking that Covidien had the right formula for outperformance.

BEHAVIORAL COACHING TIP

Your mood can affect how you process information about a company. If you're in a good mood (cognitive ease), you may be less suspicious and vigilant. If a company's story sounds too good to be true, you might want to put your guard up a bit with cognitive strain.

Users, Choosers, Payers, and Profiteers

Now that you've got your guard up, let's dive into the research process and try to better understand what makes a company tick. It can be tempting to take different research approaches for different companies or industries, but I'd argue that a more systematic method can help to limit external bias. Glossy investor relations slides or a slick presentation on cable TV may convince you to rush out and buy a stock.

However, there are plenty of unbiased tools that can help us cut through the hype and figure out if a company is improving or declining, such as strengths, weaknesses, opportunities, and threats (SWOT) analysis and Porter's five forces.[4] I encourage investors to run each new stock idea through these two frameworks.

After getting a basic understanding of your company's risks and merits, another tool that Thaler discusses is asking four basic questions about a company: "Who uses? Who chooses? Who pays? Who profits?"[5] Answering these four questions can get you to the heart of a business and also may reveal the dynamics behind key stakeholders. Going back to the idea of an economic web of bias, these four questions touch on incentives and motivations among a company's regulators, primary and secondary customers, competitors, and suppliers.

Covidien provides an interesting example of users, choosers, payers, and profit-seekers in a splintered US healthcare system. Covidien, now part of Medtronic, primarily sold medical devices to hospitals. This business model seems straightforward enough, but when you start peeling back the layers, you may find some hidden bias that can impact risks, merits, and growth prospects.

Let's start with *Who chooses?* In the case of Covidien, it depends. For some high-end medical technology such as orthopedic implants or heart valves, surgeons or medical specialists often control the selection process. Bias can play into these decisions if, for example, surgeons choose devices they trained on in a fellowship or residency. Are the surgeons choosing the best product, or are they defaulting to the one they've used the most? Alternatively, for more commoditized disposable products, hospital administrators or purchasing managers often make the final decision. Are these purchasing managers buying the most effective products or the cheapest devices? Bias may creep in here as well.

Who uses? The answer here depends as well. Surgeons generally use high-end implantable devices, but nurses or patients might use other common products such as needles or high-tech hospital beds. Medical technology companies need to figure out who end users are and what their incentives are. Do nurses want to get through as many patient visits as fast as possible? Do patients want to avoid pain?

Who pays? Covidien's diverse customer and end-user base parallels a complex arrangement of payments and profits that relates to the economic web of bias discussed earlier. If we follow the money in the healthcare sector, we usually start with a patient copay and an employer payment to a health insurance company. The insurer or government agency (Medicare or Medicaid) pays the hospital, and the hospital pays the device company. Private insurers want the hospitals to use high-quality medical products so that patients can get better and avoid high-cost retreatment, whereas government payers may suffer from political bias. Separately, small-town hospitals or big hospital networks can make direct payments to medical device companies.

Who profits? This also gets messy fast. Hospitals and insurers can be for-profit or nonprofit. Some hospitals hire third-party buying groups to scale up their purchasing power, and these high-volume purchasers also want a cut of the profits. Finally, the medical device company also has to satisfy shareholders by earning a profit. Suppliers have to decide on the right balance of research and development (R&D) spending to create safe and effective products while also allowing some money to fall to the bottom line.

Thaler's idea of *Who uses? Who chooses? Who pays? Who profits?* came out in 2008, a year after I invested in Covidien following the 2007 Tyco spinoff, so I was unable to use this four-question framework in my research process. However, my research helped me avoid external bias and answer these questions: (1) Covidien had loyal users, (2) the company's relatively cheap products flew under the radar screen of hospital choosers and payers, and (3) hospitals, insurers, and Coviden could all make profits when using Covidien's technology.

You may walk away from this discussion about Covidien and the fractured world of healthcare money flows with feelings of confusion, dismay, or frustration. Fortunately, many other companies and industries are less complex and more understandable. However, trying to dig deeper into the incentives that drive purchasing, use, and profit-seeking may help you better predict future company and stock performance.

BEHAVIORAL COACHING TIP

External bias can impact your ability to predict a company's success or failure. Push back against this bias, and take a systematic approach to researching a company, such as a SWOT analysis and Porter's five forces. If possible, go deeper and try to root out incentives and biases that can make or break a company by asking *Who uses? Who chooses? Who pays? Who profits?*

System 2 Due Diligence

Trust, but verify.
—Suzanne Massie, advisor to President Ronald Reagan

If you've switched your mind from cognitive ease to cognitive strain and you are answering tough questions like Who uses? Who chooses? Who pays? Who profits?, you are making progress toward something I call *System 2 due diligence*. Due diligence is a legal term meaning the reasonable efforts a buyer generally takes to comprehensively appraise the assets and liabilities of a potential purchase. Going with the preceding quote, even if we trust our prior research on a company or theme, now it's time to verify.

A System 2 approach to due diligence combines many of the reflective System 2 concepts we've already discussed, including taking the outside view and using cognitive strain while avoiding confirmation bias, multitasking, the availability bias, and WYSIATI. In a way, System 2 due diligence is a way of verifying or confirming your initial answers to Thaler's questions about users, choosers, payers, and profit-seekers.

Due diligence can be difficult, like taking a college final exam or looking carefully at a house you're about to buy. During a mentally challenging process, like due diligence, our brains can get tired and tempt us to take shortcuts, such as System 1 thinking. However, one way to fight back against System 1 thinking during the due-diligence process is to take the outside view and seek out a variety of experts or professionals who can help us really understand a company's risks and merits.

Although this book generally focuses on buy-side investors, we can look at sell-side investment research for examples of System 2 due diligence. When I was a sell-side equity research analyst at Bear Stearns in the early 2000s, I followed medical device companies, and due diligence was a big part of the job. At a bulge bracket firm such as Bear, management determined research bonuses on basically two factors: trading revenues and research rankings in an annual survey from a magazine called *Institutional Investor*.[6]

Generally the best way to generate trading commissions or earn a high ranking is to start with good due diligence as a way to come up with a differentiated stock call. Let's say that the majority of investors believed that a new Medtronic pacemaker was going to grow revenues and take market share. However, if the Bear Stearns team did some good due diligence and came to the conclusion that the Medtronic pacemaker would be a flop, we could generate investor interest and trades through Bear Stearns along with a higher research ranking. In a similar way on the buy side, due diligence can help investors come up with a contrarian view and either buy low or sell high.

We've established the idea that really good (System 2) due diligence is a way of doing investment research, but what's the best way to get started? As mentioned earlier, interacting with experts and professionals can be a good way to really understand a company's risks and merits or assets and liabilities. During my time at Bear, I did many channel checks with specialists, such as surgeons and oncologists, and had companies guide me through the use of robotic surgical systems and medical implants.[7]

When doing System 2 due diligence, the primary objective is to figure out the top two or three issues or growth drivers for a stock and then dig into the debates for each issue. Ideally, talking to smart people on both sides of these debates can help you grasp the upside potential and the downside risk of investing in the stock.

As you're doing System 2 due diligence and speaking with experts, it's important to seek out professional sources with opinions that differ from your own to avoid confirmation bias. Howard Marks reminds us that "[w]hen all of the facts and opinions you hear confirm your own beliefs, mental life is very relaxed, but not very enriching."[8] System 2 due diligence should be taxing, like a good workout, if you really want to understand what's driving a stock.

In a way, System 2 due diligence may be the most important behavioral coaching suggestion in the entire book. This is because in this part of the investment process you are going deep and acting like a reporter trying to get to the bottom of a story. If you get the story right, there's a good chance that you may get the stock right, even if you buy the stock a little too late or sell a little early.

To be fair, you need all the screening and early research to get you to the due-diligence step. However, if you go the extra mile and take a System 2 approach to due diligence, you may see your stock outperform. Even if the stock disappoints, you'll have a deep understanding of what drove the downside, and your research might lead you to a new idea.

Case Study: Covidien and System 2 Due Diligence

As I began to ramp up my research on Covidien, I spoke with the company sell-side analysts and did channel checks or due diligence with customers, competitors, or suppliers as a way of understanding Covidien's risks and merits.

One channel check was with a purchasing manager who bought Covidien's products. This manager mentioned that some of the company's product packaging was inferior to that of a competitor and that Covidien was late to the game in making improvements. I came away thinking that this could be an opportunity for Covidien to improve its overall product quality after spinning out of Tyco.

BEHAVIORAL COACHING TIP

At this point in the research process, you know a lot about a company that you think you'd like to invest in. Now comes the tricky part of confirming or verifying your assumptions. Use the other System 2 behavioral coaching tips you've already learned (outside view, cognitive strain, single-tasking) to help avoid a lazy due-diligence process (inside view, WYSIATI, confirmation bias). A better due-diligence process can lead to higher conviction in an investment and potentially greater returns if the investment thesis proves correct.

MANAGEMENT

Our deep research continues in this section as we pivot from a broad approach to a personal focus on the people running the companies we may invest in. The idea of an economic web of bias comes into play here because CEOs are normal, flawed, emotional people just like anyone else. By understanding company managers, we can anticipate some of their behavioral biases and perhaps do a better job of predicting a company's growth prospects.

One housekeeping note here. Throughout most of this book, I use case studies to describe some of the behavioral coaching tips. The goal is to go a little deeper with one company or one stock and show how several behavioral finance concepts impact that company. However, as we discuss management teams in this section, we will take a shotgun approach and review several different CEOs, companies, and stocks. Hopefully, the variety of case studies will shed light on how biases and emotions can impact CEOs across different industries.

CEO Impact on Company Performance

When picking stocks, many investors want to know who's running the show. A leader with a good track record might have a better chance of exceeding investor expectations. But does the past predict the future? A behavioral finance approach might suggest caution here.

Kahneman points to economic research implying that, on average, CEOs have a fairly modest influence on corporate performance. If you lined up leaders of successful and disappointing firms, you might expect the winning CEOs to beat their loser rivals 100 percent of the time. However, the literature suggests that the true success rate is only 60 percent. In a world of random chance, good and bad CEOs would succeed or fail 50 percent of the time, so the fact that good CEOs only succeed 60 percent of the time should dampen our enthusiasm.[9]

What's going on here? Kahneman suggests that a few behavioral themes color our impression of hard-charging CEOs. When we see a successful CEO join a new company, we are prone to overestimate his or her chance of influencing corporate performance.

Outsiders, such as investors, often exaggerate the potential impact of a CEO because, as Kahneman suggests, we like a clear and simple story explaining why a business failed or succeeded, even if this is an illusion.[10] Part of this misconception could be because we get the cause-and-effect relationship backward. A failing business might lead a CEO to become rigid and confused rather than the other way around.

A couple of examples may help here. I focused on management quality when I recommended that my firm buy Danaher shares in 2011 after the company said it would acquire Beckman Coulter, a medical diagnostics company. I viewed Beckman's management as mediocre compared with Danaher's CEO, and my investment thesis was that

Danaher's team could clean up a mess at Beckman, allowing the combined company to exceed investor expectations.

This Danaher thesis played out favorably in the short term, but there are certainly other examples where successful CEOs crash and burn. I've recommended another stock, Arch Capital (which is a property casualty and reinsurance company), on and off since 2010 in part because of the management team's track record.

However, I exited Arch in 2019 because I had concerns that good managers were getting into a risky new business, mortgage insurance. Fear that a recession in 2020 would pressure the mortgage market led the stock to decline sharply, supporting the research discussed earlier that a CEO's abilities may have only a modest impact on corporate performance.

BEHAVIORAL COACHING TIP

Use caution if you pick a stock primarily because of the management team's track record. CEOs often have a more modest impact on corporate performance than we believe.

Overconfidence

Have you ever met someone who was frequently wrong but always confident? Feeling overly confident is one of the flagship emotions that can get us in trouble. Howard Marks points to overconfidence as "the mother of all psychological biases" because it afflicts "most of us much of the time."[11] Where does overconfidence come from? Ignorance and laziness may play a part, as noted in a quote from Charles Darwin that, "ignorance more frequently begets confidence than does knowledge."[12]

This high-profile psychological bias is on display in CEO communication styles, whether in print or on radio or video, because these managers often appear highly confident. On TV, sharp-dressed executives use the art of persuasion and industry-specific terminology to make you think that they are smart and have a plan to grow their company.

What makes these CEOs seem so confident, and should we believe any of what they are saying as we do deeper company research? Kahneman suggests that high confidence or overconfidence boils down to a *coherent story* rather than a true story.[13] Next time you see a CEO on TV, listen as he or she generally tells a persuasive story rather than answering direct questions.[14]

When an interviewer asks Pepsi's CEO why the company is losing market share to Coke, the CEO might tell a nice story of why Pepsi lost ground and what steps the company is taking to regain share. You can almost bet that if the same interviewer asked Coke's CEO about the cola wars, the Coke CEO would also tell a coherent story about what drove the market share gains over Pepsi and why those factors will help Coke maintain or expand market share.

If we dig a little deeper into CEO communication, we'll notice that the executive's coherent story often takes the inside view, which should weaken the CEO's credibility. Going back to the cola wars, the Pepsi CEO might say that the company is developing new flavors or packaging and that these strategies will put Pepsi on a *glide path* to recapturing market share from Coke.

While this may be a coherent story, it's missing the outside view. A more believable story might be something like this: Pepsi's CEO provides customer data showing a preference for new flavors and packaging, while test markets are already indicating market-share gains. If the Pepsi CEO can prove that Coke is unlikely to respond to Pepsi's new flavors and packaging, that would suggest an even more coherent story using an outside view.

Why are CEOs so confident? There are probably many reasons, but in the context of investment research, we may want to focus on a tension between optimism and overconfidence. Many CEOs believe that their companies will succeed, and to quote Kahneman, "Optimism is the engine of capitalism."[15] Kahneman goes further by saying, "Overconfidence is a curse. It's a curse and a blessing. The people who make great things, if you look back, they were overconfident and optimistic—overconfident optimists. They take big risks because they underestimate how big the risks are."[16]

So which CEOs should we believe? Howard Marks suggests that a "real expert's confidence is reason-based and proportional to the weight of the evidence."[17] If CEOs are truly experts on their companies and industries, then we can look at their reasoning and evidence to judge potential overconfidence.

Another way of spotting overconfident CEOs, in my opinion, is the idea that actions speak louder than a coherent story. Let's say Coke has been beating Pepsi for a decade, but we only look back at what Coke has done well and ignore other flaws or mistakes. If we only look at successes, we may be missing out.

Kahneman reminds us that you can find examples of failure just about everywhere. Understanding Coke's successes and Pepsi's failures might help us evaluate the coherent stories coming out of the Coke and Pepsi CEOs. If Pepsi has been losing share for 10 years and now exudes confidence about plans to beat Coke, we should be suspicious and vigilant (going back to the idea of *cognitive strain*).

The quote at the beginning of this section ("frequently wrong, but always confident") can apply to lots of high-profile professionals who make forecasts for a living. In the case of CEOs, one way to quantify the *frequently wrong* part is to look at the executive's ability to manage investor expectations over time. Quarterly earnings results are one way of measuring a CEO's track record. If a CEO's company missed quarterly earnings estimates more than 25 percent of the time, for example, that CEO would fall into the category of frequently wrong but always confident.

BEHAVIORAL COACHING TIP

CEOs are generally optimistic, and they use coherent stories to show confidence. Be cautious if you are considering a stock whose CEO (1) has a disappointing track record, (2) uses an inside view in his or her coherent story, and (3) underestimates strategic risks.

Overconfident CEOs Who Build Empires Are Especially Risky

I meant no harm. I most truly did not. But I had to grow bigger. So bigger I got.

—Dr. Seuss, *The Lorax*[18]

The preceding section encouraged using caution when we spot CEO overconfidence. Now let's go into a special case that should raise more red flags. Confident leaders may think that they can leverage their success on a small scale by acquiring other companies and applying their management techniques across a large enterprise.

Using a concept we discussed earlier in this chapter, investors should shift into cognitive strain and be suspicious and vigilant when they see confident CEOs doing deals. The critical piece of the puzzle here is to look at what kind of acquisition is on the table.

Research from consulting firm McKinsey points to historical data that give probabilities of deal success based on the kind of deal. Historically, acquiring a struggling competitor or doing smaller "tuck-in" deals often succeeds, whereas larger transformational deals often flounder.[19]

The concepts of *base rates* and *stereotypes* may be helpful in looking at confident CEOs doing deals. In essence, confident CEOs with a successful track record may create a stereotype where investors believe that the next deal will fit into a pattern of success. However, I recommend sticking with historical data across all CEOs (*base rates*), which paint a much bleaker picture of potential outcomes, especially for large acquisitions.

A classic example of the confident CEO making a splash with a large deal occurred when AOL bought Time Warner in 2000. Investors initially thought that AOL's Steve Case would expand his internet success to traditional media, but the deal quickly ran into a buzz saw. Interestingly, I would argue that AT&T's confident CEO Randall Stephenson made the same mistake when he bought Time Warner in 2018, years after the failed AOL merger.

BEHAVIORAL COACHING TIP

Use caution when a confident CEO announces a large acquisition. Management confidence may lull investors into believing that the deal may have greater odds of success than history would suggest.

CEO Holdings and Large Acquisitions

Let's go a little deeper into CEOs doing deals with a focus on how invested the CEO is in the parent company. This section gets a little messy because there is some potentially conflicting research, but let's press on to see what investors can learn about personal financial incentives that might drive a manager to do a deal.

In one corner, we have Daniel Kahneman, who suggests that CEOs who own lots of stock in their companies often have a worse track record with large acquisitions. Kahneman argues that overly optimistic CEOs might buy more company stock and take on excessive risks, such as issuing debt instead of stock. These bullish CEOs often pay huge sums for acquisitions that can crush shareholder value.[20]

In the other corner we have academics worried about the opposite end of the spectrum where CEOs have low ownership. Colin Camerer, a behavioral economist who worked closely with Richard Thaler, sees warning signs when a *caretaker* CEO with low equity holdings has incentives that encourage empire building rather than home-grown innovation.

Caretaker CEOs can include interim or temporary leaders or perhaps CEOs nearing retirement.[21] Research from Michael Mauboussin, an investment strategist and finance professor at Columbia University, supports this idea, suggesting that CEOs with insignificant stock holdings "have limited incentive to build value because he or she would not benefit directly from that increase."[22]

Are these two views of CEO equity holdings and acquisitions really at odds? Perhaps the best lesson for investors is to be cautious with the extremes. An overly optimistic CEO who owns boatloads of company stock might take on too much risk with a big deal. In contrast, a temporary CEO with little stock but incentives to get bigger might also do a bad deal.

An example of a caretaker CEO with low holdings doing a large deal could be Randall Stephenson at AT&T. Stephenson owned roughly 0.04 percent of the stock at the time he announced his departure in 2020, following the large Time Warner deal in 2018. I viewed AT&T stock as having downside risk in this time period, and the CEO's actions and shareholdings were part of my investment thesis.

BEHAVIORAL COACHING TIP

Use caution when a CEO with unusually high or low personal stock holdings does a large deal. Optimistic CEOs who own lots of stock might be taking on too much risk, whereas CEOs who own little stock may want a quick bonus from a deal before retirement.

Incoming CEOs and Sunk Costs

Another way to evaluate management when you are researching a stock is to look at CEO change. What can a new CEO bring to an old company? New blood, a fresh set of eyes? Because this is a behavioral finance book, I would argue that a new CEO often brings less emotional baggage and might make more shareholder-friendly decisions, especially related to bad projects.

Kahneman suggests that the old CEO is encumbered by prior decisions and sunk costs. If a project is failing, the old CEO would rather gamble the firm's resources or kick the can down the road than shut down the project and earn a permanent stain on his or her record.[23] CEOs trapped by these sunk costs would rather throw more good money at a bad project for a slight chance of success as opposed to taking a sure loss by shutting down the disappointing project.

If you spent $50 million on a bad project, you could shut it down and write off the $50 million, or you could spend millions more trying to bail out the bad project. Behavioral finance theory suggests that it's better to shut down the $50 million project and invest the new money in a completely different project with greater expected returns.[24] Kahneman argues that a new CEO can avoid the *mental accounting* of good and bad projects by ignoring sunk costs and having a less biased approach to future opportunities.

In my investment career, I've seen several examples of new CEOs shutting down bad projects or businesses that have a poor fit. Darius Adamczyk became CEO of industrial conglomerate Honeywell in 2017, and later that year he decided to spin off less attractive businesses in climate control and transportation. Danaher's CEO Tom Joyce took over in 2014 and in 2019 spun off a troubled dental equipment business. In the banking sector, Wells Fargo hired CEO Charlie Scharf in 2019 to clean up a web of bad sales practices that weighed down prior management teams.[25]

BEHAVIORAL COACHING TIP

Be careful if you see a long-tenured CEO throwing resources at a struggling project. Alternatively, look for companies with new CEOs who are less biased by sunk costs, raising the odds of making decisions that exceed investor expectations.

DATA AND ANALYSIS

At this point in the deep research process we've done our due diligence and have evaluated the management team running our target company. The next step is to sharpen our pencils (or open up a spreadsheet) and wrap some metrics around all the qualitative data we've gathered.

There are plenty of tools to help investors build financial models, but because the focus of this book is behavioral coaching, let's turn to four suggestions from Kahneman that might help us reduce the bias in our analysis. Kahneman's recommendations generally fall into three categories: comparative analysis, forecasting, and probabilities.

A good first step, in my opinion, is head-to-head analysis. Before we jump into comparative analysis, in this section we will use a variety of company and stock examples, similar to our approach for analyzing CEOs and management teams in the prior section.

Head-to-Head Analysis

Only that traveling is good which reveals to me the value of home and enables me to enjoy it better.
                                                    —Henry David Thoreau

Comparative analysis can be helpful for thinking about our options, such as what college to attend, what stock to pick, or where to go on vacation. As we think about summer travel plans, some people love going to the same place every year, while others have wanderlust and prefer exploring new locations. What can we learn from the way we use our leisure time as we think about investment choices?

I would argue that both groups of travelers, the locals and wanderers, could potentially enjoy their vacations even more if they did some comparison shopping. Perhaps locals would find some new faraway destinations they may come to enjoy. Alternatively, locals might get turned off by long and expensive flights, foreign languages, currency exchanges, and the uncertainty of international travel but return to their favorite local spot with a better appreciation. In contrast, if the wanderlust crowd decides to take a "staycation" once in a while, they might find a greater appreciation for the comforts of home.

After you've done a lot of research on a stock, you may start to feel like a local and lose interest in comparing your stock with that of other domestic or international companies. As in the above-mentioned traveling example, it can be helpful to compare options and get a better sense of strengths and weaknesses.

Kahneman argues that head-to-head analysis produces more accurate valuations than a stand-alone approach. Consumer research looking at examples such as dinnerware and baseball cards suggests that people have lower accuracy in valuing an item in isolation. Our System 1 thinking might make a superficial judgment about the single item because we're unable to do comparative analysis.

However, when comparing two different sets of dinnerware or baseball cards, consumers do a better job with System 2 analysis and get closer to the actual value of the item. Comparison shopping for household goods as well as stocks may help you identify a better purchase price.[26]

Case Study: Lowes and Home Depot

I've generally favored Lowes (LOW) over Home Depot (HD) for two reasons: (1) the potential for Lowes to catch up to Home Depot's growth and profitability and (2) valuation. Although both home-improvement retailers have exceeded investor expectations, I've used head-to-head analysis as a way to test my investment thesis for favoring Lowes. If at some point Lowes fully catches up to Home Depot and investors reward the company's progress with a higher valuation, I may need a new or different reason to own Lowes. Until then, head-to-head analysis of a close competitor will continue to help my investment process.

BEHAVIORAL COACHING TIP

Head-to-head analysis can help you better understand your target company, and it can produce a more accurate valuation relative to stand-alone analysis.

Four-Step Process for Prediction

It's tough to make predictions, especially about the future.

—Yogi Berra

Ready for some math? I've tried my best to focus on logic and high-level behavioral concepts, but a little math can help us reduce bias that enters into financial projections, such as estimating a company's future profits, which stocks often chase. A quantitative framework may help us avoid emotional attachments to a CEO, product, or industry and reduce the chances of forecasting overly bullish growth prospects for a company or a stock.

Berkshire Hathaway's vice chairman Charlie Munger suggested that emotional bias may have led the company to remain in the newspaper business well after the industry's fundamentals began to deteriorate. Munger noted that emotions may have gotten in the way of cold, hard analysis when he said that "the decline was faster than we thought it was going to be, so it was not our finest bit of economic prediction. To the extent we miscalculated, we may have done it because we both love newspapers."[27] In essence, we need all the help we can get as we try to reduce bias in our prediction of future earnings and stock prices.

What can we learn from these mistakes as we try to remove emotions and biases that may push our predictions to the extreme? Kahneman recommends a four-step process that can bring bullish views down to earth or give a dose of realism to an overly bearish perspective.[28] First, we try to understand historical patterns, or *base rates*. Let's say that we've made a ton of money investing in risky software stocks, potentially making us overly optimistic about the next stock pick. However, put aside any personal experience and look across the board at the probabilities of growth or success for all software stocks.

Winners such as Microsoft and Salesforce can offset losers such as Webvan or Pets.com, using extreme examples. This is the base rate. For discussion purposes, let's say that the average software company generates a base rate of 10 percent sales growth each year.

The next step is to fall back on your intuition and, using our earlier example, speculate on how you feel the next software stock will perform. Yes, behavioral economists actually allow you to use System 1 thinking once in a while. Step two recommends that you make an educated guess based on your impression of available evidence.

Let's say that you are looking at Zoom Video Communications (ZM), a company providing web-based video conferencing for work, school, and personal use. In 2020, the worsening coronavirus pandemic triggered social distancing, working from home, and remote learning, factors that drove a spike in demand for Zoom's technology. A general impression based on this evidence might lead to an expectation that Zoom's revenues will grow faster than those of its peers for some time. In this case, let's say that you think that Zoom can grow its revenues 50 percent per year.

Step three curbs your emotional enthusiasm by bringing back System 2 thinking on the concept of correlation. This is probably the most difficult step in the process because it requires you to understand how one variable can affect another. Kahneman uses an example of the relationship between a student's reading ability and his or her grade-point average. If you think strong readers get good grades (and vice versa), then you would anticipate a high correlation.[29]

Using our example of Zoom Video, if you think that the 2020 pandemic and work-from-home trend will continue for years, then you might predict a high correlation, say 75 percent, between remote work and Zoom's revenue growth. Using this math, every 10 percent increase in people working from home drives a 7.5 percent increase in Zoom's revenues. If you are worried about a big competitor coming into the market and taking share from Zoom, you might have a more pessimistic correlation estimate, perhaps below 50 percent.

The final step puts all the pieces together and develops a forecast that attempts to reduce our bias. We start with our base rate, which in this case is 10 percent sales growth for software stocks. Then, at the other end of the spectrum, we write down our educated guess from step two, which is 50 percent sales growth for Zoom Video. Finally, we adjust our educated guess up or down based on the correlation we came up with.

Let's recap. We have:

1. A base rate of 10 percent growth for all software companies.

2. A general impression that Zoom can grow revenues at a 50 percent rate.

3. A correlation estimate of 75 percent, which means that we think that Zoom can maintain high market share.

In step four, we estimate Zoom's revenue by putting these three data points together. The distance (or difference) between the 10 percent base rate and our optimistic guess of 50 percent is 40 percent. Let's multiply 40 percent times the 75 percent correlation step, giving us 30 percent. Now take the 30 percent and add it to our base rate (10 percent) to get a less biased prediction for Zoom Video's growth, which is 40 percent.

Yes, there's a bit of math here, but essentially we started with a bullish growth projection (50 percent) and used the four steps to remove bias and add some cold, hard facts, dialing down our original estimate to a more realistic 40 percent rate. The bottom line here is that Kahneman's four-step process can moderate overly optimistic or pessimistic forecasts.

BEHAVIORAL COACHING TIP

When trying to predict how a stock will perform, consider using Kahneman's four-step process for removing bias. Start with a base rate, then come up with your own guess, look for correlation, and finally bring your guess closer to the base rate using the correlation.

Reference Class Forecasting

A bird in hand is worth two in the bush.

—OLD PROVERB

This proverb suggests that it would be better for a hunter to keep one bird in his or her hand rather than drop the bird and risk trying to get two that are in a bush. The proverb may have relied on historical patterns, or a *reference class*, that suggests that hunters have a low chance of getting two wild birds in a bush. Perhaps we can use this proverb as we continue researching potential stock picks.

Before getting into details with reference class forecasting, let's look at a potential problem that this concept might solve. When decision makers plan for the future, they are often wildly optimistic. Investors also suffer from this bias, called the *planning fallacy*, as we create an investment thesis.

One way of avoiding this behavioral risk is to follow a three-step process called *reference class forecasting*. This process is similar to Kahneman's four-step prediction model we just reviewed, but I discuss it here to give you another approach for reducing bias and getting a more realistic forecast.

In some ways, Kahneman's four steps for improving prediction can help when there is a high degree of uncertainty, such forecasting Zoom Video's sales after a global pandemic. In contrast, reference class forecasting may be a better approach when the window of uncertainty is a bit tighter, such as predicting growth for mature industries.

The theme for both reference class forecasting and Kahneman's four steps to prediction is taking the outside view and looking at real-world data rather than using your personal impression or hunch, an inside view. With these themes in mind, let's jump into reference class forecasting.

Step one involves identifying a *reference class*, which is similar to a base rate.[30] Let's use Intel, a semiconductor company, as an example. Intel in 2019 disappointed investors when it said that additional research-and-development (R&D) spending for a new semiconductor product cycle would depress profits. The question for investors was how quickly could Intel launch the new microchips and cut back on the spike in R&D costs, likely boosting profits and the stock price.

Step one in the Intel example would be identifying a reference class of other semiconductor companies that also jacked up R&D spending to push out a new product cycle. Step two involves gathering data. For simplicity's sake, let's say that most semiconductor companies take two years in hurry-up mode when trying to develop a new product cycle. Let's also say that, historically, the added R&D expenses lower the company's overall profit margins by 3 percentage points.

Now we've identified a reference class and we've gathered data on historical examples. The final step is to compare our new situation, Intel, with the reference class. How is Intel's situation different from prior examples? Let's say in this case that Intel's strategy is more difficult than the historical pattern because Intel is trying to launch a brand-new product cycle by developing a chip that's 50 percent smaller and faster than usual.

Using these metrics, we can take the reference class data, which were two years and a 3 percent hit to profit margins, and adjust for the Intel-specific strategy, which is a 50 percent increase in complexity. This analysis might suggest that it would take Intel three years (50 percent more than usual) to develop the new chips and cost shareholders a 4.5 percent hit to profit margins (also 50 percent more than average). In other words, we are going to penalize Intel with a prediction that its aggressive plan for a new product cycle will have worse results than average.

BEHAVIORAL COACHING TIP

Reference class forecasting is a three-step process that can help you reduce errors of bias in prediction, especially for companies in more mature industries. First, find a reference class, then figure out how your company differs from the reference class, and finally adjust up or down your prediction by the differences between the two.

Put Weights on Variables in Decision Making

Most people are lazy and think things are gonna happen, not gonna happen, or maybe.

—Amos Tversky[31]

The whole point of this chapter is to go deep, use analysis, and remove bias as you research a potential stock idea. The final section of this chapter focuses on quantifying difficult questions. The opening quote for this section suggests the complete opposite of what we're discussing here.

The lazy System 1 approach to picking stocks, using Tversky's three categories, might think that the stock's *gonna go up, it's not going up, or maybe*. Behavioral finance techniques can allow us to do a much better job with prediction and forecasting complex investment puzzles. In my view, picking a stock is what Kahneman refers to as a "global evaluation of a complex object."[32] How can we evaluate all the complexities of a stock and avoid falling into a trap of System 1 thinking?

The final concept in this section focuses on breaking down complicated questions, such as *should I buy this stock?*, into smaller pieces and then thinking about probabilities for each part. Before we get to some stock examples, let's start with some noninvestment questions to illustrate how bias and laziness can impact our approach to judgment and decision making.

When the Bailey family goes shopping for a new vehicle, what determines our purchase decision? Is it the gas mileage, the look, the performance, or maybe the price? System 2 thinking would focus on each of these four variables, but lazy System 1 thinking might go something like this: "Well, we like the SUV's look and feel, so we'll buy it even though it's expensive and a gas guzzler."

A better approach might be to give weights to each of these variables. Let's say that price and fuel efficiency are actually more important than look and feel. If these two factors actually are 50 percent worse than you expected, perhaps you should look for a different SUV.

A nonfinancial example is asking if you like your daughter's school. A lazy response might be a yes or no answer, but a System 2 approach could go deeper and look at the school's teachers, the commute time, the availability of extracurricular activities, and the pros and cons of alternative schools. Putting weights on these variables might help you come to a different decision than an emotional System 1 approach.

Let's apply this approach to an investment idea. The first step is to break your stock pick down into a few variables. Let's take a closer look at what might drive shares of Estée Lauder (EL), a global developer of beauty products, such as skin care, cosmetics, hair care, and perfume. For this example, let's assign weights to three variables: sales, expenses, and investor sentiment.

Kahneman recommends that we should overweight variables that have more likely outcomes.[33] For simplicity's sake, let's say that Estée Lauder has a track record of consistently beating investor expectations for sales but a more mixed record for expenses. Also, let's imagine that investor sentiment for Estée Lauder stock is above average relative to the trailing five-year period.

In this case, I might assign a 70 percent probability for sales, a 30 percent weight on expenses, and 10 percent for investor sentiment. So will Estée Lauder shares go up or outperform the market? Well, I have high confidence that sales will beat Wall Street estimates, I have modest confidence that expenses will stay in check, and I have little confidence that investor sentiment will remain above average.

Now let's put these variables together. Let's say that, historically, investors respond favorably when Estée Lauder's revenues surprise to the upside. Based on my weights and probabilities, I'm moving forward with Estée Lauder as a potential stock pick because I think that good sales will outweigh risks of mediocre expenses or potential changes to investor sentiment.

One way to remove bias during the complete research phase is to break your stock down into smaller pieces (variables) when trying to predict whether fundamental improvements for the company will boost the stock. Put weights on these variables and give higher (lower) weightings for variables that have higher (lower) probabilities.

Is There an Alternative to Logic, Data, and Analysis?

A spreadsheet leaves no room for miracles.

—RORY SUTHERLAND[34]

It would be a lot easier to predict things if the future is like the past, but bias (such as lazy System 1 thinking) can create prediction errors. We can use historical data, numerical research, and logic to reduce these errors. However, just to stir the pot, some investors see a healthy tension between logic and magic when forecasting company profits or stock prices.

Why magic? Michael Arone, an investment strategist with State Street Global Advisors, believes that consensus views stem from logic and analysis. However, Arone suggests that if you want to beat the market, you have to take a nonconsensus approach because "[i]f everyone is doing it—being logical—then it won't generate a profit for investors."[35]

However, sometimes illogical (or magical) things happen and lead to massive market changes. Logic and analysis likely failed to anticipate the rise of the internet in the 1990s, the housing boom and bust of the early 2000s, or the fall of the energy sector in the 2010s. Arone suggests that sometimes you need to sprinkle a little magic, or illogic, into your investment process in a concept called the *illogic premium*.

Let's take Amazon for an example. In 2015, the stock was trading around $500, as investors focused on the company's e-commerce growth. However, using some illogic, or hoping that Amazon CEO Jeff Bezos could work his magic, investors might anticipate some new growth driver creating a premium valuation for the stock.

In fact, Bezos did work his magic, and Amazon Web Services (cloud computing) ramped up starting in 2015, helping drive the stock up nearly fivefold ($2,400) by 2020. Considering Arone's illogic premium and the Amazon example, perhaps we can take a nuanced approach to prediction that combines historical trends as our base case while also remaining open to a pattern break or something illogical happening.

BEHAVIORAL COACHING TIP

In most cases, behavioral finance concepts such as base rates, probabilities, and scenario analysis should help with stock selection. However, if a company appears to be on the verge of a major transformation, give yourself the liberty of thinking more creatively about possibilities. Build a long-term financial model and see if the valuation today makes sense using discounted cash flows or earnings.[36]

Summary

Congratulations! You've made it through one of the tougher parts of the investment life cycle. The deep research phase is a pretty intense way of understanding how a company works, evaluating the people running the company and then using financial modeling to make sense of your qualitative research. Here's a quick summary of this chapter's deep research themes.

Getting Started

- Remain suspicious and vigilant while avoiding cognitive ease as you seek out information and sources to help you understand a company or stock.

- Get a more objective understanding of how a company operates by using frameworks such as SWOT analysis and Porter's five forces and answering the following four questions: Who uses? Who chooses? Who pays? Who profits?

- Take a System 2 approach to due diligence by seeking out experts who can support or refute your views of a company's growth prospects.

Management

- Use caution when assuming that management teams can drive success for a company and its stock. Good CEOs often beat bad ones only about 60 percent of the time, just 10 percent ahead of random chance.

- Be careful putting your faith in overconfident CEOs who tell coherent stories, take an inside view, omit the outside view, have bad track records, or underappreciate risks.

- When overconfident CEOs pursue large acquisitions, investors should focus more on historical rates of deal success and failure rather than on the CEO's coherent story about the deal.

- CEOs with unusually large or small holdings have an unfavorable track record with large acquisitions.

- It's easier for a new CEO, relative to an old one carrying emotional baggage, to shut down a bad project. This kind of major restructuring can turn a company and stock around.

Data and Analysis

- Head-to-head comparisons can reduce bias compared with a rifle-shot analysis when looking at a company or stock.

- Use a four-step process for reducing bias when predicting how a stock will perform, especially for a high-growth company. (1) Start with a base rate, then (2) make your own guess, and then (3) estimate a correlation between your guess and the base rate that can (4) bring your guess closer to the base rate.

- When looking at more mature industries, consider a three-step process of reference class forecasting as a way of reducing errors of bias. Identify a reference class, see how your company is different from that class, and then bridge the divide by adjusting your prediction up or down by the differences between the reference class and your company.

- Remove bias from your complete research process by assigning weights to variables that drive the stock. Give higher weights to variables that have a greater probability of success.

- Your best bet is to stick with cold, hard facts, figures, and analysis, but on rare occasions when companies are changing rapidly, consider a more creative approach to what a business could look like in three to five years. Then build a financial model and see if the valuation is reasonable.

4

Craft an Investment Thesis

It ain't what you don't know that gets you into trouble. It's what you know for sure that just ain't so.
—Attributed to Mark Twain

We've just come through a tough slog battling emotions and bias in a research process that gets us comfortable recommending a stock. Now we need to craft a story about why we should own this stock. Perhaps we expect the stock to beat the market or do better than peers, or maybe the stock adds diversification or helps us offset risks in other parts of our portfolio. In a way, we have to tell a coherent story about how our stock achieves some kind of goal without falling into the overconfidence trap that we read about in Chapter 3.

Going along with the opening quote attributed to Mark Twain, we have to be careful when we create an investment thesis because things can and do go wrong. However, if we use some behavioral coaching tools, we can go into a stock purchase better prepared in case problems arise.

Howard Marks uses the term *investing scared* as a way of coming up with a scenario for how your stock might outperform while also considering downside risks. Marks recommends that you "do thorough due diligence, employ conservative assumptions, insist on an ample margin of safety in case things go wrong, and invest only when the potential return is at least commensurate with the risk."[1] This is a pretty good summary of how we can turn a weakness, such as emotions and biases, into a strength as we craft an investment thesis.

Before jumping into the Kahneman and Thaler behavioral finance tools, it may be helpful to give an example of one way to set up an investment thesis. There are many ways to come up with an investment thesis, but I generally follow a structure where I set a goal and then line up risks and merits that could decrease or increase the chances that the company hits my stated goal.

Often my goal is that the company meets or exceeds investor expectations over time, using metrics such as sales, profits, and cash flows. For my investment process, I usually look for companies that are changing over time and have the ability to beat investor expectations as the business transforms, hopefully for the better. After describing how the company will beat investor forecasts, I lay out risks that could prevent the company from achieving these projections as well as merits that could allow the company to blow past long-term goals.

Having laid out one approach to creating an investment thesis, let's dive into some tools that can help us sharpen up our analysis of the upside and downside of a stock. Along the way, the process of writing a good investment thesis may lead you to a different decision, such as buying at a different time, buying a different stock, or going back and doing further research.

Before getting into the details of what can go wrong with an investment thesis, let's review some of the broader themes we'll be discussing. This chapter starts out with a warning that noise can cloud our judgment, suggesting that we are creating an investment thesis under imperfect conditions.

We then list about five different ways in which people make extreme forecasts. Next, we try to push back on this tendency to make extreme forecasts by discussing a *pre-mortem*, a method of poking holes in an investment thesis as a way to make it more realistic. Finally, we pass the baton from the investment thesis to the trade by focusing on a pattern where, even with extreme predictions, many investors chicken out and fail to make bold choices.

Writing an investment thesis can seem daunting, especially with all these warnings, and I apologize if this section takes away from the excitement and creativity that come with telling a story about the future. However, I hope that some of these themes can help you put together a logical and insightful investment thesis while avoiding some of the mistakes I've made and seen.

Judgment and Noise

The first step in crafting a good investment thesis is acknowledging that we as investors are trying to draw concrete conclusions from a chaotic ocean of events, data, and opinions. In other words, our job is to see through all the noise out there and try to find signals. Although most of this book talks about behavioral biases, this section highlights how nonbehavioral factors such as messy data can influence our investment decisions.

Chapter 1 focused on the differences between internal and external bias, and I would argue that noise is an external factor that causes an internal bias. Kahneman's bottom line is that anytime humans are making a judgment, noise likely clouds the person's ability to make the best judgment or decision.[2] Kahneman presents examples of noise distorting judgment in situations where the underlying data can be messy on the one hand (where you might expect errors), or black and white on the other (where more accurate decisions should result).

In the insurance industry, for example, underwriters have to make judgments on premiums, or the cost of the insurance, even though the data can be messy and complex. One study showed that underwriters using the same data came to different conclusions, in fact, showing 56 percent divergence. Perhaps some of the noise in the data led the underwriters to *see* different things in the data just as museum goers may see different things in the same work of art.

Kahneman indicates that the "underwriters are wasting their time."[3] Going further, he asks, "How can it be that people have that amount of noise in judgment and not be aware of it?" If noise prevents businesses from setting accurate prices, that's a problem.

Noise can distort judgment in cases that appear much simpler than insurance underwriting. Kahneman cites biometric examples in which the underlying data should be fairly binary. However, experts looking at the same set of x-rays, DNA data, or fingerprints can come up with different judgments, even when you would expect greater certainty in these decisions.

For investors, the concept of noise adds another pitfall that stock pickers should recognize as they work through the investment life cycle. In fact, the combination of noise and judgment can be particularly worrisome when you are trying to pull diverse sets of data together to craft an investment thesis for a company.

In my view, there are two ways investors can deal with noise, or messy and complex data. If we detect a lot of noise as we create an investment thesis, we may need to roll up our sleeves and go back to some of the analytical tools we discussed in Chapter 3. Alternatively, if the noise prevents us from making a reasonable analysis, perhaps it's time to pass on the stock and look for something else where we can get to a higher conviction in an investment view.

Amazon.com presents a good example of hazards that can emerge when creating a pithy investment thesis when surrounded by noisy financial and market data. As one of the largest companies in the world, Amazon creates challenges for investors trying to summarize why the stock might outperform.

Amazon's core growth drivers in early 2019, as I was updating my investment thesis, included e-commerce, cloud computing, and a burgeoning expansion into online advertising, among others. Going back to my investment process of secular change and exceeding expectations, I focused on Amazon's growth drivers that were in the early stages of expansion, and online ads seemed to fit the bill.

Noise and judgment came into play in two ways. First, Amazon's less than transparent reporting created some noise as I tried to estimate quarterly online ad sales. Amazon reported ad sales in an *other revenue* line, which also included sales unrelated to advertising. This combined reporting creates noise for investment researchers. Second, Amazon's online ad sales were fairly volatile because the business was just getting off the ground, and I had trouble seeing through the boom and bust quarterly reporting, another example of noise.

Despite the noise involved in Amazon's ad business, I made a judgment that over time the company's ad sales would likely exceed investor expectations and boost profits for the overall company. Time will tell if my investment thesis can overcome the challenges of cutting through the noise in Amazon's reporting, but early signs are promising.

When crafting an investment thesis, be cautious that noise doesn't distort your judgment. If the level of noise seems excessive, you may need to lower your level of confidence in the portion of the thesis that the noise is impacting.

Extreme Investment Thesis Risk 1: Bold Forecasts and the Inside View

Hope is not an investment thesis.

—JOE HEALY[4]

Writing an investment thesis can be a humbling task. We've just checked our ego at the door with the idea that noise can impact our judgment. Now we're going to outline a string of other risks that can blow an investment thesis off course. The common theme for these five risks is a tendency for investors to make bold or extreme predictions as a part of the investment thesis. In this section, we'll touch on ways in which the inside view can lead to an extreme investment thesis.

Why do investors make optimistic or extreme projections when they pick stocks? More broadly speaking, Thaler underlines the idea that "people make forecasts that are too extreme,"[5] with an example of pro football scouts who are trying to judge the future potential of athletes. These scouts "are too willing to say that a particular player is likely to be a superstar, when by definition superstars do not come along very often."[6]

How can our tendency to make extreme forecasts lead to overly bullish investment views? The quote at the top of this section comes from my director of research when I worked at Legg Mason. Joe's point is that emotions can cloud our forecasts and lead to bad decisions. If we are recommending a stock or if we own it, we hope it goes up, and this emotion can lead up the food chain to hoping that our investment thesis works out. Joe taught my team to remove the emotions and stick with facts, analysis, and probabilities.

Hope generally stems from an inside view and can lead to an overly optimistic investment thesis. Thaler and Kahneman point to an example of a group of authors trying to estimate the time needed to finish a new textbook. The authors got "caught up in the optimism that comes with group endeavors" and made an extremely aggressive timeline for finishing the book.[7] When hope and the inside view creep into our investment thesis, we can have overly aggressive assumptions for a company's fundamentals that then inflate our price targets.

Amazon presents a case study of how the inside view can lead to a bold forecast and investment thesis. As discussed earlier, I expected Amazon's ad business to exceed investor expectations. However, I probably took more of an inside view as I developed my investment thesis. I relied heavily on Amazon's historical ad sales and growth rate as a guide to the company's future results.

Contrary to my investment thesis, Amazon's ad sales disappointed in early 2019. Looking back at this short-term forecasting mistake, I should have taken more of an outside view and done more due diligence before projecting a surge in Amazon's online ad sales.

BEHAVIORAL COACHING TIP

When creating an investment thesis, be aware that an inside view can lead to bold forecasts and a potentially unrealistic investment thesis. An outside view can help reel in an overly bullish thesis.

Extreme Investment Thesis Risk 2: The Planning Fallacy

Everybody has a plan until they get punched in the mouth.
—MIKE TYSON[8]

Whether you are competing for boxing victories, business market share, or investment performance that beats a benchmark, you generally need a game plan. As the opening quote suggests, many boxers have to scrap their plan once the punches start flying. Similarly, in business and finance, a marketing plan or investment thesis may need a plan B as you bring in competition and real-world market dynamics. A more realistic investment thesis may help you manage expectations and perhaps get you closer to your investment goal.

We've just reviewed an idea that most people make extreme forecasts, suggesting that we may fall into this trap when we write an investment thesis. Now let's take things up another notch with the concept of the *planning fallacy*, in which we often anticipate the best-case outcome, rather than a more likely possibility.[9]

A classic noninvestment example of the planning fallacy is in the construction industry. Time and time again, builders and developers lay out a schedule and budget that seem destined to end up delayed and well over budget. A best-case proposal might help win a deal, but unfortunately, reality often sinks in, creating cost and scheduling overruns.

The planning fallacy comes into play frequently as investors work toward an investment thesis. If you are looking to buy a stock on the idea that a company will meet or beat investor expectations, are you anticipating the best-case outcome or a realistic possibility?

Often company management teams will guide investors toward financial targets for future sales, profits, or other metrics. However, a little System 2 thinking might wonder if the planning fallacy is creeping into management's projections, especially if your investment thesis hinges on this guidance. Looking at a company's history of meeting or beating guidance metrics can give investors a sense of how realistic the future guidance might be.

My investment thesis with Amazon gave me a reminder that the planning fallacy is alive and well. As mentioned in the preceding section, I expected Amazon's online ad sales to help the company beat Wall Street's profit estimates. Unfortunately for me, Amazon's ad sales disappointed in the first quarter of 2019, possibly because of the noise in the system that we discussed earlier.

Fortunately for me, my investment thesis also anticipated that Amazon's other businesses in e-commerce and cloud computing would continue to perform well, and those two divisions did indeed help to offset the poor ad sales. My experience with Amazon is a good reminder to diversify your investment thesis. If you put all your eggs in one basket, the planning fallacy can lead to a meaningful downside. However, if your investment thesis is more of a three-legged stool, you have a better chance of avoiding the pitfalls of the planning fallacy.

If your investment thesis anticipates improving company fundamentals, keep in mind that the planning fallacy often means that your realistic outcome is actually the best-case outcome. Multiple independent catalysts can support a good investment thesis and reduce concentrated risk in one part of a company, which may fail to play out as seen in the planning fallacy.

Extreme Investment Thesis Risk 3: Possibility and Certainty Effects

So far we've taken a sober approach to drafting an investment thesis, acknowledging that noise in the system can cloud our judgment and that we often anticipate a best-case outcome rather than a realistic outcome. Because this book is about investing and finance, let's look at some tools that can help us quantify whether our views are realistic or too bullish.

Taking the planning fallacy a step further, we are now going to assign some probabilities to our investment thesis as a way of figuring out if we are being realistic or overly optimistic. We'll also discuss how bias creeps in and makes us overweight rare events, such as the best-case scenario, and underweight more likely, or realistic, outcomes.

Kahneman uses a dramatic healthcare example to describe how we feel about the difference between a 5 percent chance of amputation and a 10 percent chance. Both are terrible outcomes, but in theory, we should feel better about the 5 percent chance. However, in reality, many people freak out over small risks and will pay a huge premium (more than an expected value) to completely remove the risk. This desire to overpay to remove all risk is called the *possibility effect*.[10]

Imagine how this could play out for investors if a company has a small risk of a major problem. Perhaps most investors will become risk averse and run away screaming because they can't stomach a tiny chance of a massive disappointment. This could create opportunities for value buyers who swoop in to acquire cheap stocks that are left for dead by mainstream investors.[11]

Whereas the possibility effect describes our feelings about unlikely events, the *certainty effect* describes how people respond when outcomes are almost 100 percent likely. Even if a bad event is almost certain, we cling to a tiny shadow of hope that we will be among the lucky ones.[12] If there was a 95 percent chance that a stock will go down on pending news, investors might become risk seeking and hope to avoid the loss. These investors might hold onto the stock by copying the classic movie line that "it's so crazy, it just might work!" However, overly bullish investors hoping for a Hollywood ending often suffer.[13]

Going back to Amazon, I can look at my investment thesis of online ad growth and see whether it falls into the possibility effect or the certainty effect. In the very short term, my thesis likely suffered from the possibility effect. This is because I looked at rapid online ad growth in 2018 and drew a straight line to continued expansion in 2019.

I saw a small possibility of a big upside surprise for Amazon's online ad sales. However, hope or greed (along with noise) may have clouded my judgment, making my 2019 ad sales forecast less likely. Unfortunately for me, Amazon's first quarter 2019 online ad sales disappointed investors, suggesting that I should have been more aware of the possibility effect.

BEHAVIORAL COACHING TIP

When working on an investment thesis, consider whether you are overweighting unlikely events or underweighting more likely events. Use caution with these extreme events because they can make investors either risk seeking or risk averse in anticipation of gains or losses.

Extreme Investment Thesis Risk 4: Impact of Vivid Experiences

The preceding section warned us that humans have a tendency to expect rare events or ignore highly likely outcomes. Let's say that Amazon has been growing profits at a rate of 25 percent per year for about three years. If we expect Amazon to shift gears and grow profits of 50 percent per year, we should ask ourselves if this is a realistic scenario.

This example of Amazon's accelerating earnings growth is fairly unemotional and lacks juicy details. However, what if Amazon made headlines by acquiring a rival such as Netflix, Facebook, or Costco, triggering a massive response from the economic web of bias (i.e., cable news, governments, other tech CEOs, Wall Street analysts, etc.)? Vivid images of vocal experts talking about the new Amazon might lead investors to overweight the chances of Amazon doing much better, such as doubling its growth rate to 50 percent using the earlier example. Kahneman suggests that fluency, vividness, and the ease of imagining can impact the way we think about probabilities and outcomes.[14] Dramatic memories may lead to dramatic predictions.

Another example of vivid images impacting an investment thesis is Boeing. In late 2018 and early 2019, two recently designed Boeing 737 Max-8 planes crashed, killing nearly 350 passengers and crew members. These disasters were tragic, likely triggering a natural emotional reaction of sympathy for the victims and their families. In cases like these, many companies struggle as they try to understand what went wrong and then correct the mistakes.

Investors in Boeing in 2019 may have been biased by vivid images as the investors weighed the probability of a turnaround. As emotional as these cases can be, investors should try to let the facts guide their investment expectations. If emotions and vivid images seem to be creeping into your investment thesis, perhaps passing and looking at a different stock might be a better option.

BEHAVIORAL COACHING TIP

When developing an investment thesis, use extra caution if your analysis involves emotional outcomes or dramatic events. Vivid images can make us think that low-probability events are more likely.

Extreme Investment Thesis Risk 5:
Expecting Short-Term Pattern Changes

History doesn't repeat itself, but it often rhymes.
—Attributed to Mark Twain

Is it realistic to expect a slow-growth company to suddenly hit the gas and start gobbling up market share? An investment thesis that anticipates this kind of short-term pattern break may end in disappointment.

Rapid acceleration, related to growth markets, can be another type of extreme investment thesis. Let's dig a little deeper to see why these kinds of pattern breaks are less likely.

Investors and sales executives love the idea of growth markets. Surging demand for your product will ring the cash register and earn you a promotion. However, one of my most memorable takeaways from a marketing class in business school was the idea that *there's no such thing as growth markets, just an endless search for new customers.*

Many investors may think that companies can easily toss a new product into a growth market and magically create shareholder value. In contrast, a more realistic approach is to turn this idea around and focus on the hard work that goes into finding new customers and revenues. I recommend taking the latter approach when creating an investment thesis, with the premise that a business selling one additional widget or finding one more customer is a challenge rather than the default.

So far this chapter has reviewed four reasons why an extreme investment thesis can lead to bad outcomes. We've now arrived at the fifth and final warning sign, which gets into behavior patterns. Essentially, expecting rapid changes in companies or management teams can prove costly for investors.

During my career, I've seen many stocks come crashing down when investors bet heavily on the latest and greatest product cycle, service, demographic change, acquisition, regulatory change, or new CEO. High investor expectations can collide painfully when betting that a mediocre corporate track record can magically become a Wall Street darling.[15]

I would argue that individual and corporate behavior patterns, such as buying and selling, drive macro trends. Investors can go against the grain and anticipate dramatic shifts away from prior patterns, but this is a risky endeavor. Howard Marks suggests that "the forecasts that produce great profits are the one that presciently foresee radical deviations from the past. But that kind of forecast is, first, very hard to make, and second, rarely right."[16]

Behavior patterns run deep in the healthcare industry, highlighting the dangers of an investment thesis that predicts rapid uptake for new drugs and devices. Highly regulated industries, such as healthcare, often lead decision makers, such as nurses, doctors, hospital administrators, and insurance executives, to avoid risk. Breaking with a proven workflow may create health or efficiency gains, but at the cost of potentially harming patients or taking on legal liability.

New medicines and medical technologies often struggle to gain market share because doctors remain in their comfort zone with older products. Often new healthcare treatments see early adoption in academic medical centers with lots of resources. However, more remote community–based doctors may take a wait-and-see approach before ordering the latest cancer drug, hip implant, or diagnostic test.

Some investors may expect big pattern changes for companies that straddle multiple industries, such as CVS Health, a company that sells consumer retail products along with prescription drugs and health insurance. Investors owning CVS Health shares in early 2019 likely anticipated meaningful behavior change as a part of their investment thesis.

CVS in 2018 spent $69 billion buying health insurer Aetna, potentially as a way to keep up with rivals UnitedHealth and Cigna. CVS in 2019 began experimenting with a new retail approach called HealthHUBs, which are larger than usual retail stores offering a wide menu of primary care services and an Aetna insurance sales kiosk.

A favorable scenario for CVS would be for a consumer to buy Aetna insurance and then use low-cost CVS HealthHUBs for primary care needs. Aetna insurance would profit because the HealthHUBs are cheaper than other providers (e.g., doctors, hospitals, or walk-in clinics), and CVS might benefit if patients got prescription drugs at the pharmacy or bought other consumer products at the front of the store.

A key concern for this investment thesis is that it requires patients and consumers to meaningfully change their behavior patterns. What if a patient likes his or her primary care doctor more than an unknown provider in a retail CVS location? What if the CVS HealthHUB location is inconvenient for the patient? Also, what if the patient is unable to access Aetna insurance through his or her employer? What if Aetna's rivals discourage patients from using CVS HealthHUBs?

Despite these concerns, the CVS–Aetna partnership eventually may create shareholder value. However, in examples such as this, where the investment thesis rests on meaningful behavior change, investors should think long and hard about their time horizon.

Another way of looking at this idea of behavior change is to think about customer loyalty. In healthcare, orthopedic surgeons might train on Stryker or Zimmer implants for years and then prefer to stick with the same supplier for the rest of their careers. At the other end of the spectrum, consumers may favor a particular brand of toothpaste, deodorant, or razor because they are comfortable with a brand they've used for much of their adult lives. An investment thesis that banks on a rapid switch in orthopedic implants or personal care brands might disappoint.

In some ways, this behavioral coaching concept runs counter to my investment process in which I look for situations where investors have yet to fully appreciate major changes in a business over time. In fact, I'd argue that most businesses change gradually over the long term because employees, managers, and competitors often stick with existing work patterns. Although genuine business transformation can be less common, investors can find meaningful opportunities if they set up realistic expectations.

My investment thesis for Amazon's online advertising business tries to thread this needle of slow behavior changes for both consumers and businesses. Google and Facebook currently dominate the online ad market, but Amazon appears to be capitalizing on consumer loyalty to Amazon's e-commerce site. As consumers shop on Amazon, the company gradually inserts ads related to the consumers' browsing and buying patterns. Rather than trying to take consumers away from Google or Facebook, Amazon simply tries to show targeted ads to its existing shoppers.

I favor this type of growth model, where Amazon's online ad business requires minimal behavior change among e-commerce shoppers. My investment thesis also rests on Amazon's track record of setting up and entering new businesses. In contrast, I've had less confidence that other brick and mortar retailers can quickly and successfully enter brand-new markets.

From a broader perspective, this discussion of short-term pattern breaks reminds me of a comment I heard at an investor meeting sponsored by Celgene, a biotech company that Bristol-Myers Squibb later acquired. During the meeting, a top Celgene executive said, "[T]he future is not something you enter, but rather something you create." The idea here is that Celgene had to follow up its drug approvals with the blocking and tackling needed to encourage doctors and patients to use its biotech drugs. In the biotech sector and across the market, a good investment thesis takes a realistic approach to forecasting pattern changes for new products, services, or markets.

Be careful if your investment thesis requires some economic decision maker or organization to meaningfully and quickly change behavior patterns. Large-scale changes in consumer or producer behavior patterns often take longer than many investors expect and can lead to disappointing results.

Give Your Investment Thesis a Pre-mortem

Before embarking on a project, imagine receiving a message from the future: the project failed, and spectacularly.
— TIM HARFORD, *FINANCIAL TIMES*[17]

I often tell my kids that if they complain about something, they need to offer a solution. I've just *complained* about the many ways investors can get in trouble by creating an extreme or bold investment thesis. So what are some good ways to solve these problems and avoid these behavioral traps?

In general, Kahneman recommends conducting a pre-mortem before making major decisions as a way of dialing down "overconfident optimism."[18] Kahneman's idea of a pre-mortem is a way of actively crafting a story of why your decision was a disappointment before you make the final decision. In contrast, a post-mortem can be helpful to see what you learned from a decision, but by then it's too late to go back and change your mind.

For investors, this predecision activity can help identify flaws in the investment thesis. If you work on a team, it can be helpful to have more than one investment professional conduct a pre-mortem and then compare notes as a way of avoiding groupthink. Also, if your investment thesis has specific targets, such as earnings forecasts or price targets, your pre-mortem can tell a story about why the company failed to hit these targets a year later.

Using my Amazon example, I can conduct a pre-mortem with a focus on the company's online advertising business. I could say that Amazon's online ad segment disappointed for the following reasons:

1. A spike in 2018 sales set up difficult 2019 comparisons.

2. Google and Facebook lowered their pricing to compete with Amazon.

3. E-commerce shoppers preferred to do their browsing on other sites and do their buying on Amazon.

4. A recession led to lower overall advertising activity, depressing Amazon's ad sales.

5. Amazon decided to put its ad business on the back burner and focus on other areas.

6. Amazon's ad business generated meaningful sales, but startup costs depressed the profit contribution from the ads.

After writing a pre-mortem, it can be helpful to debate each point with another investment professional on your team. If the pre-mortem concerns seem more likely than the merits of your investment thesis, it could be time to reevaluate. In my experience, the pre-mortem generally takes some of the emotional excitement out of the thesis (which is probably a good thing), but it's rare that a pre-mortem will completely shut down the stock idea.

BEHAVIORAL COACHING TIP

Once you finish your investment thesis, give it a stress test by conducting a pre-mortem. Try telling a story of why your thesis failed, and you may help tone down an overly optimistic forecast and better understand the company's risks.

Transitioning from Investment Thesis to Trading: Bold Forecasts and Timid Choices

My best advice, I think you would be happier if you reduced your expectations.

—CHARLIE MUNGER[19]

So far in this chapter we've spent considerable time talking about a tendency for investors to make bold forecasts, such as bullish earnings predictions and upside price targets. If we think a stock is going through the roof, we might buy a lot of it, putting our money where our mouth (or mind) is. This bias could lead to financial losses if our bold forecast for a stock turns out to be wrong and if we've acted on our bold forecasts.

In a real-world example, let's say that we think that Amazon's profits next year will exceed Wall Street estimates by 20 percent. If stocks chase earnings and investor sentiment (measured by the stock's PE ratio) is stable, then, in theory, Amazon's stock price also could go up by 20 percent over the next year. If our bold forecast of a 20 percent return in one year looks attractive, we might make Amazon a big part of the portfolio, perhaps 5 percent or more.[20] In this example, we've made a bold choice to go along with our bold forecast.

Our Amazon purchase might seem like a logical choice for someone who thinks that the stock is about to move up. However, in an ironic twist, Thaler explains that most people actually make *timid* choices to go along with their *bold* forecasts. An economic system of rewards and punishments in most companies leads many professionals to become risk averse or make timid choices. A bold decision that succeeds generally gets you a small reward, whereas a major flop will get you fired.[21] The Amazon bull is more likely to chicken out and buy a small position rather than a big one.

Interestingly, during the transition from investment thesis to trading, investors could make two mistakes that actually offset each other. If we make an overly bullish prediction for a stock, our second bias kicks in and hits the brakes as we benefit from a timid choice in purchasing the shares. This could be the only example in this book where our behavioral biases protect us from getting into even more trouble. As we transition from investment research to trading, we'll dig into the implications of our timid choices.

BEHAVIORAL COACHING TIP

Because many investors make bold forecasts and timid choices, try to make a realistic investment thesis. This should give you a better starting point as you move to the next phase of acting on your prediction.

Summary

- When writing an investment thesis, be aware that noise in the market can limit the strength of your thesis.

- Ask yourself if your investment thesis relies on an inside view, which can lead to bold or extreme forecasts. An outside view can nudge your thesis back toward reality.

- Be aware of the planning fallacy and consider the odds and consequences of your investment thesis. Are you hoping for the best-case outcome or a more realistic outcome? Does your thesis take an all-or-nothing approach, or are there several upside catalysts in case the planning fallacy impacts part of your investment thesis?

- When working on an investment thesis, consider whether you are overweighting unlikely events or underweighting more likely events.

- Vivid images can make us think that low-probability events are more likely as we develop an investment thesis.

- Think twice if your investment thesis requires some economic decision maker to meaningfully change his or her behavior.

- Conduct a pre-mortem as a way to flesh out any underappreciated risks or overly bullish projections.

- Develop a realistic investment thesis to avoid falling into the trap of bold forecasts and timid choices.

5

Decide on Timing and Sizing of Trade

Case Study: Salesforce.com

Salesforce.com (CRM), a software company developing tools for digital sales, service, and marketing.

———

What can investors learn from a Disney song? As a father who raised young kids during the 2010s, I've seen Disney's *Frozen* enough to memorize most of the lines. While most of the dialogue is lighthearted, one line that stuck out to me as I was writing this book was from the song "Fixer Upper" that talks about making bad decisions when you're angry, fearful, or stressed out. I think the song gives kids and adults some good advice about when and how to make good choices.

For adults working in groups, on tight deadlines, and dealing with major decisions, you can imagine colleagues who are mad, scared, and stressed out. Professional investors collaborating on investment and trading decisions could do well by heeding the "Fixer Upper" advice!

To this point, we've focused on the research and investment thesis that makes up the initial stages of the overall portfolio management process. However, we're now ready to transition from words to actions and go from individual research to group investment debates as we prepare for our initial trade.

Speaking of actions, this part of the investment process generally involves a healthy debate, perhaps between an analyst and a portfolio manager or among members of an investment committee.[1] Generally, these debates focus on a yes-or-no decision for a stock, as well as the timing and size of the purchase. These debates also can get spirited and emotional, potentially leading to decisions that we may regret.

The goal of this chapter is to identify emotional triggers that can take away from a healthy debate over a potential investment. Hopefully, these behavioral coaching tools can be a "Fixer Upper" for our portfolio and help structure a good debate over how much of a stock to buy and when to buy it.

Bold Forecasts and Timid Choices Part Two

In Chapter 4, we ended with a double bias in which we often think big but act small. As we transition from investment thesis to prepping for a trade, it's important to keep this double bias in mind. Hopefully, Chapter 4 has helped you to think *real* instead of big.

Ideally, a debate format can help to fight back against bold forecasts and timid choices, which often suffer from the inside view. A group of investment professionals can apply an outside view and expose flaws in the timing and size of a stock purchase or sale.

Let's say that an analyst is recommending Salesforce because she thinks the company will exceed Wall Street earnings estimates by 20 percent next year, a bold forecast. Additionally, let's imagine that the analyst is proposing that the firm buy a 1 percent position in Salesforce, a relatively timid choice[2] that may reflect concerns that Salesforce could have a higher risk/return profile than a more mature tech company such as Apple, Intel, or Cisco.

In this case, an investment committee can ask tough questions about the analyst's earnings projections to see if an outside view either supports or challenges the analyst's assumptions. If the committee's debate concludes that Salesforce might beat Wall Street estimates by say 10 percent, then a 1 percent holding in the portfolio might be more appropriate. However, if the analyst defends her arguments and the committee gets on board with high odds of a durable profit stream that exceeds Wall Street expectations, then the committee might recommend a bolder choice, such as a 2 percent or greater position size.

BEHAVIORAL COACHING TIP

If you have high conviction about an idea, make it a significant part of your portfolio, such as a weighting of 2 percent or more. This is where it's helpful for a committee to come in and apply the outside view and suggest potentially a higher weighting.

Uncomfortable Recommendations

The nail that sticks out gets hammered down.

—JAPANESE PROVERB

When I was in high school in the late 1980s and early 1990s, Japan seemed to be taking over the world as Japanese investors bought Rockefeller Center in New York and as the Nikkei nearly hit 40,000. As a young, ambitious person interested in business and finance, I decided to chase the "hot dot" by learning Japanese in college and studying abroad in Tokyo as a way of hitching a ride on Japan's long-term growth.

Why was I so confident that Japan's multidecade run would continue? Because the crowd said so. I followed the comfortable advice of economists and business reporters even as the Nikkei started falling and as emerging markets started rising. Looking back, perhaps I should have taken a contrarian view and made a less comfortable choice in language studies and plans for future career options.

So what does all of this have to do with pitching a stock to an investment committee? For one, chasing the hot dot can feel like a comfortable path, but it can often be the wrong one, as I learned the hard way by betting several years of my life that Japan would continue to be an attractive market. One of the things I observed while living in Japan was a homogeneous culture where locals often frown on straying too far from the crowd.

The Japanese proverb at the opening of this section hints at swift and painful consequences to being different. For investors, we often face similar pressures to follow the crowd. In this chapter, we'll continue to look at behavioral coaching tips that can help us avoid these emotional traps.

In the preceding section, we talked about a tendency for investors to make bold forecasts and timid choices. Ideally, such investors can leverage some of the benefits of taking an outside view, leading to a bold choice to go along with a bold forecast.

The preceding section also discussed an example where an investment committee embraced a risky stock idea, Salesforce, and went with either a low- or high-conviction weighting. However, in practice, committee debates over non-blue-chip stock recommendations can get quite spirited. In my experience, investment committees often struggle with adding new stocks to a portfolio when the new stock is less widely known or if risks seem greater than the average stock in the existing portfolio.

However, if you want to beat the market, you have to do something different, such as taking big positions in relatively smaller stocks, buying deep value, adding to a growth stock in the early innings,[3] or owning securities that are excluded from a market benchmark. Salesforce, for example, was about 1 percent of the S&P 500 in late 2020. If you owned a 5 percent position in CRM, and if the stock went up 20 percent in 2020 while the overall market went up 10 percent, your portfolio likely had a better chance of going up more than 10 percent, or beating the market.

Alternatively, you could own a non-blue-chip stock, such as an energy pipeline master limited partnership (MLP). The S&P 500 generally excludes MLPs. If your energy pipeline stock goes up more than 10 percent in 2020, then you have a better chance of beating the market.

The problem in my experience is that doing something different often means doing something uncomfortable. Howard Marks suggests that "all great investments begin in discomfort, since the things that everyone likes or feels good about are unlikely to be on the bargain counter."[4] You have to take on risk if you're trying to beat the market, and these risks can turn into lengthy and potentially uncomfortable debates in an investment committee.

Still, I would argue that the analyst or investment researcher owes it to clients to identify nonconsensus stocks that can help a portfolio meet or exceed market benchmarks. If the analyst goes with blue-chip stock recommendations and *hugs* the market index, it can be difficult to justify active management fees that are above passive index expenses.

Why do investment teams feel pressure to take the easy way out and favor comfortable recommendations? John Maynard Keynes said decades ago that "worldly wisdom teaches that it is better for reputation to fail conventionally than to succeed unconventionally."[5] Clients may criticize you more if you fail with an unusual tech investment compared with something well known such as IBM. Additionally, David Swenson, who managed Yale University's endowment, suggests that unconventional investing "requires acceptance of uncomfortably idiosyncratic portfolios, which frequently appear downright imprudent in the eyes of conventional wisdom."[6]

I would summarize these themes with the suggestion that a professional investor's job is to make uncomfortable recommendations and push back against the conventional wisdom. If our mandate is to meet or exceed a benchmark, then we need to try something unconventional. To be fair, we also need to flesh out the upside and downside risks of our uncomfortable recommendations as we may be getting into unchartered territory.

BEHAVIORAL COACHING TIP

Clients are paying for value-added research and portfolio management, which often means making bets that can be uncomfortable because they differ from the crowd. Today's unconventional stock recommendation can become tomorrow's blue chip.

Difficult Questions and Lazy Answers

At this point in the investment life cycle, we've done our homework on a stock, and we're prepared to debate the merits and risks of an initial purchase. The goal of this chapter is to sensitize investors to bias and emotions that can emerge during investment committee debates about the timing and size of the trade. For this section, we'll lean on Kahneman's System 1 (automatic or lazy) and System 2 (reflective and insightful) thinking models.

During investment committee discussions, I've noticed a pattern where difficult System 2 questions often lead to lazy System 1 answers. Frequently, the investment research person (usually an analyst) gets nervous or emotional after hearing a System 2 question, and he or she responds with a lazy or automatic System 1 answer. As you can imagine, this can lead to a dysfunctional debate where good questions linger unanswered. Investment committees might miss out on good buying opportunities or fail to dig up hidden risks.

Let's walk through an example of this difficult question, lazy answer pattern and try to figure out why people act like this. In 2016, my team was looking at buying Salesforce stock, but we had concerns about the company's acquisition strategy. Specifically, media reports speculated that Salesforce might buy Twitter (TWTR), a move that my committee viewed with caution. We felt that Twitter, a social media product, would distract Salesforce from its core business of developing sales, marketing, and service software.

The difficult question was, "Should we buy Salesforce stock now?" However, as the director of research, I was defending the idea, and I probably got nervous and shifted to System 1 thinking with my response. The correct answer to "Should we buy Salesforce now?" is a comprehensive approach to all the risks and merits of the business as well as a valuation analysis. Unfortunately, I got nervous, and my System 1 response was a narrow focus on concerns that Salesforce would overpay for Twitter.

We passed on Salesforce in 2016 because we believed that a Twitter acquisition would depress Salesforce shares. Unfortunately for us, the deal failed to materialize, and we missed out because Salesforce's share price doubled between 2016 and 2019 when we later made our first Salesforce purchase. Of course, the opposite could have happened, and we would have felt much better about our investment debate. The bottom line here is that all members of an investment committee should be vigilant for this pattern of difficult questions and lazy answers.

When discussing an investment idea, avoid the temptation to answer a difficult question with a lazy answer. Tough questions demand thorough answers, and this type of debate can help committees make better investment decisions.

Hunger and Bad Decisions

The line between hunger and anger is a thin line.
—JOHN STEINBECK, *THE GRAPES OF WRATH*

A local clergyman once told me that when people are hungry, angry, lonely, and tired, bad things happen. Connecting this story with the opening Steinbeck quote suggests that there might be a thin line between hunger and bad decisions.

Have you ever been grocery shopping on an empty stomach? Did you end up with any impulse purchases? Most people probably would answer yes. Even though picking groceries and picking stocks are two completely different kinds of purchases, hunger can lead to bad outcomes in both cases.

Why do people make bad decisions on an empty stomach? Kahneman relates a study of parole judges who tended to grant prisoners their freedom 65 percent of the time after a meal. However, within the two hours after eating, the judges granted parole less and less until it reached nearly zero just before their next meal or snack break.

Kahneman suggests that hungry (and probably tired) judges likely fell back on the easiest or default option of refusing to grant parole.[7] Perhaps the judges lacked the extra mental energy needed for focused System 2 thinking. For investors, the same pattern can play out.

If hungry decision makers prefer to take the easy way out, then investors might make the same mistake. Let's say that an investment committee is deciding between a consensus choice and a controversial option right before lunch. Hungry investors might default to an easier choice, such as recommending the sale of a loser or buying the crowd favorite, such as a blue-chip stock like Microsoft.

However, the better alternative, amid a chorus of growling stomachs, might be to eat something and then take more time to debate the risks and merits of each investment choice. Removing the emotions tied to hunger might allow more time to pick a less widely known stock, such as CRM, or hold onto an underperforming stock that has recovery prospects.

I generally recommend scheduling investment meetings, which may include some debates, after lunch, and this timing generally helps avoid the empty stomach, bad decision problem. However, if you anticipate a spirited debate, it may be best to schedule a meeting around mid-morning, say 10 a.m., when committee members are still sharp but not yet hungry for lunch.

BEHAVIORAL COACHING TIP

Be careful making investment decisions on an empty stomach. You usually default to the easiest option.

Halo Effect and Groupthink

Whenever you find yourself on the side of the majority, it's time to pause and reflect.

—MARK TWAIN

Mark Twain knew a lot about how people think and act. It may be a stretch, but Twain's quote seems like good advice for committees making important decisions. Kahneman suggests that one of the biggest problems with open discussions is that the group often falls in line with those who start the meeting with powerful and confident opinions.[8] Teams that fall into groupthink often lose the benefit of the *wisdom of crowds*, which requires lots of independent thinking.

When investors make group decisions, emotions and politics can enter the equation. Junior committee members might want to support the boss, whose idea can have a *halo effect*, potentially blocking out other ideas. Because most employees show respect and deference to the person signing their paycheck, a halo effect occurs when the team members favor the leader's ideas over other ideas.

A good way to avoid the halo effect and groupthink is for each member of an investment committee to write down his or her opinion about a potential trade ahead of a discussion. This extra step can provide a better diversity of insights and give junior committee members a way to save face during a debate.

For example, let's say that a junior analyst or portfolio manager thinks a controversial stock such as Salesforce is a buy and puts his opinion in writing ahead of a group meeting. This step allows the junior member to either stick with his initial buy recommendation or tell the committee that he originally favored a buy but after listening to the discussion now feels that a sell has more merit. I believe that this type of dynamic discussion can lead to better outcomes compared with a one-sided meeting where everyone *follows the leader*.

BEHAVIORAL COACHING TIP

Committee members should write down their opinions before discussing an issue, a move that avoids the halo effect and groupthink.

Basic Assessments

Know what you own.

—PETER LYNCH[9]

When investors think of Peter Lynch, a well-respected portfolio manager at Fidelity Investments, they often think about Lynch's idea of owning businesses that you understand. If you are shopping at the grocery store and find a new product that you think might be a big seller, perhaps you should buy the stock of the company making the product, for example. This creates a superficial investment process where *good company = good stock*.

But is stock picking really that easy? Kahneman might view the idea of good company = good stock as a *basic assessment* rather than an in-depth, rigorous System 2 approach to decision making. With casual (and sometimes lazy) System 1 thinking going on, we are almost like passive security cameras, watching the world go by without any specific goals or intentions.[10]

A basic assessment is like a passive radar system constantly evaluating what's going on internally and externally. When making big decisions, would you rather use a reactive approach or take a more pro-active and organized stance? Investment teams that pick stocks using basic assessments can run into trouble.

Investment firms often use committees to pull in a diverse group of resources and insights. Committees can include analysts with compre-hensive knowledge of a stock or industry as well as portfolio managers or strategists with a good sense of market cycles, themes, and changes in sentiment.

In my experience, efficient investment committees give equal air time to each member, allowing a diversity of opinions on the risks and merits of a potential trade. However, good committees require each member to acknowledge where his or her area of expertise begins and ends.

Analysts may know a company from soup to nuts but have a vague sense of market trends. In contrast, portfolio managers often have strong opinions about the big picture (markets and asset classes) but have less intimate knowledge of a particular company's financial state-ments, customers, competitors, or suppliers.

Using System 2 thinking, investment committee members can identify their own limitations and work with peers to fill the gaps. Analysts can avoid making market calls, and portfolio managers can realize when they are making a basic assessment of a stock rather than a comprehensive System 2 analysis.

With our Salesforce example, some investors might make a basic System 1 assessment by noting that a potential Salesforce–Twitter deal might get messy and depress growth for the combined company. However, a System 2 approach might look at probabilities of a bad deal as well as current valuations. A low Salesforce stock price might create an attractive risk/reward opportunity suggesting a modest downside if the deal goes through and a meaningful upside if Salesforce were to decide against buying Twitter.

BEHAVIORAL COACHING TIP

Investment committees should avoid making decisions that stem from a basic assessment of a company or stock. Take a more comprehensive System 2 approach to buy/hold/sell debates.

Probability Neglect

When we see a bad outcome, we often fall into a trap of thinking that something bad could happen at any time rather than thinking clearly about probabilities. If an airline delays our most recent flight, we might take a more pessimistic view toward all our future travel plans. A vivid image or experience can color our judgment about the frequency of bad outcomes.

Another behavioral economist, Cass Sunstein, discusses an experiment where participants had either a 1 percent chance or a 99 percent chance of suffering a "short, painful, but not dangerous shock."[11] The economic angle here is that the trial allowed participants to pay money to avoid the shock.

Perhaps surprisingly, the 1 percent group paid a median of $7 to avoid the pain, while the 99 percent group only coughed up $10. In other words the 1 percent group likely neglected to think about the probability of the painful shock. They felt willing to pay a relatively high price for protection from a relatively rare risk.

In a similar example, let's say that you had a 1 percent chance of missing your flight. What would you pay to guarantee that you made the flight and arrived at your destination on time? Would you pay $10? How about $1,000? What would you pay if there was a 50 percent chance of missing the flight?

Researchers suggest that when an "outcome triggers strong negative emotions, people tend not to think a whole lot about the issue of probability."[12] Kahneman refers to this pattern as *probability neglect*, where our level of concern becomes detached from the probability of danger.[13] We can also see probability neglect on the flip side, where people often succumb to glitzy marketing about favorable outcomes, such as winning the lottery, and neglect to consider the nearly impossible odds of winning.

For investment committees, probability neglect can lead to bad decisions. If investors overweight the probability of bad outcomes, they might miss out on an attractive risk/reward tradeoff. If bad outcomes are rare, then perhaps it's worth taking a chance on an investment.

In the Salesforce example, my committee was concerned that a Twitter acquisition would be a bad deal. A history of large, messy transactions, such as the AOL–Time Warner merger, likely focused our thoughts on the numerator (or number of bad deals).

However, a better approach would be to look more broadly at the denominator, which includes a list of good deals, bad transactions, and canceled mergers. If bad deals turn out to be a small percentage of both actual and speculated mergers, then buying Salesforce stock might be a better idea, especially if the stock is telling you that other investors expect a bad outcome from a Salesforce–Twitter merger.

BEHAVIORAL COACHING TIP

When looking at risks of a potential investment, avoid the risk of probability neglect and frame the debate in terms of a numerator (bad outcomes) and a denominator (all outcomes).

Rare Events

So you're telling me there's a chance?
—Jim Carey, *Dumb and Dumber*

The preceding two behavioral coaching tips focus on ways in which investors make sweeping generalizations about a company or stock rather than a comprehensive System 2 approach to risks and merits. Rare events present another variation on this theme of personal experiences coloring our judgment.

In the preceding section we talked about bad outcomes, such as a delayed flight or a bad acquisition. These events happen fairly frequently. However, what about rare events that can create an even more lasting impression on an investment decision maker? The problem for investors is that our brains struggle to process rare events.[14] Essentially, we tend to overweight a rare event that we have experienced while underweighting a rare event that we've yet to experience.

Employees owning shares of AIG, WorldCom, or Enron experienced a rare event when their sense of financial security went down the drain. These shell-shocked individuals might never buy company stock from a future employer, potentially missing out on attractive retirement benefits. For investment committees, personal experiences can lead to overweighting the probabilities of rare events and create unnecessary risk aversion.

Rare events also can have an opposite effect on people who have never experienced the event. Someone who's never run out of gas might feel just fine driving with a nearly empty tank. This lucky driver is underweighting the possibility that the gas light means that the car will come to a screeching halt before he or she can get to the closest gas station. In a similar way, investment committees can underweight rare events for personal reasons and risk becoming overly bullish.

In our Salesforce example, a team member experiencing a rare event, such as owning AOL Time Warner, might push harder against buying Salesforce by overstating the risk of a combination with Twitter. Alternatively, an investor who's never lost money due to a bad acquisition might be overly bullish on Salesforce and downplay any risk from a Salesforce–Twitter deal.

BEHAVIORAL COACHING TIP

Our experiences with rare events can lead investment committees to over- or underweight the probabilities of these events happening again. Take a broader perspective and try to frame the potential risk and reward of rare events.

Multiple Gambles

Many people may think of investing as a series of binary decisions. Should I buy or sell this stock? Yes or no? While there are many investment styles, research suggests that taking a broader view of multiple investment choices often produces better results.

Kahneman suggests that people become less risk averse when they consider multiple gambles. For equity investors, stocks have been a favorable bet for decades because annual total returns historically have been in the 8 to 10 percent range.[15] By looking at several investment bets at once, we can reduce the odds of losing by combining favorable gambles.[16]

Would you accept a coin toss bet where you win $100 on heads but lose $50 on tails? Many risk-averse people would pass because the pain of losing can be twice the joy of the gain. But what if you did this bet 10 times? Many people feel more comfortable when considering multiple favorable gambles. For investors, this pattern may allow portfolio managers, who often deal with multiple gambles, to stomach more risk than analysts, who generally focus on one stock at a time.

For investment committees, the idea of multiple gambles suggests mixing analysts and portfolio managers to help reduce loss aversion. However, translating the idea of multiple gambles into an investment process can be tricky because often the idea generators would rather look at binary decisions. As a former analyst, I'm guilty as charged here.

During the first 15 years of my investment career, I was an equity analyst covering industries such as healthcare, insurance, and technology. Analysts tend to go deep but focus on a small number of securities or potential gambles. Portfolio managers, in contrast, tend to look across a broader range of investment choices but stay at a high level.

In my experience, analysts tend to present investment committees with binary choices. Buy this stock or sell that stock. Fortunately, portfolio managers often come to the rescue and provide a greater perspective on different investment or trading options.

Using a hypothetical example, let's say that an investment team was struggling with buying a high-growth but expensive stock such as Salesforce. Rather than simply deciding to buy or sell Salesforce, a multiple-gamble approach might compare Salesforce with another growth stock such as Netflix.

If the investment committee thinks that both stocks are expensive but Salesforce looks relatively more attractive, the team could decide to sell Netflix now, raise cash, and then wait for a better buying opportunity on Salesforce, for example. At a minimum, multiple gambles help investors think in relative terms, perhaps leading to better decisions.

BEHAVIORAL COACHING TIP

Approach each investment decision from a broader perspective of multiple gambles rather than a binary buy/sell focus on one stock. In this way, you'll reduce the chances of becoming too risk averse by looking at one stock at a time.

Principal–Agent Alignment

The customer is always right.

—Harry Gordon Selfridge,
John Wanamaker, and Marshall Field

Professional investors provide a valuable customer service, threading the needle between risk and return so that clients can achieve their desired goals. However, professionals need to consider how bias and emotion can enter the equation because principals (customers) and agents (stock pickers) may have different incentives.

Tensions can rise in two areas. First, agents (professional managers) can act in their own self-interest and maximize their own welfare rather than putting their clients (principals) first. And second, principals and agents have an information asymmetry. Clients are unlikely to know everything that professional investors know.

How can professional investors be on the lookout for principal–agent misalignment? Professional stock pickers need to make sure that they have a good sense of their risk mandate, or how much risk their clients are comfortable with. When investment firms and savers are on the same page, stock pickers can find a sweet spot in terms of risk and reward.

However, when clients punish their investment managers for risks that fail to pay off, a wave of risk aversion can sweep over the stock-picking process, potentially leading to a vicious cycle of bad financial outcomes. Alternatively, professional investors might become risk averse and take the easy way out because they are worried about job security. Picking mainstream stocks might be easy, but it can also lead to disappointing performance for clients.

Richard Thaler suggests that one way of encouraging principal–agent alignment is to create a framework where principals will reward agents for taking the right amount of risk with information available at the time of the decision even if the decision turns out to lose money after the fact.[17] One way of creating this framework is to establish a risk framework with new clients. Strategies that segment clients into higher and lower risk groups can create better principal–agent alignment so that professional investors know what kinds of stocks they should be researching and buying.

In this chapter we've talked about the purchase decision for a high-growth company, Salesforce. My investment process generally takes a multiyear approach, which can allow short-term choppiness from higher risk/return stocks such as Salesforce. This process tends to have a good fit with clients seeking long-term performance knowing that there may be near-term volatility.

A good way to create and maintain this principal–agent alignment is to consistently run a diversified portfolio where lower-risk stocks can balance out riskier investments. This can create a virtuous cycle where clients feel comfortable even if a risky stock underperforms the market because they know that the overall portfolio generally will still be intact.

BEHAVIORAL COACHING TIP

Investment firms should have an open dialogue with clients about risk taking. When investment professionals and clients see eye to eye, stock pickers can take an appropriate level of risk without fear of punishment if the risk fails to pay off.

Risk Aversion in Group Settings

In the 1980s song "Every Breath You Take" from The Police, Sting describes watching someone very closely, noticing every time they breathe and every word they say. How do you think most people act when others are watching them *very* closely? Because investing is all about risk taking, we can take this question further to see if investors have the same approach to risk in public as they do in private.

You might think that some Wall Street types crave the spotlight because they show off their stock-picking skills in a group setting. However, it's more likely that professional investors follow the opposite pattern and become more risk averse in public than in private.

Game shows can be a good way to test how people take on risk in public settings, according to Richard Thaler. In one study, a group of students played a simulated game show but made "private decisions on a computer in a laboratory."[18] In contrast, another group of students made decisions in front of a crowd, and this second group showed much more risk aversion.

In my experience, investors also take a more risk-averse approach when, after every word you say, a full table of people are watching you. Going back to our Salesforce example, my team may have become more risk averse as we made a group purchase decision. My committee publicly debated a fear that the Salesforce CEO was becoming an empire builder, and this concern may have created a risk aversion that played into our decision to pass on the stock.

BEHAVIORAL COACHING TIP

Because investors can become risk averse in public settings, consider a smaller prep session before you get to a larger committee meeting. In this way, a smaller group may feel less risk aversion relative to the broader group.

Encourage Open Debates Without Fear of Punishment

In the movie *Glengarry Glen Ross*, Alec Baldwin plays a hard-charging sales manager who tells his team of underlings that prizes for an upcoming sales contest include a new Cadillac for first place, some steak knives for the runner-up, and in third place, you get fired. In this high-pressure sales culture, the boss loves winners and hates losers.

As you can imagine, these love/hate emotions can lead to bad business decisions that help the salesperson at the expense of customers, employees, and the firm. In the investment business, a culture of fear also can lead to a dysfunctional investment process.

This chapter is all about setting an investment committee up for success by avoiding emotions, biases, and System 1 thinking, which can lead to bad investment decisions. As we wrap up this chapter, we focus on leadership and culture for investment committees as a way of improving the odds of outperformance.

Richard Thaler recommends that businesses create a culture that's the complete opposite of the toxic emotions we see in *Glengarry Glen Ross*. When employees "feel that making evidence-based decisions will always be rewarded," regardless of the outcome, firms can increase "the flow of new ideas" and reduce "the risk of disasters."[19] Thaler encourages managers to create a professional setting where workers "observe, take data and speak up,"[20] without fear of getting penalized.

In my opinion, these four factors can create a virtuous cycle, especially for professional investors debating buy and sell decisions. The critical issue for avoiding a toxic decision-making process, in my view, is establishing a level of trust among investment team members.

Investment researchers start the process by observing, taking data, and creating a compelling case for buying or selling a stock. Earlier in this chapter, we argued that investment analysts or researchers often make controversial recommendations. Putting these pieces together, a stock picker needs to know that he or she can come to the table with an uncomfortable recommendation without fear of retaliation.

Trust goes both ways, however, because other senior members of an investment team also need to believe that the researcher did the proper due diligence (observing and taking data). Highly functional investment teams, in my experience, have both hard-working data-gathering researchers and trusting committee members who are prepared to discuss controversial stock ideas without threats of penalty.

When my team looked at buying Salesforce a few years ago, I was fortunate to have a level of trust between the research side and the rest of the committee. I made my case for buying Salesforce after observing and analyzing data, and while the other members of the team respected my analysis, they decided that an expensive purchase of Twitter might take Salesforce stock down. I spoke up and respectfully disagreed with the rest of the team, without fear of penalty, and the majority still decided to avoid purchasing Salesforce. The level of trust on both sides allowed my team to agree to disagree and move on to other stock ideas.

BEHAVIORAL COACHING TIP

Senior members of investment teams should encourage a level of trust that allows researchers to observe, take data, and speak up without fear of penalty.

Summary

- Many investors make bold forecasts and timid choices. Leverage an investment committee to help decide if a bold forecast is realistic, and if it is, go for a bold choice (2 percent or greater position size) rather than a timid choice (less than a 2 percent weighting, for example).

- A professional stock picker's job is to make emotionally uncomfortable recommendations on both the buy and sell sides. Thorough due diligence and a coherent investment thesis can give stock pickers greater conviction as they debate nonconsensus recommendations with an investment committee.

- Investment committees should watch out for difficult questions that lead to lazy answers. Encourage a healthy debate with System 2 thinking for both questions and answers.

- Avoid investment committee meetings right before a meal, such as lunch, because hunger may lead members to an easier decision rather than the best decision.

- Better debates often stem from independent thoughts. Writing down buy, hold, or sell recommendations before an investment committee vote can reduce groupthink and the halo effect.

- Investment decision makers should avoid relying on basic assessments. Companies and stocks are complex and require a good System 2 analysis ahead of a buy or sell decision.

- Some investment committees focus on risks and pass on potentially attractive investments through probability neglect. A better approach is to frame a numerator of bad outcomes relative to a denominator of all outcomes.

- Investors may overweight the probability of rare events if they have personal experiences with these types of events and vice versa if they've never experienced a rare event. Ideally, investment committees should frame rare events relative to more likely events as they make buy and sell decisions.

- Avoid making binary buy/sell decisions. Consider multiple gambles as a way of comparing different investment options.

- Try to establish a good alignment between stock pickers and clients on risk tolerance. Professional investors need the freedom to take on some risk without worrying that clients will punish them if the risks fail to pan out.

- Consider debating investment decisions in small groups. Larger groups are more likely to become risk averse.

- Encourage investment researchers to observe, take data, and speak up during team meetings without fear of punishment.

6

Make Initial
Purchase

*Time in the market is more important than
timing the market.*

—WALL STREET ADAGE

A t this point in the investment life cycle, it's
time to stop talking and start trading. We've
done a lot of System 2 thinking to get us to
the point where we know what stock we're buying,
when, and how much. The actual trade should be
the easy part, right? It depends. Unfortunately for
many stock pickers, and most decision makers for
that matter, when the rubber hits the road, we often
hesitate and second guess our decisions on timing.

This chapter walks through some of the mental pitfalls that can make investors look like deer
in the headlights before they hit the "buy" button. Fortunately for those reading this book, we
can anticipate some of these barriers to getting a
trade done and perhaps become more efficient in
the overall investment process. By getting the trade
done, we can own a stock for a long time (time in
the market), which often rewards investors more
than trying to time the market perfectly.

Mild Procrastination

Done is better than perfect.

—POPULAR MOTTO AT FACEBOOK[1]

This quote comes from a poster at a Facebook office, and I think it summarizes the company's views of procrastination. If you've seen the movie *The Social Network*, you'll know that Mark Zuckerberg and his team worked their tails off to start the company. If Zuckerberg waited for everything to be perfect, the fortunes of Facebook and early rival MySpace might have been reversed.

We start out this chapter with some good news and some bad news. The good news is that many investors only suffer from a mild form of procrastination before an initial trade. The bad news? In my experience, emotions and biases can lead to more delays when trading around existing holdings as well as a final sale. But because we are on the topic of procrastination, we'll discuss the bad news later.[2]

Let's talk about why investors might face a mild form of procrastination ahead of an initial purchase. In my experience, investors may feel confident in knowing what stock to buy and how much to purchase, but then the confidence melts away as procrastination sinks in. Investors may decide to wait for the stars to align perfectly before getting the trade done.

We'll get into some behavioral reasons for procrastination next, but first an example. In mid-2007, as the housing bubble was starting to pop and the stock market was approaching a prerecession high, I recommended that my team buy a medical device company called Covidien.

Early tremors from the great financial crisis earthquake started in August 2007 as markets fell 9 percent in six weeks. Investor fears rose as big funds (such as BNP Paribas) halted withdrawals, and insurer AIG projected that risky subprime mortgage delinquencies were spreading to safer prime borrowers. In the middle of these prerecession jitters, my team asked if I was sure I wanted to buy Covidien now.

A mild form of procrastination started to set in. Should we wait for markets to dip and then buy the stock at a lower price? Or if the economy and markets seemed headed for a downturn, perhaps we should start buying defensive stocks, such as a utility?

We decided to buy Covidien in August 2007, and while it was a bumpy initial ride, the stock ended up outperforming broader markets over a number of years. Overcoming procrastination bias can be challenging, but my experience with Covidien and other stocks suggests doing your work and moving ahead with action steps.

BEHAVIORAL COACHING TIP

Often a mild form of procrastination can kick in and delay your initial purchase. However, if you've done your work on a stock and your team is ready to buy, go ahead and make the trade because, historically, time in the market offsets trying to time the market perfectly.

Opportunity Costs

In the movie *Jerry Maguire*, Tom Cruise's character, a sports agent, is trying to get his client, Rod Tidwell, played by Cuba Gooding Jr. to make a big decision and sign a contract. Tidwell is sick of waiting and screams to his agent on the phone that he wants to see the money before signing on the dotted line.

In a similar way, we just made an argument that many investors get stuck waiting for the perfect time to buy a stock rather than plowing ahead and taking action. A behavioral finance theme that may be triggering this procrastination is the idea of *opportunity cost*. Essentially, are you going to wait for a better deal or, as in the movie *Jerry Maguire*, are you going to stop waiting and make a trade?

When we make financial decisions and choose option A, we often give up the opportunity of choosing option B, especially when there are budget constraints. Decision makers might ask themselves: Should I take Uber or the subway? Should I buy my ticket now or wait to see if prices come down? Should I buy a cheap, beaten-up stock? Or should I pay up for a high-growth stock that keeps rising?

For many investors, the mental gymnastics of choosing between stock A and stock B can become a vague and abstract exercise "compared to handing over actual cash."[3] While we are debating stock A versus stock B, there is a vague and abstract opportunity cost because we have yet to make a purchase. However, after we pay $10,000 to buy stock A, we get immediate and quantifiable feedback on our action, as well as what that $10,000 would have done if we bought stock B.

Going back to the Covidien example, my team decided to fork over actual cash and take an initial position in the face of choppy pre-recession markets. As discussed earlier, we had a vague and abstract sense that all stocks might decline ahead of a broader downturn.

The opportunity cost of waiting to buy Covidien is that the stock might go up, and we would have to buy at a higher price. In our case, we were wrong in the short term, but we made the right decision over the long haul.

Covidien fell nearly 10 percent between August and December of 2007, worse than the overall market. However, the stock came roaring back and more than tripled on improving growth and after Medtronic bought the company for a premium in 2015. By comparison, broader markets rose about 60 percent between August 2007 and early 2015.

If vague and abstract opportunity costs can delay our initial purchases, what are some ways to avoid these pitfalls? In my experience, cold, hard facts, data, and analysis can remove some of the mystery that may surround these opportunity costs. Going back to 2007, a scenario analysis might help an investment committee consider the upside and downside of buying Covidien immediately, buying it later, buying something else, or just sitting on cash ahead of a potential downturn.

BEHAVIORAL COACHING TIP

Investors often struggle with vague and abstract opportunity costs as they approach initial stock purchases. Data and analysis can help investors quantify these opportunity costs, perhaps allowing greater confidence in handing over real cash for an investment.

Outside Lag and Portfolio Impact

In Chapter 2 we discussed the idea of an inside lag, or a delay in recognizing a potentially attractive investment. Now that we've picked our stock and we're ready to trade, we also need to be mindful of the opposite effect, an *outside lag*.

In a way, the outside lag effect is pretty straightforward. If you think that a stock is going up, better to buy it now because it may take some time for the new stock to help lift the overall portfolio. If you have a good stock idea and you wait, it will get tougher to drive performance as cash weighs down the portfolio.

Let's say that an investment theme will play out like a baseball game, over nine innings. You may waste the first two innings figuring out the theme (inside lag), and then if you keep waiting a few more innings to buy the stock (outside lag), you will miss out on the bulk of the investment opportunity.

As investors think about timing of initial purchases, it's important to remember the compounding effects of both the inside and outside lags. In essence, most investors will experience a delay as they recognize a favorable business trend. Then we may see an additional delay in portfolio impact as we make an initial purchase.

Let's use the Covidien case as an example of both the inside and outside lags. Covidien is a bit of a special case because the company spun out of Tyco, a diversified parent company, so the clock started ticking on a possible inside lag once Covidien fully exited Tyco in 2007.

I started my due-diligence process ahead of the spinoff to help reduce the risk of an inside lag, and we bought right away to try to avoid an outside lag. As mentioned earlier, Covidien took an initial dive after we bought it, but the stock rose into the final Medtronic acquisition price, adding to overall client portfolio performance. While I've had plenty of stocks go the other way, in this case the early research and purchase helped my team avoid the pitfalls of inside and outside lags.

BEHAVIORAL COACHING TIP

If a stock has the potential to outperform, say going from $50 to $100, investors should keep in mind that inside and outside lags will take away from the potential upside to our portfolio. The stock might run from $50 to $60 before we can complete our research. Then the stock might run from $60 to $70 before we can agree on timing and size of our purchase. If we still like the stock, we should avoid further delays and buy it at $70 so that it can impact portfolios on its way to our $100 target price.

Summary

- Avoid mild procrastination after you've picked a stock and settled on a portfolio weighting. Waiting for the perfect time generally leads to disappointing outcomes in my experience.

- Data and analysis can help investors gain confidence in making an initial purchase. Otherwise, vague and abstract opportunity costs may cloud our judgment as we prepare to hand over cash for a new investment.

- Inside and outside lags create challenges for decision making and results. Knowing that these lags exist, investors should avoid additional delays when prepared to make initial purchases.

7

Analyze Early Results and Stock Movement

And they're off!

At this point in the investment life cycle, we've done our work and taken the plunge by forking over cash to buy a stock. Now what? Should we expect the stock to go straight up? What if the market declines or the stock has some bad news right out of the gate? Did we make a mistake? Should we cut our losses before it gets worse?

Unfortunately, behavioral finance theories are unlikely to help us answer all these questions. However, some behavioral coaching tips might reduce our anxiety and help us frame the next step in the investment life cycle.

In my experience, there is a learning curve for investors who own individual stocks for a number of years. This pattern suggests that investors know less about a stock at the beginning of the investment life cycle. If we are less knowledgeable about a stock and we get disappointing results after an initial purchase, we might be more willing to just sell and walk away.

The goal of this chapter is to help investors take a System 2 approach to dealing with a stock that goes down shortly after purchase. Perhaps these behavioral coaching tips can help you to hold onto stocks that had a rocky start in a portfolio.

On a side note, if your stock trades up nicely in the days and weeks after your first purchase, you can skip this chapter and move on to Chapter 8. However, if your luck is like mine, you may see some initial choppiness once you become a new owner of a stock, and this chapter may help you avoid selling too early or at a loss. Even if your stocks are up, reading this chapter may better prepare you for potential declines on the next stock you're reviewing.

Why Is the Stock Moving?

> *Adversity does not build character, it reveals it.*
> —Southwest Airlines CEO Gary Kelly[1]

Sometimes running an airline might feel like managing a stock portfolio. Between 2019 and 2020, Southwest dealt with the loss of its founder, a government shutdown, violent weather, the grounding of the Boeing 737 Max, and a nearly total collapse in travel demand amid the COVID-19 pandemic. As Southwest managed through these challenges, investors also had to deal with what to buy and sell amid market volatility and big moves in portfolio holdings.

Gary Kelly's opening quote suggests to me that investors have the ability to make good decisions even during bad times. However, I would argue that behavioral coaching can increase the odds of maintaining your character during difficult periods.

Speaking of coaching, if you're still reading this chapter, congratulations! All the work you put into researching and buying the perfect stock may have led to a disappointing initial investment. All kidding aside, frequently a volatile market or an ugly news headline can take down a stock right after you buy it.

Continuing with the coaching analogy, when a sports team starts losing, it's up to the coach to first figure out what's wrong before making changes in personnel or strategy. The same approach applies in investing. So let's figure out why our stock is underperforming before we consider any additional buying or selling strategies.

Although most of this chapter focuses on understanding why a stock is down, we can generalize the question for a stock that's made a big move up or down. Howard Marks believes that investor emotions fuel a boom/bust market cycle for stocks because "the most optimistic psychology is always applied when things are thought to be going well, compounding and exaggerating the positives, and the most depressed psychology is applied when things are going poorly, compounding the negatives."[2]

Perhaps we can apply this idea of a market cycle as we try to understand why our stock is down. Marks suggests that market psychology careens from "flawless to hopeless" rather than a more realistic middle ground where stocks are either "pretty good or not so hot."[3] If our stock is going through a rough patch and we are thinking about selling, we can avoid meaningful losses by waiting for a stock to trade from hopeless to not so hot.

Problem Solving Versus Problem Finding

Don't listen to the person who has the answers; listen to the person who has the questions.

—Albert Einstein

Are you a know-it-all or a learn-it-all? In the business world, we hear a lot about confident problem solvers who can swoop in and save the day as a company flirts with disaster. However, the idea of problem solving rests on a notion that we actually know what the problem is. Perhaps the problem solver is a know-it-all. However, sometimes the most important task is problem finding, which might be a better for a learn-it-all.

If you buy a stock and it goes down, do you need to solve a problem or find a problem? An emotional (System 1) response might quickly decide that the stock pick was a mistake and that the best way to solve the problem is to sell the stock. However, a more nuanced, System 2 approach might take a deep breath and try to understand the problems causing the stock to disappoint.

So what's the best way to start our problem-finding mission? We have to go back to two themes we've discussed previously: the economic web of bias and System 2 due diligence.

Back to the Economic Web of Bias

The economic web of bias comes into play here as we ask questions and interpret why our stock is down. Is a presidential candidate making a campaign promise to take on big business, even if the threat is unlikely to become law? Why is the media making a big deal of a declining stock on a slow news day?[4] Is a CEO doing a major acquisition to build an empire? Could an industry expert make a controversial forecast as a way to gain publicity?

As we become more aware of the potential biases, the next step is to consider some meaningful due diligence. Going to a conference, picking up the phone and speaking to experts, and analyzing additional data can help us to better understand what's really dragging a stock down.

An example may help to illustrate these themes. In June 2013, I recommended that my team buy shares in Allergan, which at the time was a specialty drug company that sold Botox for wrinkles and Restasis for dry eye. Within a week of the purchase, Allergan stock gapped down 12 percent on news that generic versions of Restasis, which made up about 15 percent of Allergan's profits, might launch sooner than investors expected.

In this case, the economic web of bias was less powerful because a new risk emerged that had a clear potential impact on Allergan's growth potential. However, let's say hypothetically that a government leader called out Allergan's dry-eyes drug for being too expensive, sending the stock down. In this scenario, we should try to consider any potential bias behind the government leader's statements.

Another Round of System 2 Due Diligence

Time to go back to the drawing board and do some problem finding. System 2 due diligence might help us understand if Allergan investors are too bullish or bearish on the generic Restasis competition. In this case, we could consider speaking with legal experts to gauge the probability of a generic entry or speak to medical groups to see if doctors would be comfortable prescribing the generic form of the drug.

After peeling back the economic web of bias and doing some extra due diligence, we can get a better sense of why the stock is down. What's more, we can potentially get an initial sense of whether investors have become too pessimistic on the stock. Once we really know what's taking the stock down, we can tie this back to our investment thesis.

BEHAVIORAL COACHING TIP

If you buy a stock and it starts to go down, hit the pause button and first try to peel back any external biases that might be twisting the story of why the stock disappointed. Then engage in some System 2 due diligence and work with experts and data to really dig into why the stock is down. This approach will help you as you consider buy, hold, or sell strategies next.

The Availability Cascade

We could talk ourselves into a recession.
—Tom Barkin, President of the
Federal Reserve Bank of Richmond[5]

In the preceding section we cautioned investors to be wary of the economic web of bias when diagnosing the reason for a stock's decline. A special case within this web of bias is a feedback loop where the media may overreact to a relatively minor problem, triggering a stock selloff, which attracts more media attention, and so on. Kahneman describes this vicious cycle as an *availability cascade* where decision makers judge the importance of an idea by how quickly and emotionally the idea enters our thinking.[6]

If your stock is down in sympathy with broader market or sector issues, you could be looking at an availability cascade. This may be especially true if your stock has improving fundamentals, but other stocks in the industry are suffering slower growth, market-share loss, or lower profitability. An availability cascade can temporarily obscure winners and losers in an industry.

A few examples may better clarify how an availability cascade can depress stock valuations. The opening quote gives an example of a potential availability cascade as seen by a central banker. Tom Barkin suggested that a growing narrative about a looming recession could lead to uncertainty that could then depress consumer confidence and spending.[7] Talk of a recession might trigger one.

We could imagine a similar pattern in the transportation sector, where the availability of information creates a cascade that influences decision makers. During an industry conference, a railroad executive might feel surrounded by competitors making pessimistic comments about their current volume and pricing trends. If the media headline from the trade show said something like "Rail Executives See Downturn Ahead," that could trigger other decision makers to cut back on economic activity, potentially hastening a recession.

This railroad example focuses on a broader availability cascade across the economy, but we can also see more targeted examples, such as the situation with Allergan's generic dry-eyes drug. If the media framed Allergan's generic drug risk as part of a broader industry trend, then investors might become more concerned and perhaps sell shares in Allergan and other branded drug makers. A big decline in these healthcare stocks could trigger another wave of unfavorable media reports and additional selling.

While these railroad and pharmaceutical examples are somewhat hypothetical, we can also see an availability cascade in the tobacco industry in 2019. Amid a spike in underage use of e-cigarettes, emerging media reports suggested an association between vaping and deaths from unusual lung injuries. These data points led to regulatory restrictions on vaping companies such as Juul Labs.

The cascade continued as shares in Altria, which owns a large stake in Juul, also declined as the deaths mounted and the news cycle worsened. By the end of 2019, scientists were unable to confirm whether tobacco vaping actually triggered the lung injuries and deaths. However, this availability cascade led to disappointing results for Altria shareholders.

BEHAVIORAL COACHING TIP

If your stock declines and you read lots of unfavorable media headlines associated with the selloff, be aware that an availability cascade may be impacting investor sentiment and the stock price. As discussed in the preceding section, some System 2 due diligence may help you separate media hype from reality as you consider your next move with the stock.

Loss Aversion

This may hurt a little.
—WHAT MY DOCTOR SAID BEFORE GIVING ME A FLU SHOT

The preceding two sections focused externally on what factors are driving a stock into the red. Now let's turn inward and examine our responses to these financial disappointments and losses. The next three sections build on our emotional reactions to economic losses, such as a stock that's declining. Hopefully, we can try to manage our emotions around losses and make rational investment decisions backed up by research, data, and analysis.

Kahneman describes *loss aversion* as the pain of small losses being worse than the pleasure of small gains.[8] A simple example of loss aversion is the pain we feel after losing a dollar in a contest relative to the joy we feel if we win a dollar. In fact, Kahneman and other researchers have quantified this ratio and believe that most people feel about twice as much pain from losses as they do joy for equivalent gains.[9]

If we apply this concept to investing, we might find that researchers (analysts) and portfolio managers who look at prices too much also may suffer loss aversion. If we looked at 100 days of stock trading, we might have a few more up days, relative to down days, say 60 days in the green and 40 days in the red.[10] If investors look at prices every day, then they should be happy for 60 days and sad for 40. However, if loss aversion kicks in, the 40 down days will outweigh the 60 good ones, based on Kahneman's two-to-one ratio for loss pain versus the joy of gains.

So what can investors do about loss aversion? Be prepared. After an initial purchase, if your stock goes down, preparing for the pain of a loss might help you to gather your thoughts more calmly. With better preparation, you can reduce the emotions and biases that might prevent you from moving on to the next step of doing more analysis and considering your next buy, hold, or sell strategy.

Using a healthcare analogy, we can think about this idea of preparing for an uncomfortable or painful sensation. If we compare the pain of losing money to actual physical pain, we can think about medical professionals who try to calm our emotions before a procedure. If a doctor prepares us by saying that a flu shot may hurt a little, sometimes the actual injection pain is less than we expected. Perhaps this preparation can help investors who see lots of red on their screens.

Going back to our Allergan example, the stock decline on rising generic competition triggered an emotional response from my team. We just spent time discussing the purchase, and then we bought the stock right before a big gap down. Loss aversion was alive and well for my team, but luckily for us we decided to hold on, despite the initial disappointment. Another drug company called Actavis later acquired Allergan, sending the stock well above our purchase price.

BEHAVIORAL COACHING TIP

Right before you buy a stock, be prepared to feel the emotions of loss aversion in case the stock drops. Anticipating this type of emotional reaction may help you to more rationally move on to the next steps in the investment life cycle.

Myopic Loss Aversion

The preceding section focused on the pain we feel from losses in general, but investors often can suffer additional anguish by taking a short-sighted approach to recent equity losses. This *myopic loss aversion*[11] can compound the effect of recent losses.

Richard Thaler describes experiments that control how frequently investors observed performance and then looked at how risky or cautious those investors became. As you might imagine, checking your portfolio frequently exposes you to the brutal volatility of short-term market movements. However, investors refraining from an obsession with short-term performance actually felt more confident taking on more risky holdings.[12]

There are a couple of ways to handle myopic loss aversion. If your stocks or overall markets are creeping lower day after day, consider turning off your screen to avoid seeing intraday price movements. If markets are in a rough patch and heavy selling pressure is driving equities lower, perhaps take the high road and abstain from looking at your portfolio's results for a few days. Alternatively, you can create a risk policy, such as a procedural rule that you will avoid selling when the market (or stock) declines a certain percentage, say 5 or 10 percent.

In our Allergan example, we might have felt even more pain from the gap down in the stock if we spent time staring at other stocks that declined that day. One way to reduce the emotional pain of the Allergan decline would have been to shut off the screen and start digging into what drove Allergan's underperformance.

Myopic Loss Aversion and Framing

Attitude . . . is a choice.

—PAT SUMMITT[13]

Pat Summitt coached the University of Tennessee women's basketball team for decades and retired with the most wins in college basketball history. Her comment on attitude is a good fit for basketball players dealing with ups and downs during the season but also for investors managing through stock market ups and downs. If you're in the dumps because of a recent loss, consider reframing your attitude and getting back out there.

Our final stop on this journey is a focus on how to frame our emotional response to losses. Our earlier example suggested that stocks might go up 60 percent of the time and down on 40 percent of trading days. We argued that if we stare at our screens every day, the pain of losses would more than offset the pleasure of up days.

However, what if we try to bring in a different frame for the problem of myopic loss aversion? Instead of looking at daily ups and downs, perhaps we can take the long view and look back over decades or even look ahead toward our long-term financial goals as a way of putting near-term volatility in perspective.

If your stock has been around for a while, consider pulling up one or two decades' worth of average annual returns. If your stock has generally performed at or above the broader market for a number of years, this perspective may reduce the pain of a short-term loss after an initial purchase. If your stock has a shorter trading history, consider looking at longer-term results from similar companies in the same industry.

The main point here is that stocks historically go up alongside corporate profits. Frame your recent losses as a minor detour from a fairly consistent path upward. To be fair, you can also take a recent loss as an opportunity to revisit and test your investment thesis. Are the recent losses a minor detour or a major deviation?

Another approach to myopic loss aversion and framing comes from Thaler, who suggests looking way ahead rather than looking backward. Thaler suggests that investors who look at annual stock results will be risk averse, but those who look at 30-year forward expected returns may have better results.[14] Thaler's views suggest that a multi-decade time horizon can help optimize risk and return. In my opinion, this long-term forward view may help investors avoid emotional selling after an initial decline.

When Allergan declined just after we bought it, it would have been easy to consider retreating and exiting the position. However, framing the situation over Allergan's history would bring up other examples of the company overcoming challenges, such as potential competition for Botox. What's more, a broader frame would demonstrate Allergan's consistent annual earnings growth that helped drive attractive stock performance for years. Looking ahead, we could argue that Botox's barriers to entry could drive durable growth for Allergan a decade or more. This favorable view on long-term fundamentals may help investors avoid the urge to sell after the slightest disappointment.

BEHAVIORAL COACHING TIP

Investors can push back against a tendency to get emotional after initial losses by broadening the frame beyond daily stock movements. Ten or more years of historical results can give investors confidence in longer-term trends for a stock. Additionally, looking ahead at expected results over decades can reduce the urge to sell a stock that's just dropped.

Optimism and Setbacks

We cannot change the cards we are dealt, just how we play the hand.

—RANDY PAUSCH[15]

If most of this chapter has felt like a root canal, cheer up! We're about to talk about how optimism can help overcome some of the natural tendencies to get down on ourselves after a disappointment, in this case a stock decline.

Whether it's playing cards, investing, or dealing with the complications of modern life, we often have to pick ourselves up after disappointments. When my son Andrew was 14, he showed me how people can take an optimistic approach despite a string of setbacks. During the COVID-19 pandemic and lockdowns of early 2020, Andrew decided that he wanted a *quarantine puppy*. I told him that our home needed a gate before we could get a dog, so he spent several weeks building one by himself. Andrew suffered many setbacks during the gate construction, but he had grit and showed me a memorable example of optimism and reaching your goals.

Kahneman suggests that optimists are generally resilient in the face of setbacks,[16] and I saw that in my son's gate project. For investors, I would argue that a healthy dose of optimism can help in responding to initial losses after a purchase. Optimism and confidence may overlap a bit here, reading into Howard Marks's suggestion that it "requires confidence to hold onto a position when it declines—and perhaps add to it at lower prices—in the period before one's wisdom becomes clear and it turns into a winner."[17]

Another well-known behavioral economist, Dan Ariely, suggests that optimists and pessimists focus on different things. Pessimists might feel "overwhelmed by the magnitude of problems that seem impossible to solve."[18] However, optimists focus on things they can change and progress they've made toward current and future goals. With a sense of hope, optimists "strive for goals that are attainable, know the pathway to achieving those goals,"[19] and take actions needed to reach their objectives.

How can we apply Ariely's comments to dealing with a poor initial investment? Here are some ideas:

1. **Have a sense of hope.** Because stocks have historically increased well above inflation, our diversified portfolio, including the recent disappointment, should also exceed inflation over time.

2. **Focus on the progress you've made.** Consider reviewing your portfolio's historical performance (but avoid anchoring). Even if you have trailed the broader market, you're likely well ahead of inflation.

3. **Strive for reasonable goals.** Managing a diversified portfolio can help winners offset losers, such as the stock you just bought.

4. **Know the pathway to reach those goals.** Try to own at least 30 stocks in a portfolio and also use behavioral coaching recommendations to help reduce mistakes.

5. **Take positive actions to get there.** If you have a highly concentrated portfolio, add some diversification. If the stock you just bought has declined, review your investment thesis and look ahead to the upside and downside scenarios. If the investment thesis failed and you see more downside than upside, sell and move on to other new stock ideas. Alternatively, if your investment thesis still holds and you see more reward than risk, hold onto your stock.

If we go back to the Allergan example, it would have been easy to become pessimistic after the initial 12 percent drop in the stock. However, I was lucky to have a dose of optimism back in June of 2013, and I decided to reduce the emotional impact of the loss by calmly reviewing my investment thesis and considering upside and downside scenarios.

I came away thinking that Allergan was more likely to go up than down, and I maintained my position in the shares. Essentially, I saw the 12 percent stock drop as a signal that investors expected nearly a 100 percent chance that Allergan's Restasis sales would drop to zero. However, I also believed that Allergan's legal maneuvers could delay competition, allowing Allergan to switch patients to a new version of its drug. If either of these options succeeded, Allergan's revenues likely would exceed investor expectations and drive the stock higher.

If a recent stock decline gets you down, run through Ariely's five steps. Pat yourself on the back for what you've already accomplished, stay diversified, and look at future risk and reward potential for the stock that's having challenges.

Summary

- If your initial stock purchase declines, try to look through the economic web of bias to figure out why the stock is off. Next, try to confirm your views through System 2 due diligence.

- Unflattering media attention can trigger waves of selling as part of an availability cascade. Additional System 2 due diligence can help dissect the actual reasons for the stock's decline.

- Be prepared to feel worse about losses relative to the satisfaction you feel about gains of a similar magnitude. Good preparation can help you to avoid making a rash, emotional decision after an initial decline in a stock you've just purchased.

- Short-term, or myopic, loss aversion can create emotional swings if your stock declines after an initial purchase. Turning off your screen or setting a risk policy may lead to better decisions coming out of the stock's downturn.

- Framing myopic loss aversion can be a way to reduce emotional ups and downs after a stock takes a dip. Consider looking at multiple years of historical results for your stock as a reality check or look ahead at longer-term financial goals rather than shorter-term metrics.

- Optimism can help you work through a stock that's down. Remember your past successes, stay diversified, and think calmly about the upside and downside potential for your stock that's just declined.

Consider a Follow-on Trade

Sell in May and go away.

Would you rather try to beat the market once or twice? When we do tactical, or short-term, trades around a long-term holding, we are basically trying to beat the market twice in a short period of time. This chapter will walk you through the behavioral pitfalls of trying to beat the market twice as you round up or round down a long-term holding.

At this point in the investment life cycle, we've done our homework, created an investment thesis, executed a trade, and monitored some initial movement in our stock. If all goes according to plan, we can sit back and watch our stock gradually reach our price target. However, as you can imagine, things rarely go exactly according to plan, as Murphy's law states.

What happens if our stock gaps up quickly? Or what if the stock underperforms? This is the part of the investment life cycle where you may consider trading around a long-term holding. For buy-and-hold investors, this is a tricky part of the process because you have to make two good decisions. If you trim a holding now, will you be smart (or lucky) enough to buy back at the right time? Alternatively, if you add to a position now and it goes up, will you really trim it back later at a higher price?

The "sell in May and go away" theme provides a good analogy to trading in and out of stocks that you view as core holdings over a number of years. Historical data suggest that the Dow Jones Industrial Average performs better in the November to April period relative to the May to October time frame. Some investors believe that slow summer trading volumes and perhaps distractions in the back-to-school period in the early fall may lead to disappointing investor sentiment, driving underperformance in the six months from May to October. The media do a good job of drawing attention every spring by reminding investors of the possible benefits of selling in May and going away. Using the idea of confirmation bias, which we discuss in Chapter 2, we can see why the *best-six-months theory* comes up every year.

Many investors may be looking forward to getting away for a summer holiday, and if the media suggest that you can make money and enjoy a vacation at the same time, then perhaps investors will pay more attention to the sell in May and go away idea. In a similar way, if the media tout a new medical study showing that chocolate is good for your health, then the confirmation bias may lead many consumers to make a mad dash for the candy aisle.

On May 1, 2019, I had a chance to refute the sell in May and go away idea on the PBS *Nightly Business Report*, partly for behavioral reasons.[1] I mentioned that investors have to make two good decisions but that other behavioral biases, such as overconfidence and anchoring, can come into play.

Overconfidence may lead investors to think that they can make two smart decisions (sell in May and buy in November) when actually pulling the trigger and trading may be more emotionally difficult. For example, if you sell stocks in May and the Dow Jones Industrial Average is at 26,000, what happens if the market rallies and you have to buy back into stocks in November with the Dow at 27,000? The pain of anchoring to 26,000 may prevent investors from getting back into the market.

On the *Nightly Business Report* episode, I proposed an easier option for investors as a way of getting around some of these behavioral issues. Rather than sell in May and go away, I suggested *always remember, buy in November*. For buy-and-hold investors, buying in November requires only one decision rather than two. Investors who have accumulated cash during the summer and fall can put some of that money to work in November as a simpler way of following the best-six-months strategy.[2]

So what can we learn from the sell in May and go away idea of market timing? Basically, making two good decisions is really hard because it doubles the chances that a behavioral bias leads to a bad decision.

Pivoting back to individual securities, I would argue that in a similar way, fewer trades are generally better than more as a way of cutting down on the probability of a bad decision. This chapter will walk you through some good ways to think about trading in and out of long-term holdings, but in general, I recommend using a high bar for making these trades.

Mistakes and High-Risk Situations

Reaching for yield is really stupid. But it is very human.
— WARREN BUFFETT[3]

Investors make mistakes in both bond and stock markets as risk levels rise. Warren Buffett made the opening comment as investors continued to chase risky bonds, pushing their prices up and their yields down. We can apply a similar warning for equity markets when mainstream investors chase trends or themes.

Kahneman recommends that decision makers learn to recognize situations where mistakes are likely and when the stakes are high.[4] If emotions are rising and lots of bias creeps into a situation, put your guard up and get a second opinion because other people are often better at recognizing our potential mistakes in high-risk situations than we are.

In my experience, high-momentum stocks and markets create a toxic scenario where investors are more likely to make big mistakes. Chasing a stock that has suddenly doubled or tripled can create a sense of euphoria, and acting on this emotion with a big purchase can lead to major losses.

Alternatively, emotions and biases tend to spike during bear markets and when individual stocks are down 20 percent from prior peaks. During these major corrections, you could be feeling lots of emotions and getting lost in a sea of bias as you try to figure out your next move. I would argue that the stakes are high in this situation because if you decide to sell your stock during a bear market, you could be looking at a permanent loss of capital. Investors who sold during the downdraft of the Great Recession (September 2008 to March 2009) may still be struggling to reach long-term savings goals.

A related scenario occurs when a sector of the market falls into a major decline (~20 percent or more). In this case, investors also may fall into behavioral finance traps with high stakes because selling could lead to permanent capital losses. An example here might be the bear market that hit energy stocks in early 2016.

XLE, which is an exchange-traded fund tracking energy, fell from the low $80s in May 2015 to the low $50s in February 2016 as commodity supplies rose and prices fell. It may be easy to look back on this situation and recommend avoiding sales during sector bear markets, but history suggests that waiting for a modest rebound in sector performance generally is a better option.

BEHAVIORAL COACHING TIP

Learn to recognize situations where mistakes are likely and when the stakes are high. Put your antenna up and get a second opinion from a colleague when you notice these factors coming together. Try to avoid making big moves, especially selling as markets decline, which can permanently reduce capital.

Favor Base Rates over Stereotypes

Don't judge a book by its cover.

—OLD ADAGE

In the preceding section, we warned investors to be highly sensitive to situations with lots of money on the line and when mistakes are increasingly likely. As investment teams debate trading around an existing holding, one possible mistake is using stereotypes (judging a book by its cover) rather than hard data. Sometimes stereotypes can be accurate, such as the idea that most tech stocks exhibit high growth. However, stereotypes also can be misleading and distract people from obvious facts or historical trends, also called *base rates*.[5]

As we discussed earlier, many investors lost money in energy stocks in 2014 and 2015, creating a stereotype that energy stocks could be a dead-end investment. Should investors believe the stereotype and sell remaining energy stocks? A better option would be a System 2 approach using data and base rates as a way of framing a conversation about trading around a loss-making energy position.

Selling energy stocks at the bottom of a bear market for oil prices proved disappointing in early 2016. Historically, low oil prices lead to supply cuts, which boost commodity prices and can drive energy stocks higher. A base-rate approach proved superior to stereotypes in this case. Holding depressed energy stocks rather than selling at the bottom would have generated a 34 percent return between late January and late April 2016 as oil prices recovered.[6]

Another example of stereotypes and base rates might be asset bubbles, such as internet stocks or housing-related investments leading up to the Great Recession. In the late 1990s, internet stocks earned a reputation as high-flying investments year after year as technology companies attracted more eyeballs than profits. Similarly, in the early 2000s, home builder stocks performed well because investors believed a stereotype that house prices never decline.

However, using base rates, investors might take a more cautious approach to these types of momentum investments. For 1990s internet stocks, base rates for revenues and profits might offset the momentum stereotypes. Additionally, base rates for home prices in the early 2000s would have shown that home prices, construction, and sales were well above historical trends.

One stock my team debated in 2019 was UnitedHealth (UNH), a diversified insurance and health services company. We considered adding to an existing UnitedHealth position after the stock fell on fears that a presidential candidate might push patients out of private insurance and into a Medicare single-payer system.

Stereotypes might suggest selling UnitedHealth because of a rising risk to the company's core business. However, we favored base rates and looked at historical examples of massive regulatory threats to industries. We came away thinking that a Medicare single-payer system had a low probability of becoming law, and we held our existing UnitedHealth position.

Be cautious if your investment team seems to be making conclusions based on stereotypes. Base rates are a much more powerful tool for debating a buy-or-sell trade for an existing holding.

Formulas Versus Intuitions

A memorable scene from the 1977 film *Star Wars* shows Han Solo, Luke Skywalker, and Princess Leia falling into a giant trash compactor inside the evil Death Star. As the walls start closing in on the rebels, Han Solo wonders aloud that he has a sinking feeling about their next move. Under these kinds of stressful situations, do we go with our gut, or can we use data, math, and formulas to solve problems?

Investing can involve a mix of art and science as numbers and ratios bleed into a messier set of constraints including tradeoffs, incomplete information, and time pressure. While there may be some art to investing, behavioral economists might push back if we rely more on gut feelings than data. Jedi knights might use the Force, but investors probably should stick with math and formulas to accomplish the mission.

Kahneman in particular highlights the stark contrast between intuition and formulas as decision-making tools. If we use our intuition when we are predicting something like future stock prices, we put too much weight on our impressions and too little weight on other data sources. Formulas, in contrast, reduce intuition bias and can generate more reliable predictions.[7]

To be fair, we can see examples of famous and successful decision makers who seem to favor intuition over formulas. Softbank founder and venture capitalist Masayoshi Son likes to "feel the force" when sizing up an opportunity, and New England Patriots coach Bill Belichick prefers to "evaluate what I see" rather than use analytics. Still, there are likely many more business and sports failures that stemmed from using intuition rather than analytical tools such as formulas.[8]

Continuing with our UnitedHealth example, my team also favored data, analysis, and formulas rather than intuition as we evaluated a buy/sell decision. Intuition might lead to a feeling that a particular candidate, such as Elizabeth Warren, might have a good chance of becoming president, leading to pressure on health insurers, but our analytical approach used a formula to consider our decision.

In the fall of 2019, a decline in UnitedHealth's stock price indicated to us that most investors saw a rising probability that Warren would become president and pressure the private health insurance industry. We took a different view and saw a low probability of a single-payer health system and an inexpensive stock price for UnitedHealth, prompting us to maintain our position.

Sunk Costs and Odds of Success

When a stock you own goes down, you may have a chance to buy more of it at a better price. However, this is where System 1 emotions come into the equation, especially if you are highly optimistic about the stock's upside potential and you anchor or fixate on the stock's purchase price. In contrast, a System 2 approach considers the purchase price to be a sunk cost, or something you're unable to change.

If you buy nonrefundable tickets to a sporting event and there is a terrible snow storm the night of the game, would you brave the weather or just write off the money you paid for tickets? The sports tickets are a *sunk cost* because you're unable to get a refund. In a similar way, the price you pay for a stock is nonrefundable at the purchase price. If your stock falls, you should look ahead to potential upside or downside and look out for any excess optimism creeping into your calculations.

For example, if you bought UnitedHealth stock for $100 and the shares decline to $80 because politicians are talking about a single-payer health system, you should think about potential gains and losses from the $80 level. If UnitedHealth could be worth $40 under a single-payer system or $160 in a status-quo scenario, what would you do? Would you consider UnitedHealth at $160 to be a $60 gain ($160 future price less the $100 purchase price)?

A System 2 analysis would ignore the $100 sunk cost (purchase price) and see the potential for a double ($160 future price less the $80 current price). Moving from theory to practice, my team decided to hold UnitedHealth shares because we expected more upside than downside from the depressed market price (similar to the $80 level earlier).

Sometimes it's better to hold, but be careful if anchoring prevents you from folding. Kahneman suggests that decision makers often throw good money after bad because they are uncomfortable admitting defeat for a risky project. The old (bad) money is a sunk cost. If the decision maker is overly optimistic about the project's odds of success, he or she will waste more money on a bad project.[9]

Because stock picking carries inherent risk, Kahneman's comments suggest to me that investors should sell a stock that's lost money (a sunk cost) when they have overly bullish investment forecasts and price targets. How do we know if our investment forecasts are overly bullish? We can use some of the concepts discussed elsewhere in this book:

- Conduct a four-step process for prediction. (Chapter 3)

- Put weights on variables in decision making. (Chapter 3)

- Perform a pre-mortem. (Chapter 4)

- Use formulas, base rates, and checklists. (Chapter 8)

BEHAVIORAL COACHING TIP

Decision makers should quit a risky project with a sunk cost if they become overly optimistic about the project's odds of success. As investors, we should focus less on a stock's purchase price (a sunk cost) and spend our energy on upside and downside scenarios for the stock, being vigilant for any excess optimism in our analysis.

Hope Versus Experience

One of the keys to great investing results is "sitting on your ass."
—Charlie Munger[10]

My family accuses me of being an overly safe driver. Frequently, I hear a chorus of backseat voices shouting, "We would get there faster if Mom was driving!" However, to my family's dismay, I believe that slow and steady wins the race, and this can be true for both investing and driving.

Overly aggressive drivers hope to get to their destination sooner, but experience teaches us that bad driving can lead to expensive, time-consuming, and potentially dangerous accidents. The lead-foot driver is making a tradeoff between hope and experience.

We see the triumph of hope over experience elsewhere in society, including second and third marriages, as well as restaurateurs who think their new concept will succeed where others (in the exact same location) have failed. Hope drives overly optimistic CEOs to take on debt and overpay for acquisitions, leading to value-destroying deals.[11]

Hope often overshadows experience among aggressive investors and traders. We may hope to gain a few points in our portfolio by quickly trading in and out of positions. However, going with Charlie Munger's quote, perhaps we should ask ourselves if we really need to make a trade. Are we hoping the trade will benefit the portfolio, even if experience teaches us that sitting tight may be a better option? Think back to your prior experience. Did you buy low and sell high when trading around a position?

In my experience, trading around existing holdings can be a tricky business and may lead to additional frustration if the timing turns out to be poor. For many buy-and-hold investors, excess trading can trigger additional behavioral pitfalls, such as anchoring, regret, and risk-seeking.

What can we learn from all these examples? Kahneman suggests that excess optimism and hope can lead us to ignore experience and take on more risk than we realize.[12] The trick is channeling the right amount of optimism and hope to guide our efforts without losing track of reality.

BEHAVIORAL COACHING TIP

Before trading around an existing holding, consider the themes of hope versus experience. If you've experienced challenging or disappointing trades in the past, use caution if you hope that the next trade will be different. Less frequent trading may help you focus on situations where you have higher conviction.

Focusing Illusion

Don't sweat the small stuff.

—RICHARD CARLSON[13]

Have you ever shopped for a car or done a home renovation? It can be an all-encompassing ordeal in some cases. Looking back on your car-buying and home-improvement experience, do you think that your life would be radically different if you bought a Ford instead of a Honda? What if you chose light gray paint instead of beige for a living room? My guess is that your quality of life would be similar in all these scenarios.

So why do we get all tied up in knots for these relatively unimportant decisions? Kahneman discusses the idea of a *focusing illusion* to describe what leads people to obsess over fairly minor decisions. In essence, when we focus on one part of our life, such as car shopping, an illusion takes over, and that small thing becomes a big thing. Kahneman suggests that we push back against these focusing illusions with the idea that "nothing in life is as important as you think it is when you are thinking about it."[14] In other words, don't sweat the small stuff.

UnitedHealth provides an example of how investors might get caught in a focusing illusion. When my team reviewed adding to our position, we discussed a downside risk where a political candidate called for serious cuts to private health insurers such as UnitedHealth. This conversation could have taken on a life of its own and led my team to make a drastic decision, such as selling our entire position to avoid the risk. Fortunately for me, we decided to hold as fears of eliminating private health insurance receded, boosting the stock.

How can investors escape a focusing illusion? One option is to have a separate team meeting that allows plenty of time to discuss a particular trade. In this way, your team can avoid feeling rushed to make a decision, even if you are under the illusion that this individual trade is highly urgent.

Broad framing also may help your team fight back against the temptations of a focusing illusion. Examples here might include (1) consider the relative importance of your stock compared with the overall portfolio, (2) do a head-to-head analysis of your stock with a similar security, and (3) consider more than one trade to see which alternative is more important or timely.

If you are debating a possible trade around a stock you own, be aware of a focusing illusion that can inflate the importance and urgency of the trade. Take your time and look at alternatives. There may be other trades that are more relevant for your overall portfolio.

Breakeven Effect

What can investors learn from the Kenny Rogers song "The Gambler" about knowing when to hold or fold your cards? If you walk into a casino with $100 and you start losing, do you feel an urge to keep playing until you at least break even? Some investors hold their cards (or stocks) and try to break even during a calendar year when instead they should walk or run away.

Earlier in this chapter, we discussed the sell in May and go away investing theme. This idea focuses on beating the market in a calendar year. But why do calendar years matter if you are trying to consistently meet or exceed a market benchmark over a multiyear time frame? In my experience, the external web of bias, especially the media, feeds a System 1 temptation to focus on short-term performance.

If you want to improve your diet, you know you should order a salad, but the smell of a grilled burger tempts you to order it. We know that we should think about the long term for our investment decisions. However, our emotional focus on the short term, supported by media comments on year-to-date winners and losers, may tempt us into System 1 short-term thinking.

How can we push back against a cycle where we should think long term, but short-term temptations keep popping up, especially if our year-to-date performance trails the broader market? The *breakeven effect* is one concept that may help us redirect our investment focus back to the long term.

Thaler refers to the breakeven effect as occurring when decision makers become risk-seeking as they try to catch up to some kind of benchmark or dig themselves out of a perceived hole.[15] Gamblers who are losing at the casino might feel a wave of desperation crash over them as they become more risk-seeking and try to win back the money they've lost.

In the investment world, mutual fund portfolio managers often take on more risk in the last quarter of the year if they are trailing a performance benchmark such as the S&P 500 as they try to break even with the broader market by year end.[16] Risk-seeking for investors might include selling a stock just because it's performing poorly and buying a stock that's up, going against the idea of buying low and selling high.

What would you do if you owned a tech stock that's up 10 percent between January and October, but the overall tech sector is up 20 percent in the same period? Or what if your Pepsi shares are underperforming Coke on a year-to-date basis, and you see investors on TV explaining with high conviction why Coke is a much better stock than Pepsi? These are situations where the breakeven effect can kick in.

In general, I would recommend three ways of countering the breakeven effect. One is to take a deep breath and remind yourself that you are in this for the long haul and that short-term results will be noisy. Second, if your stock is meaningfully trailing a benchmark over a short period, I would stop and reevaluate your investment thesis. If you still think that the stock is attractive over the long term, stick with it. Alternatively, if some System 2 analysis suggests that your investment thesis has broken down, perhaps it's time to consider owning a different stock with more upside potential.

A third way to avoid pitfalls related to the breakeven effect is to use caution when potentially trying to chase year-to-date winners. Use broad framing (discussed in Chapter 1) when thinking of buying stocks that are up in a short period of time.

Going back to our UnitedHealth example, there have been times when the stock has underperformed peers or the market on a year-to-date basis, and I've felt an emotional urgency to do something to catch up. As discussed earlier, the stock trailed broader markets on a year-to-date basis in mid-2019, prompting me to consider taking action.

As a first step, I reviewed my long-term thesis and felt that it was intact. Second, I looked at valuation and decided to propose buying more of the shares on a short-term drop in the stock. In this case, my logical System 2 thinking won out, but I'm sure that there will be many other times when the breakeven effect will tempt me to think short term and become risk-seeking as a way to play catch-up.

If your stock or portfolio is trailing a benchmark on a year-to-date basis, pause, review your investment thesis, and push back against a temptation to take on greater risks to catch up to the benchmark.

Self-Control

So I made a New Year's resolution to lose 10 pounds. . . . Only 15 more to go!

—JIM SUVA, CITIGROUP TECHNOLOGY ANALYST[17]

In the preceding section we talked about how the media can inflame our emotions, especially if our stock or portfolio is underperforming. Let's stick with the theme of the external web of bias and dig deeper into ways to protect ourselves from its emotional effects.

This chapter is all about dealing with movement in stocks you already own. So far we've pointed out several emotional System 1 pitfalls that can lead us to make bad trading decisions on these stocks. Self-control is another theme that may help us in this part of the investment life cycle.

Thaler suggests that we can improve our self-control by removing "the cues that would tempt [us] to do something stupid."[18] People trying to stop smoking might want to avoid public spaces where there are lots of smokers. If you're trying to eat healthier, keep all the "sinful" foods out of arm's reach.

For investors, if a stock that you own is going through a rough patch and the media are having a field day bashing the company, resist the temptation to sell immediately. Turn off CNBC and log out of your quote screen. These kinds of self-protective measures can keep System 1 thinking at bay and allow your System 2 analysis to evaluate the situation.

Earlier in this chapter we described a steep decline in UnitedHealth shares in mid-2019 as new regulatory risks emerged. The media piled onto this rough patch and speculated that government-run health insurance might put private insurers out of business.

As a self-control mechanism, I tried to avoid any of these emotional media stories about the looming cliff coming for UnitedHealth. Fortunately, I switched to System 2 analysis and maintained my position as the shares recovered. If I had had poor self-control, I might have sold at the bottom that year.

In my experience, the theme of self-control is especially important during the four times of the year when companies report earnings. One dramatic example here was Facebook (FB) in late July 2018, when the stock fell nearly 20 percent after reporting disappointing quarterly earnings. The media piled on as headlines focused on the worst one-day loss of market value of any stock in history (nearly $120 billion). In this case, I decided to use some self-control measures, and I turned off my quote screen.

To be fair, Facebook stock continued to fall for another five months, but the stock did recover the next year. In this case, short-term traders made money by selling after the 20 percent decline, suggesting that emotional selling would have temporarily done better than self-control and holding the stock. However, long-term investors using a System 2 approach saw better returns by holding onto Facebook stock after the 20 percent crash.

BEHAVIORAL COACHING TIP

When your stock is moving intraday by more than 10 percent and emotions are high, practice good self-control and consider removing cues that might lead you to make a bad decision. Turn off the TV and the live quotes and stick with analyzing the facts and long-term trends as you consider your next move.

Mental Accounting and Narrow Framing

This chapter is all about figuring out what to do with a stock you currently own. Should you sell your winners, or are they just getting started? Should you cut your losses or double down if your stock enters the doldrums?

We've discussed several biases that can cloud our judgment as we try to make these investment decisions. In this section, we will flag two forms of lazy thinking called *mental accounting* and *narrow framing*, which can combine to produce disappointing portfolio results.

As discussed earlier, investors do mental accounting when they divide up their assets into artificial categories, such as "savings money" and "play money," when in fact it's all the same. We've also reviewed the idea of narrow framing, where investors focus on only one thing at a time rather than taking a broader view. As you might expect, Kahneman recommends avoiding these pitfalls.[19]

Mental accounting can cause lots of problems for investors as they consider trading around existing positions. In this section, we'll discuss how investors treat their losers differently from the rest of their portfolio holdings as they consider trading around positions. This is in contrast to another form of mental accounting that can impact the way we treat our winners.

Investors who have a narrow focus might look at only one part of their portfolio at a time. Making matters worse, these investors might make a second mistake and create artificial labels for each part of their portfolio. One of these labels might be "losers," and another might be "winners." Some investors try to justify holding onto losers by hoping that the winners will offset the pain and disappointment of the losses.

This line of flawed reasoning might lead you to think that if one stock is down, you can feel okay about it because you'll make it up somewhere else in the portfolio. As you can imagine, the best approach from a behavioral finance perspective is to own a portfolio full of your best ideas.

Using the UnitedHealth example, narrow framing and mental accounting might label the stock as a loser in mid-2019, with the hope that a winner would provide an offset. A better approach would be to ask tough questions about UnitedHealth after it becomes a loser. Do you think that the business or investor sentiment will improve? Or are you holding the loser because it's okay for a portfolio to contain some winners and losers?

As discussed earlier, I did some analysis and decided that investor sentiment would likely improve for UnitedHealth later in 2019. Fortunately for me, my loser became more of a winner, although Kahneman would prefer that we avoid using these labels!

BEHAVIORAL COACHING TIP

Avoid taking a narrow approach to portfolio management that uses mental accounting to label stocks as winners and losers. Rather than hope that a winner will make up for a loser, do the work and either sell a true loser or buy more of it if you think that it will turn around.

House-Money Effect

On my honeymoon in 1952, my bride, 19, and I, 21, stopped in Las Vegas. I saw all of these well-dressed . . . people who had come . . . to do something that every damn one of them knew was mathematically dumb. And I told Susie, I said, we are going to make a lot of money.

—WARREN BUFFETT[20]

Several themes in this chapter, such as mental accounting and narrow framing, sunk costs, hope versus experience, the breakeven effect, and self-control, deal with behavioral pitfalls that can cloud our judgment when we consider buying more of a stock after it falls. However, emotions and shortcuts also can impact our thinking when we debate buying more of our winners. Speaking of winners, let's turn to the "Oracle of Omaha" to see if we can learn from the mistakes that winning gamblers make as they relate to taking on even more risk.

I attended the Berkshire Hathaway Annual Meeting in the spring of 2019 and heard Warren Buffett tell the story in the opening quote about gambling and his honeymoon. Buffett appears to be making a point that some gamblers will keep playing even if they are unlikely to win. If Buffett is right, how can we apply this idea to trading around stocks we already own?

Let's stick with the gambling analogy for a minute. In Las Vegas, some gamblers will set their winnings aside and label it "house money," or cash they won from the house (the casino). These gamblers may treat their house money differently from the hard-earned money they brought with them to the casino.

In fact, gamblers may be more risk-seeking with their house money because they view it as almost free. These gamblers are using mental accounting to separate money into different categories, such as money I earned from my job and money I won at a casino, even though it's all the same. However, when you are risk-seeking, the odds may be stacked against you. Warren Buffett may have seen some gamblers betting their house money while he was on his honeymoon, leading to his opening quote.

Richard Thaler's research supports Buffett's honeymoon story, noting that risk-averse people become risk-seeking after they win house money.[21] Investors may also fall into a trap of mental accounting and see recent gains as house money, leading to risk-seeking activities such as buying more stocks.

I've seen the house-money effect exert its influence during debates about trading around smaller positions that have performed well. In mid-2019, my firm owned a small amount of Nike (NKE) stock, about 1 percent of total equity assets. Nike performed well, and we debated buying more of the stock to make it a full position.[22]

Nike was a bit of an anomaly for our firm because it was an unusually small position. The stock always seemed expensive, and we kept waiting for the right time to buy more of it. After Nike shares went on a run in early 2019, we felt the house-money effect, and we had the temptation to buy more of it.

However, we again reviewed the stock's valuation and looked at some of the macro trends, such as potential Chinese tariffs on US apparel companies, and we decided against buying more. In the short term, perhaps we should have embraced the house-money effect because Nike continued to go up after we decided against buying more. As a modest consolation, we tempered our emotions on Nike with the reminder that you win a few and you lose a few.

BEHAVIORAL COACHING TIP

If one of your stocks is moving up, you may treat your recent gains like house money in a casino and engage in risk-seeking behavior, such as taking on more equity exposure. Avoid this mental accounting shortcut and treat all your equity assets the same way. Think twice before quickly buying more of a stock that's outperforming the market.

Overconfidence and Excess Trading

Less is more.

—Ludwig Mies van der Rohe

Throughout this chapter, we've looked at shortcuts and emotions that can lead us to bad trading decisions for stocks that we already own. But what if the best decision is to sit tight and simply hold onto our current portfolio a bit longer? In a way, the idea of trading suggests that I have confidence that buying or selling my stock is better than keeping my current position. If we need confidence to trade, could there be a risk of overconfidence that could cloud our judgment?

We discussed the idea of overconfidence in Chapter 3 in the context of company management teams and empire builders. However, let's turn the focus back on ourselves and ask if we are being overconfident as we consider more stock trades.

When we trade, we are actually making a bet that our idea is better than the other party's. If we are selling and the other party is buying, each side has high confidence that it is right and the other side is wrong. But what if the other party is pretty smart, just like us? Maybe both sides are onto something, and perhaps the trade is a bad idea.

The idea of overconfidence is another reason why we should double-check our work and make sure that the data support the trade. Going the extra mile on analysis might help us avoid excess trading. Richard Thaler's work supports a theory that overconfidence can lead to too many trades, although, to be fair, Thaler admits that it's difficult to prove in practice.[23]

An example of less is more for stock trades comes from Bill Miller, whom we discussed earlier in the book. In an investor letter, Miller described how his fund outperformed in the final three months of 2019 by saying, "In the fourth quarter [of 2019], we did our favorite thing to do in markets: nothing."[24] Miller also added, "No new names and no elimination of holdings from the portfolio. This doesn't happen as often as it should."[25] Perhaps Miller used his behavioral edge as he held tight to high-conviction stocks rather than trade around them.

Going back to a specific stock example with UnitedHealth, we can see one approach to overconfidence and excess trading. As described earlier, my team debated buying more UnitedHealth stock after a downturn in mid-2019. However, because we already owned a substantial position (perhaps 2.5 percent of equity assets), we decided to pass on the trade.

We realized that if we took our position up to 3.5 percent and then the stock appreciated, we might be looking at an oversized position of 4 percent or more,[26] potentially leading us to trim. As a buy-and-hold investor, I was looking at potentially buying and then selling UnitedHealth shares in rapid succession. The themes of overconfidence and excess trading led me to pass on buying more of UnitedHealth in mid-2019.

Investors should respect the downside risks of overconfidence and avoid too many trades.

Checklists and Speaking Up

Most of this chapter has focused on biases and emotions that can lead us to make bad trades for stocks we already own. This section will outline a fairly simple tool and process that can help identify and minimize some of these behavioral finance risks as we prepare for the next trade.

Richard Thaler recommends setting rules, following them, and speaking up when someone breaks them as a way of limiting bad decisions.[27] This framework can help high-risk professionals, such as surgeons, pilots, and mountain-climbing guides, avoid life-threatening mistakes. Tragically, Thaler points to the deadly consequences when KLM pilots in 1977 and Mt. Everest guides in 1996 remained silent after their colleagues failed to follow a checklist.[28]

If checklists are good enough for pilots, surgeons, and Nobel Prize winners, then perhaps they are good enough for our investment process. I decided to put Thaler's theory into practice by creating an investment checklist for my team.

A member of my research team, Zach Weiss, and I debated quantitative and qualitative items for a checklist and especially the subjective items, which could allow one of us to break the rules. We've settled on a checklist with about 15 steps, although in an effort at constant improvement, we've been refining the checklist over time.

We put our checklist to the test with UnitedHealth in September 2019, and using our 15 metrics, we came away thinking that the stock offered meaningful value. The checklist gave high marks for the company's fundamentals (i.e., margins, profits, and upside surprises) and also pointed out that the stock's valuation was well below average at a time when the broader market was getting expensive.

A cheap stock with good or improving fundamentals is generally a rare find, and the checklist increased our conviction that we needed to own a big position in UnitedHealth in late 2019. As described earlier, we decided to maintain our large holding rather than buy even more, but the checklist helped us gain comfort with our bet that UnitedHealth would meet or beat the broader market.

Taking a step back, in some ways this entire book is one massive checklist. The book's 100+ steps provide a checklist for the entire investment life cycle. Hopefully, these 100+ items can provide consistency to your investment process and allow healthy debates if all your team members understand the rules and speak up if someone breaks them.

BEHAVIORAL COACHING TIP

Checklists can be a great way to take some of the emotion and inconsistency out of your investment process, especially if you are considering trading around a stock you already own. Follow the rules and speak up if someone breaks them.

Sandwich Recommendations

In *Hamilton: An American Musical*, Aaron Burr's character shows off his diplomatic skills during the song "My Shot" when he recommends that his genius associates (Hamilton, Jefferson, and Lafayette) keep their voices down as a way of avoiding trouble and increasing their choices. Can we lean on Burr's advice and stay out of trouble as our teams debate stock trades?

After running through all the heavy behavioral finance theories in this chapter, this final segment offers some lighter fare. Because this chapter is about how to prepare for team discussions on a stock, let's look at a way of taking some of the emotions out of these debates. In my experience, emotional team debates can lead to more System 1 thinking and potentially bad decisions or hurt feelings.

As your team gets into heated debates about trading around a stock you currently own, consider a *sandwich recommendation* as a way of bringing down the heat. After listening intently to a team member's proposal, you can mention something favorable about a proposed trade, then a concern, and then finish with another merit. This good, bad, good approach allows constructive criticism to improve the investment process rather than create division. Just as the diplomatic Aaron Burr did in *Hamilton*, more smiles and fewer words can help improve group dynamics.

When my team debated the investment merits of UnitedHealth in 2019, our final decision was essentially a sandwich recommendation.

My team voted against buying more, but the discussion told me three things: (1) we like the investment idea, (2) we have concerns with buying more, and (3) because we already own a lot of UnitedHealth, if the stock goes up, clients will see a benefit.

This approach made me feel much better than if the team had simply vetoed the trade and said, "We're cautious." As a research director, I feel more comfortable suggesting nonconsensus or controversial trades if I know that my team will make sandwich recommendations during debates.

BEHAVIORAL COACHING TIP

When debating trades around an existing position, consider sandwich recommendations that start with a compliment, then include a criticism, and finally wrap up with another favorable comment. This good, bad, good approach can help the team make less emotional decisions.

Summary

- Seek external advice if you recognize situations where you're more likely to make a mistake, such as when emotions and biases are running rampant, and be extra cautious when the stakes are high. This toxic combination can come into play as investors consider selling into a bear market.

- Stereotypes are a convenient shortcut for making buy/sell decisions for existing holdings. Try to limit the use of stereotypes in group discussions and rely more on data and base rates.

- Formulas are better than intuitions for making big decisions such as trades.

- Avoid the temptation to throw good money after bad (a sunk cost) if you are uncomfortable admitting defeat for a risky project and become overly bullish about an investment's prospects.

- Favor experience over hope when considering trades around an existing position.

- Avoid falling into a trap called a focusing illusion where your trade seems like the most important or urgent matter. Look at the bigger picture before making the trade.

- Focus on multiyear performance rather than year-to-date results. This long-term view can help avoid a temptation called the breakeven effect where you might take on greater risks to catch up to a benchmark if your stock or portfolio is trailing the benchmark on a year-to-date basis.

- If your stock is having a big day (up or down 10 percent or more), consider a self-control measure such as turning off external triggers (TV and live-quote screens) that might lead you to make a bad decision.

- Avoid mental accounting shortcuts that create categories of winners that can balance out losers. Try to make each portfolio holding a high-conviction stock that you think offers more upside than downside.

- Investors often treat recent gains like free money (or house money in a casino) and engage in risk-seeking actions such as buying more of their winners. Use caution if this house-money effect tempts you to seek greater risk.

- When planning a trade, ask yourself whether you sense any overconfidence creeping in. Fewer trades can help push back against an overconfidence bias.

- Use a checklist as a way of treating each stock the same way as you consider trading around a stock you already own. Make sure that your team understands the checklist's rules, and encourage speaking up if someone breaks them.

- When debating trades around an existing position, consider using sandwich recommendations that say something good, then bad, and then good about a colleague's investment proposals. This approach can keep the focus on the ideas and analysis rather than letting emotions drag the team into bad decisions.

Execute a
Follow-on Trade

Congratulations, you've made it through one
of the more difficult parts of the investment
process! Debating a potential trade around
a stock you already own should be a comprehensive and rigorous process. Now we can move on to
something easier, right?

Because we've spent considerable time researching and debating our trade idea, the actual transaction should be straightforward. However, investors
(myself included) can be lazy and take shortcuts, so
even the simple trading process can run into behavioral pitfalls. This chapter should provide a bridge
over some of these problems and allow your team's
investment ideas to become actual trades.

Procrastination

Git-r-done.

—LARRY THE CABLE GUY

In my experience, procrastination can impact trading at all parts of the investment life cycle: the initial purchase, follow-on trades, and the final sale. At

this point in our journey, let's take a look at how procrastination can be a midlife crisis for a stock you already own.

Last time we reviewed procrastination, we described it as being relatively mild. That's because when you first buy a stock, you generally have less behavioral baggage, such as anchoring to a purchase price. However, now that you own a stock and are planning to buy more or trim back, I would argue that the power of procrastination is stronger because of three behavioral themes: anchoring, taking losses, and paying taxes on gains.[1]

Let's use Apple Inc. (AAPL) as an example of how the power of procrastination can impact a trading and investment process. I initially bought Apple in mid-2015 at $32 (split adjusted) on the premise that the company would meet or exceed investor expectations while the stock traded at a discount to peers. I then trimmed some of my position in September 2017 at $40 because I believed that a new iPhone launch would disappoint investors.

I recommended this modest sell in 2017 fairly quickly after the initial purchase in part because: (1) my $32 anchor was fairly close to my recommended sale price of $40, (2) I avoided losses, and (3) I had only minor tax consequences. However, the next trade would be a different story.

During most of 2019, I debated Apple's pros and cons as the stock proceeded to run up nearly 80 percent. Mild procrastination that had impacted my 2015 and 2017 trades became a major stumbling block in 2019 and 2020. I suffered from anchoring as Apple stock approached $75 and tax implications became meaningful for clients. Speaking of taxes, because broader markets rallied in 2019, clients taking tax gains on Apple were generally unable to offset those payments to Uncle Sam with losses elsewhere.

So, for better or worse, I lost the battle with procrastination as I considered trimming Apple in 2019.[2] So how can I push back against procrastination next time? Here are a few ideas, which we discuss in greater detail elsewhere in this book: (1) avoid looking at a stock's initial purchase price as a way to avoid anchoring, (2) frame a loss as a cost of doing business rather than as a permanent reduction in capital, and (3) look at paying taxes as a good problem, though this is easier in theory than in practice.

When preparing to trade around a stock you already own, be prepared for a wave of procrastination to slow you down. However, if you avoid anchoring, view losses as a cost, and take taxes as a sign of success, you might get the trade done in a more timely manner.

The Planner and the Doer

Well done is better than well said.
—BEN FRANKLIN, *POOR RICHARD'S ALMANACK*

In the Preface, we discussed Kahneman's idea of System 1 and System 2 thinking, where one person can think and act very differently based on which system he or she is using. Thaler takes a related approach in his belief that each of us can be a "forward-looking 'planner' who has good intentions and cares about the future and a devil-may-care 'doer' who lives for the present."[3] I would argue that these two ways of thinking and acting can impact the way investors trade.

In some ways, the *planner* in us uses System 2 thinking, with lots of analysis and logic, as we work through a complex decision such as buying or selling a stock. However, as we move from the planning stage to the doing step, our unemotional System 2 logic breaks down, and we become System 1 thinkers and *doers*. The compelling stock trade that we've planned all of a sudden looks risky. The doer in us whispers, "Maybe we should wait for the stock or market to fall a bit more before buying."

I would argue that the stark differences between the planner and the doer can lead to execution risk in investing and especially during trading stages of the investment life cycle. In some ways, the tensions between the planner and the doer might be worse at this midpoint in the investment life cycle relative to the first and last trades. This is so because investors often have more conviction in their initial purchase and the final sale compared with trading around existing positions.

Let's use Apple as an example of how the planner and the doer take different approaches to trading. As described earlier, I put on my planning hat as I looked at trimming Apple stock during 2019. I used a checklist and did all the rational analysis and research that a System 2 planner would recommend. I even did some System 2 due diligence and met with management at the company's futuristic Apple Park head-quarters in Cupertino as I weighed the pros and cons of selling.

However, when the rubber hit the road, the doer in me struggled to sell Apple. The doer voice told me to wait for a higher price so that I could lock in more gains, but the stock's steady rise from a low of around $37 to a high near $75 (in calendar year 2019) created emo-tional forces favoring the planner over the doer. I kept planning to trim my Apple holdings, but the doer in me failed to pull the trigger. This example is a reminder that well-intentioned trades can hit a brick wall when we have to hit the "buy" or "sell" button.

BEHAVIORAL COACHING TIP

When preparing to trade around a stock you currently own, be aware that the planner in you can set up a logical trade, but then your doer personality can take over and delay or cancel the trade.

Group Compliance and Trading

The next two themes continue to focus on trading execution, but they broaden the discussion to teams with client-facing advisors or portfo-lio managers. My prior comments in this chapter on procrastination and the tensions between the planner and the doer focus on the person or team that develops research and trading ideas. However, there can be another layer of execution challenges when investment ideas move from theory to practice across a larger firm.

The following examples may apply most to wealth management firms or registered investment advisors (RIAs), where trading strate-gies start with an investment team and then move to a broader group of client-facing advisors to complete the trade. In some firms, client-facing advisors have a considerable amount of discretion to fully or par-tially participate in a group trade. In my experience, getting closer to full participation in a trade can help clients reach a consistent level of performance and reduce the risk of behavioral pitfalls in the future.

For example, let's say that my investment team recommends trim-ming Apple positions across the board and some client-facing advisors comply fully, whereas others recommend holding back on the sale. If Apple shares go up or down significantly, advisors may anchor to the recommended sale price, potentially creating emotional divisions within the team of advisors. In my experience, if an investment team has high conviction in a trade, it's generally more efficient to get as close to full trading compliance as possible.

What are some ways to achieve high compliance in a group trade? Thaler suggests that "if you want people to comply with some norm or rule, it is a good strategy to inform them (if true) that most other people comply."[4] One way to do this is to highlight your firm's historical group compliance rate for trades.

Going back to our case study, when discussing the Apple sale with your team, say that "in prior trades, we've had 80 to 90 percent participation, and we would like to keep this streak going." A carrot-and-stick approach also can work after the initial trade. If you tell noncompliant advisors in private that 80 to 90 percent of their peers just trimmed Apple holdings, perhaps these advisors will get on board and you'll get compliance above 90 percent.

BEHAVIORAL COACHING TIP

When executing a trade with a broader group of client-facing advisors who have discretion over the trade, consider informing the group that most of their peers plan to complete the trade for the majority of their clients.

Trading Friction

If you want to encourage someone to do something, make it easy.

—RICHARD THALER[5]

In the preceding section, we discussed ways of improving group compliance in a trade. However, there are plenty of other barriers, road blocks, and speed bumps for investment teams as they attempt a group trade. These trading barriers create friction that can slow a trade or reduce participation. This is where Thaler's opening quote comes in. If you think that a trade will benefit clients, do your best to reduce trading friction and make it easy for client-facing advisors to complete the trade.

Some of these trading frictions might be in your control, whereas others may be more difficult to change. One way to make the trade easier is to frame the trade as the default option and require your client-facing advisor to actively opt out if they choose.

Thaler believes that people are more likely to go with the default option, suggesting greater participation in a group trade if you frame the choice this way. In one example, an employee retirement savings program switched the default choice from opt in to opt out and saw participation jump from 49 percent to 86 percent in the first year.[6]

Other trading frictions, such as taxes, commissions, glitchy software, and trading errors, may be tougher to control, but you can still try to reduce them. Some advisors know that their clients want to avoid paying taxes on gains, potentially reducing group compliance in selling a stock where many clients have gains.

Going back to our example, if you recommend trimming Apple and it happens to be near the end of a calendar year, consider pushing the trade into the new year as a way of delaying a potential tax bill for clients. This approach might improve overall compliance in a trade. Technology has been a big help in reducing trading friction because software has cut the amount of time a professional has to spend executing trades. Good software also can reduce trading errors.

Historically, broker commissions also have created trading friction, but a price war among the online brokers has led to a march toward zero commissions for most highly liquid US stocks. While the absolute dollar amount of the commission cut ($5 to $10 per trade) may be small, this race to zero removes another trading friction that historically has led some advisors to opt out of a trade.

BEHAVIORAL COACHING TIP

When planning a group trade, try to reduce friction that can limit full participation. Frame the trade as the default option and also try to minimize near-term tax implications for trades as ways of reducing overall friction.

Framing a Choice: Status Quo or Back to Zero?

At this point in the investment life cycle, we've planned and executed a trade for a stock we own, so we're ready to move on to other stocks, right? I wish it were that easy! There's one last step in a good investment process that can be a bridge between finishing one trade and starting to look at the next one.

Before jumping to this bridge between trades, let's look at Thaler's concept of *status quo or back to zero* as a way framing our investing and trading actions. At a basic level, when we take action, we've changed something. What do we do next? Do we keep acting the same way (status quo), or do we go back to what we were doing before? And how should we frame this choice?

We discussed framing choices in the preceding section on group trades, and we'll use the concept again here as we think about what to do after a trade. In general, our post-trade options are (1) maintain the new status quo or (2) go back to a prior baseline, or back to zero.[7]

Using a simple example, if we walk from point A to point B, we have created a new status quo. Do we go back to point A or stay at B as we think about our next move? Thaler believes that most people have a status-quo bias in which inertia often wins out. A good way to push back against this inertia is to quantify the pros and cons of the status quo compared with going back to zero.[8]

If we are investing in a company-sponsored retirement plan, such as a 401(k), do we passively invest the same percentage every year (status quo), or do we go back to zero and make an active decision on how much to invest every year? The way we frame this investing choice can have a real impact on our savings goals, and as you can imagine, people often save more when their 401(k) is on autopilot. Thaler's work on framing choices to encourage retirement savings was a key contribution to his Nobel Prize.[9]

Speaking of framing an investment choice, let's look at choices that emerge as we trade around stocks we own. If we're trading one stock at a time, we'll end up with at least three changes after the trade: (1) more or less cash, (2) more or less stock relative to cash, and (3) more or less exposure to a sector.

Let's go back to the Apple example to illustrate these changes. In this example, we start out with a 100 percent stock portfolio, which includes a 5 percent Apple position. Because Apple is in the technology sector, let's say our total exposure to tech is 20 percent, including the 5 percent in Apple and 15 percent in other technology stocks. If we trim our Apple position to 3 percent from 5 percent, we've also increased cash to 2 percent, and we've cut our technology weighting to 18 percent. Here is the before and after:

- **Initial position.** 0 percent cash, 100 percent stocks, 5 percent Apple, 20 percent tech stocks

- **Action.** Sell Apple down to a 3 percent position from 5 percent

- **Position after the trade.** 2 percent cash, 98 percent stocks, 3 percent Apple, 18 percent tech stocks

Now what? We've just made four changes. Should we keep the status quo or go back to zero? When we finish trading around a stock we own, do we maintain all our prior sector and cash weightings? Or do we completely start over with a zero stock portfolio sitting in 100 percent cash and reevaluate all decisions? These are different ways of framing our choices on what comes next.

Going back to our Apple example, before our trade, technology stocks represented 20 percent of our portfolio, and let's say that tech also made up a similar 20 percent of the broader market, such as the S&P 500. If we are equal weight tech and trim Apple, we are now making a bigger bet against the tech sector and against the market overall.

What's our next move? We could buy another technology stock to get back to the prior status quo for tech-sector exposure and cash holdings. We could also expand this process to trading small- versus large-cap stocks, US versus international stocks, growth versus value, and high- versus low-dividend-paying stocks.

Trying to constantly rebalance all these sector, size, style, and geographic factors can drive even a System 2 thinker crazy! In my experience, the status-quo bias often takes over and investors do nothing, or make only slight changes, rather than doing a full portfolio rebalance with every trade.

I recommend a flexible approach to the choice of status quo or back to zero by having high and low limits for cash and sector weightings. These guardrails can help thread the needle between keeping the status quo and rebalancing back to the old weightings.

For example, if we were sitting on more cash than usual before trimming Apple, we would try to deploy the Apple proceeds back into another stock quickly, which is more of the back-to-zero approach. However, if our cash levels were unusually low before selling Apple, we might keep the new status quo as we move to a higher cash level.

When you trade around stocks you own, you rock the boat in terms of making several changes to your portfolio. Consider developing an investment process before you trade so that you can frame your choices after the trade. You can keep the new status quo, go back to zero (the old status quo), or take a balanced approach.

Summary

- Be aware that procrastination can slow your trading process as the themes of anchoring, losses, and taxes kick in.

- We can do a great job planning to trade around a stock we own, but then at the execution stage, the doer in us often takes over, leading to second thoughts and changes to our plans, such as delaying or canceling our trade.

- Investment teams often have discretion for fully or partially participating in a group trade. If you want to increase compliance with a trade, inform the group, if true, that most members historically have high participation in the trade.

- If you want to encourage your team to complete a trade, make it easy. Consider making the trade as the default option, requiring advisors to actively opt out. Also try to reduce near-term tax implications by pushing sales into the next calendar year, if possible.

- After we trade, we need to frame the choice of what comes next: do we keep the new status quo, go back to zero (the old status quo), or split the difference?

10

Review Long-Term Investment Thesis

We've traveled far as we have journeyed through the investment life cycle. Now it's time to take a long look back and also look ahead at what's next. Our investment idea is definitely hitting middle age at this point, and retirement may be around the corner. We've done our initial work, bought a stock, and possibly traded around the stock as it has moved.

Now we have an opportunity to reflect and see how many miles are left in this old car. Is our investment thesis still valid, potentially after several years and multiple trades? Should we keep our stock or move on?

This chapter starts out with some behavioral coaching tips that can prevent you from becoming a deer in the headlights. Inaction can feel comfortable for stocks we've held for some time, but it can lead to bad performance. We next take a deep dive into the endowment effect, which creates a bias to favor a stock we own, again leading to inaction.

The bottom line here is that we need to push back against the urge to set it and forget it[1] and do a comprehensive investment thesis review using some of the techniques we discussed in Chapters 4 and 8. Because this chapter is all about shaking the dust off our investment thesis, let's get to it and see what we can uncover.

INACTION

Complacency

Your margin is my opportunity.

—Jeff Bezos[2]

Many years ago, I interviewed for a stock-picking job with T. Rowe Price, one of the biggest active investment managers in the world. As you can imagine, I put on my game face and used some cognitive strain to focus on answering tough interview questions. While one of the senior investors at T Rowe was grilling me, out of the corner of my eye I noticed a little sticky note on his computer screen that had two words: complacency and overconfidence.

The fact that a big-time investor kept a constant reminder of these two behavioral finance themes on his screen left a lasting impression. I believe that these themes are also highly relevant for evaluating a long-held stock in your portfolio.

We've spent some time discussing the risks of overconfidence already, so let's unpack the idea of complacency and see if we can push back against this behavioral tendency. The quote at the top of this section gets to the idea of complacency in the business world. Jeff Bezos probably wakes up every day thinking about all his competitors and wondering who's getting lazy.

Bezos' quote suggests that Amazon will go after bloated companies that may have worked hard a long time ago and built up a high-margin business. However, if you are a competitor that's gotten complacent, you better believe that Bezos and Amazon will try to displace you faster than next-day delivery.

Amazon's success going after complacent businesses such as book stores and mall-based retailers is a pretty stark warning to avoid getting too comfortable in a competitive industry. Because Wall Street is also highly competitive, let's take the Bezos example and turn our focus back to investing to make sure that we avoid falling into the complacency trap.

In 2017, the broader market broke with historical patterns and moved up 22 percent with little volatility as investors anticipated a big corporate tax cut that would boost profits starting in 2018. Typically, markets will take a breather and fall about 10 percentage points every 33 weeks on average before resuming an upward climb,[3] but 2017 was atypical.

Some investors see this type of glide path with low volatility as too good to be true and wave a red flag that complacency is kicking in. Richard Thaler said in October 2017 that "the stock market seems to be napping."[4] Thaler was right but a bit early because market volatility kicked in three months later and the S&P 500 fell 10 percent in early 2018.

Let's go from macro to micro and look at an example of complacency for an individual stock. My firm owned AT&T for years with a notion that a blue-chip, dividend-paying, defensive telecom company was a good way to offset risk from high growth or cyclical companies elsewhere in the portfolio. However, this investment thesis set my team up for complacency.

I decided to review our investment thesis after AT&T took on massive debt to buy Time Warner and as AT&T shares slipped well below those of its competitor, Verizon, which my company also owned.[5] Any complacency I had started to melt away after the stock popped in mid-2019 as an activist investor started pushing for change. I decided that the new higher price reflected much of the good news and little of the downside risk. Despite AT&T's history as a steady-Eddie stock, I pushed back against complacency and decided to walk away.

BEHAVIORAL COACHING TIP

Beware of sloth and lethargy in your investment process. Stocks that have worked in the past can lead us to feel complacent about the future. Shake the dust off your investment thesis at least once a year to make sure that your stock still offers a compelling risk/reward tradeoff. Consider using the checklist we discussed in Chapter 8 as a way of pushing back against complacency.

Regret and Inaction

At this stage in the investment process, we've owned a stock through some ups and downs, and we may be at a fork in the road. Do we stick with our investment, or is it time to look for alternatives? In essence, we're looking at a choice of action or inaction, and this is where bias creeps in.

If we take action, such as selling our stock before a big rally and we're wrong, we feel regret. However, if we do nothing with our stock and we're wrong, we feel less regret. In fact, we know this ahead of time, according to Kahneman, who suggests that people expect to have more regret from an outcome that requires *action* versus an outcome that requires *doing nothing*.[6]

Kahneman goes deeper and compares inaction to the status quo, using the following example. Imagine two drivers, one who never picks up hitchhikers and one who always picks them up. If both drivers get robbed by a hitchhiker, which one feels more regret? The one who never picks up strangers but breaks from the status quo.[7]

Turning to a financial example, if there's a chance we might lose $1,000 in a risky bet, we would rather take that chance by doing nothing than taking action. In a sense, we often become risk averse as we try to avoid regret.

Let's go back to our AT&T example to illustrate the impact of regret and inaction. As mentioned earlier, AT&T shares performed well in 2016 and early 2017, reaching the low $40s as falling interest rates made blue-chip stocks with high dividends relatively more attractive. However, in late 2016, AT&T took on more risk by using debt to pursue Time Warner, an $85 billion deal representing about a third of AT&T's market value at the time.

Investors started to sour on the deal and AT&T's rising debt levels, especially because the rest of AT&T's business began to struggle. If all these dynamics suggest hitting the pause button and reevaluating your investment thesis, you would be right. However, this is where regret and inaction come into the equation.

As AT&T shares descended toward the high $20s, I knew that my investment thesis was in trouble, but I also struggled with selling and potentially facing regret over a poorly timed sales price. Looking back, I probably tried to minimize my feelings of regret by choosing inaction over action.

In this case, it was better to be lucky than good because an unexpected factor drove AT&T shares up. Amid my regret and inaction feedback loop, an activist investor swooped in and shook up AT&T, boosting the shares and providing a more attractive exit. In some ways, the activist investor helped me choose action over inaction.

BEHAVIORAL COACHING TIP

If you've owned a stock through several market cycles, it's probably a good time to review your investment thesis. If this review suggests taking action, such as a sale, be aware that you may feel more regret for taking action relative to doing nothing. Push back against this tendency toward inaction by using a checklist and debating buy/hold/sell options with colleagues.

Status-Quo Bias

If it ain't broke, don't fix it.

—OLD ADAGE

As we wrap up this deer-in-the-headlights section of the book, let's focus on a third behavioral shortcut that can put our investment process in a deep freeze. Just as complacency and regret for acting can lead us to rest on our laurels, a status-quo bias can steer us toward holding a stock even when buying more or a complete sell makes more sense.

Why might investors favor the status quo? Let's turn to some of the experts to find out. If we broaden the discussion to all economic decisions, Kahneman suggests that the perceived risks of making a change often outweigh the potential benefits, leading people to favor the status quo.[8]

Other economists warn decision makers to watch out for a status-quo bias for slightly different reasons. Thaler suggests that when we give up an asset, we feel a slight loss, and many people would rather do nothing or maintain the status quo rather than feel a loss. Loss aversion and a tendency to "stick with what you have, unless there is some good reason to switch"[9] can lead to inertia. The status quo can be a problem for investors because dynamic stock prices constantly make alternatives more or less attractive.

Moving from theory back to practice, we mentioned in Chapter 8 that overconfidence and excessive trading often produce bad results, so could the status quo be a good thing? Perhaps. Kahneman suggests that our aversion to losses and our preference for the status quo generally point us in the direction of small changes and away from major ones.[10] As we are reviewing our long-term investment thesis, a status-quo bias may help us tame a desire to make an overly confident buy or sell decision.

Another factor that may lead to more or less inertia in our investment review process is the issue of gains or losses for our stock. Because we are more emotional about losses, we may be more likely to sell a stock that's up 50 percent rather than down 50 percent from purchase. The status-quo bias can be more powerful when dealing with losses.

Going back to our AT&T example, my sense is that I suffered from a status-quo bias, especially toward the end of the holding period. I became pretty comfortable with my AT&T position because the stock generally drifted up after the 2009 recession ended. I had few reasons to change my holding size or consider alternatives, likely reflecting some risk or loss aversion. However, three events shook the dust off of my investment views of the company.

First, AT&T took on a mountain of debt to make two controversial acquisitions (Direct TV and Time Warner). Second, other investors sold down AT&T shares as the company's risk profile worsened. Finally, my team's new analyst brought a fresh set of eyes, and the team took a more objective approach to the stock's risk/reward profile.

As mentioned earlier, a status-quo bias may have helped me with AT&T because I sat on the stock until an activist investor got involved and helped boost the shares. However, I learned a lesson that a status-quo bias can impact my decision-making process for risky equities or more defensive companies such as AT&T.

BEHAVIORAL COACHING TIP

A tendency to shy away from risks or potential losses may lead investors to hold onto stocks until well past their expiration dates. Push back against this tendency by pulling in a teammate with fresh perspectives or consider using an investment checklist.

THE ENDOWMENT EFFECT

What do stock pickers have in common with picky eaters? More than you might think. My wife and I have had the pleasure of introducing new foods to our five children for many years, and one of the joys of having seven people around the table each night is finding meals that everyone wants to eat. When we try to get our children to eat something healthy, they often push back on the vegetable, fruit, fish, or anything other than a box of mac and cheese. Dan Ariely, a behavioral economist at Duke University, has some coaching tips for busy parents that we might also apply to stock picking.

Ariely suggests stealing a bite of the healthy green thing on the kid's plate. What happens next is an example of the *endowment effect* because kids often get mad that someone is taking away their dinner, and they want it back. Ariely says, "We tend to like things more when we perceive them as belonging to us."[11]

What parallels can we draw between good eating habits and good stock-picking habits? The next four concepts will go deep into the endowment effect as we look for ways to avoid falling into a trap of hanging onto a stock well past its expiration date because of our personal feelings about the holding.

Personal Stories and Distraction

Does this spark joy?

—Marie Kondo[12]

My family recently moved to a new house, and we got to experience the pleasure of the *keep versus throw-away decision process*. Moving is a great time to purge unwanted stuff, and our rule of thumb is anything sitting unused for over a year means trash or give away.

Perhaps another rule of thumb might come from Marie Kondo's cult of tidying up household items by asking, "Does this spark joy?" In my mind, that's a pretty high bar. Spouses, babies, and puppies come to mind when thinking of what can spark joy. However, for some investors, long-held stocks might spark too much joy, to the detriment of their portfolios.

Investors also can get tied up in knots with the keep versus throw-away decision. Thaler's work suggests that interesting personal stories surrounding our existing investments can grab our attention and cloud our keep versus sell decision.[13] For people moving to a new home, we may struggle with what to do with grandma's family heirloom, even though the item has been in a box for years. In a similar way, many investors get tied up in stories about stocks they've owned for years.

The *endowment effect* distracts us from rational decision making as we look back with fond memories on a stock that's made us money for years. Alternatively, we might remember all the ups and downs of a stock that could have been a contender. Should we keep the winner and dump the loser? Or, more important, are all the memories distracting us? The next question to ask is, what are we missing by being distracted? Thaler says that the endowment effect and its interesting stories "distract us from pervasive market forces that should be our principal concern."[14]

As investors, we should be cold and calculating as we review existing holdings and constantly look for new ones. However, the endowment effect can blur our judgment and prevent us from seeing major market changes. If these pervasive market forces are bad for our stock and good for others, we should be prepared for the keep versus throwaway decision.

Robert Shiller's work also supports the idea that interesting stories may combine with the endowment effect and influence the way we think about possessions. Shiller's concept of *narrative economics* suggests that stories can get stuck in our heads, and we may act on them, often with disastrous consequences.[15]

In the early 2000s, many decision makers believed a false narrative that house prices could only go up, leading homeowners to borrow heavily and speculate on expensive homes. This idea of narrative economics also might make us hold onto stocks longer than we should. Examples such as Enron in 2001 and GE in 2018 come to mind here because investors believed a false narrative that large, seemingly high-quality companies could never blow up.

Our example for this chapter is AT&T, and I was guilty of struggling with the endowment effect as I considered keeping or selling the stock. The company's rich history and grand plan to combine media with wireless communication became an interesting story that distracted me from powerful market forces working against the company.

I had to cut through this distraction to see market risk factors, such as a wave of streaming media competitors releasing new content and charging lower fees than AT&T's Time Warner Division. I also put aside my pleasant memories of AT&T as a safe stock as I watched the company's Direct TV unit grind lower just as the company's debt pile grew taller. AT&T was a reminder to me about the influence of the endowment effect as I reviewed my existing holdings.

BEHAVIORAL COACHING TIP

When reviewing a long-held stock, be careful to avoid the endowment effect. Our history with a stock can be so interesting that it distracts us from seeing pervasive market forces that will likely determine whether the stock will be a winner or loser regardless of the personal stories we tell about the stock.

A Premium Valuation

Our journey into the endowment effect continues as we look at how our feelings and emotions affect the way we value our investments. Thaler suggests that "people value things that are already part of their endowment more highly than things that could be part of their endowment."[16] In other words, we put a premium valuation on what we own relative to alternatives.

Thaler uses an example of sports tickets and the economic choice between attending a sporting event or selling your ticket. If you have a ticket to the Super Bowl, you can go to the game and have a valuable experience, or you can sell the ticket for a price that buyers and sellers determine.

Let's say that you bought your Super Bowl ticket for $5,000 and the secondary market price (such as Stubhub, etc.) has moved up to $10,000. Now what? You can sell now for $10,000, wait and hope that the market price goes up, or just go to the game. Often the ticket holder feels a special ownership for the ticket, and this emotional attachment makes the $10,000 market price seem too low. Perhaps the passionate sports fan would sell for $15,000 if the market price moves up.

We can apply this concept to real estate because home buyers often refuse to sell their homes for years because the endowment effect makes the sales price feel too low for the seller. Your home has interesting stories that may distract you from pervasive market forces, such as a recession, changes in interest rates, or supply/demand dynamics.

Sales prices for comparable homes in a neighborhood may suggest a price for your home that feels like an insult. Sadly, home sellers generally must take the market price for the home or sit and wait (and hope) for prices to rise. However, for stock pickers, hope is not an investment thesis, as we outlined in Chapter 4.

We've talked about how the endowment effect can create a premium valuation for sports tickets and homes, but what about stocks? I would argue that we see a similar pattern where investors who've held stocks for years think that they are worth much more than alternatives.

For AT&T, the endowment effect may have led to feelings of a premium valuation versus alternatives. I essentially felt that AT&T was worth more than a similar stock because of my distraction with the interesting stories of the company. I liked AT&T's slow and steady business model and its reliable dividend payments that provided recurring income to clients over the years.

Other defensive dividend payers, such as real estate, consumer staples, and utility stocks, seemed relatively risky and expensive to me in mid-2019. If these alternatives were cheaper, perhaps I would have sold AT&T and bought one of them. In other words, I felt that AT&T deserved a valuation premium over those alternatives.

Fortunately for me, a fresh set of eyes on my team did some additional digging and analysis on AT&T. A new perspective with less historical baggage helped me break free of the endowment effect and its connection with putting a premium valuation on AT&T. My bias created an expectation that AT&T deserved a premium valuation. However, a less biased approach brought my AT&T price target down to earth, and I later sold at what turned out to be a reasonable valuation.

BEHAVIORAL COACHING TIP

Owning a stock for a long time can lead you to think it's worth more than alternatives. Consider bringing in a new perspective (and possibly a new person) to review a long-held position, especially if your investment thesis is struggling. A new analytical approach can remove the baggage of the endowment effect and its impact on premium pricing.

Holding on Too Long

Let it go.

—FROZEN SOUNDTRACK[17]

I apologize if you've heard the *Frozen* soundtrack way too many times, but I couldn't resist, especially with a section on struggling to let go of a stock. We've just made the case that our possessions carry interesting stories that distract us from market forces and encourage a premium valuation. The next step in this emotional journey leads us into economic quicksand because investors often hit the pause button and hold a possession beyond its sell-by date even though selling might make the most logical sense.

Thaler summarizes this theme by saying that people under the influence of the endowment effect are more likely to keep an asset they already have rather than trade it.[18] Thaler backs up this prediction with a few experiments involving trading possessions for cash.

In one experiment, some participants got a lottery ticket worth $3, whereas others received $3 in cash. In a random group of people, you might expect some risk takers who want a lottery ticket and some risk-averse people who want the cash. Surprisingly, in this experiment, 82 percent of the people who started out with the lottery ticket refused to sell, whereas only 38 percent of people starting out with cash wanted to buy. This example suggests that people may hold onto their possessions for too long because emotions offset rational thinking.

Switching from lottery tickets to stocks, we can see a similar effect. For me, the endowment effect likely put my analysis in slow motion because I held onto AT&T for an extended period, especially after the Time Warner deal led to rising debt levels and new risks. Fortunately, some fresh perspectives from a new team member helped me see through the endowment effect, providing a greater sense of urgency for holding or selling AT&T shares.

BEHAVIORAL COACHING TIP

The endowment effect can make investors act like a deer in the headlights as we sit on our stocks too long. Long-held stocks often have interesting stories that distract us from market forces, lead us to assign premium valuations, and persuade us to hold the stocks longer than we should. Because time is money, consider bringing in some new analytical approaches or new team members, and push back on the endowment effect with a rational and time-sensitive buy/hold/sell discussion.

Comparing Our Asset with Alternatives

One man's trash is another man's treasure.

—OLD PROVERB

We've come to the last stop in our exploration of the endowment effect and this is where we focus more on problem solving rather than problem finding. The endowment effect casts a spell on us because interesting stories obscure what's going on in the world around us. As spellbound investors, we think that our stock is worth more than it probably is, and we hold on too long because we think the market price has yet to reach our magic number.

Those are the problems. How about the solutions? Kahneman suggests that owners, in this case shareholders, can avoid the endowment effect by viewing our goods as things that we can exchange for other valuable items in the future.[19] One way to depersonalize our holdings, as discussed earlier, is to bring in a fresh set of eyes to value the stock. Another way to push back against the endowment effect is to ask, how much do I want that long-held stock compared with others I could have instead? Framing the question in this way helps break up the emotional tension between the joy of receiving and the stress of letting go.[20]

The proverb "One man's trash is another man's treasure" comes in handy here. We may think of our long-held stock as a treasure or a collector's item, but others who have never owned the stock may think of it differently. In some ways, selling a stock is like admitting that our old treasure is now trash. Can we get rid of our old trash and find some new treasure?

The reality is somewhere in the middle because stocks are generally neither trash nor treasure, although there are a few exceptions (e.g., Amazon versus Enron). The challenge for investors who are emotionally tied to long-held stocks is to consider that there might be even better treasure out there that's superior to what we currently own.

As my team evaluated our position in AT&T shares, we had a trash versus treasure moment. We had a good run with the stock, but we saw dark clouds on the horizon as deals and debt started piling up. Fortunately, we also owned AT&T's competitor in the telecom space, Verizon.

We did a head-to-head analysis of AT&T and Verizon to provide some number crunching behind the question, "How much do I want that stock compared with others I could have instead?" We came away thinking that Verizon was closer to treasure (though more like silver than diamonds) but that AT&T was ready for the trash can.

We felt that AT&T's Time Warner deal and the massive borrowing painted the company into a corner. If Time Warner failed to produce hit shows in an increasingly competitive market,[21] then AT&T might struggle to pay down its debt or, at a minimum, face challenges in paying its dividend. We decided to dispose of AT&T and hold onto Verizon for its steadier growth and the dividends that investors treasure.

BEHAVIORAL COACHING TIP

You can limit the endowment effect through comparative analysis by asking yourself how much you want this stock compared with another one you could have. This can help take away some of the emotional pull that prevents you from selling a long-held stock.

Summary

Inaction

- Complacency can creep in for stocks you've owned for a long time, especially if they've performed well. Consider using a checklist annually to make sure that you still see the stock as attractive.

- We tend to feel more regret for action, relative to inaction, potentially leading us to hold onto stocks well past their sell-by dates. Use checklists and debates to lift yourself out of this cycle of regret and inaction.

- Be cautious of the status-quo bias, which can lead you to favor holding a stock too long rather than considering actions such as buying more or selling.

The Endowment Effect

- Stories about long-held stocks can be so interesting that they distract us from evaluating pervasive market forces that are more critical for our buy, hold, and sell decisions.

- When we own things for a long time, we often feel that they are worth more than alternatives.

- Investors are less likely to sell long-held stocks because the endowment effect creates inertia in the investment process.

- Use head-to-head analysis to push back on the endowment effect. Other stocks might seem more compelling than the one you've owned for years, even though you have emotional ties to your stock.

Evaluate a Complete Sale

We're in the home stretch! If you've made it this far, you've been through the highs and lows of picking a stock, watching it move, perhaps trading around it, and testing your investment thesis. If your investment rationale is in good shape, then you can skip this chapter!

However, if you are managing a portfolio of stocks, the law of large numbers suggests that at some point one of your investments will fall off the wagon. If your investment thesis has broken down or your stock has run through your price target, then read on. This chapter will help you evaluate whether it's time to move on by evaluating a complete sale of your stock.

Anchoring

Ignorance is bliss.

—OLD ADAGE

Sometimes less is more for investors. When we buy or sell stocks, we often try to predict the future stock price, which can drive the trading decision.

However, a little ignorance might be helpful here, especially compared with excess information that can pollute our prediction process. Focusing on the wrong kind of information can make us fixate, or *anchor*, to certain numbers or ideas.

I saw a few examples of the idea of less is more during my 15 years as an industry analyst, going deep into a few sectors of the economy with a particular focus on healthcare. In September 2014, I attended a Citigroup investor meeting in Boston, which brought together biotechnology management teams presenting to hedge fund and mutual fund specialists looking to buy or sell biotech stocks. During this conference, I saw an emotional example of anchoring.

Before we discuss the anchoring example, let's set the stage for what was going on in biotech in the early 2010s. A handful of medium-sized and large biotech companies launched new blockbuster drugs between late 2011 and mid-2015, driving a feeding frenzy for stocks such as Biogen, Alexion, Celgene, and Regeneron. With the biotech index (or BTK) up threefold,[1] the bull run got so hot that a top analyst (Mark Schoenebaum) warned that an entire class of biotech investors had yet to see a sector bear market.[2] It almost felt like a mini–housing bubble where investors thought biotech stock prices would never go down.

With this bull market in mind, let's go back to the Citigroup conference to get a sense of how the excitement of making money can lead to bad investment habits such as anchoring. During these types of conferences, CEOs or CFOs usually give 30-minute presentations and then break for five minutes to allow the next management team to load PowerPoint slides for its talk.

As investors and CEOs shuffled around during a five-minute break at the Citigroup conference, I noticed a hedge fund investor talking excitedly with a top manager at Regeneron (REGN), a biotech company developing new drugs for eye diseases such as macular degeneration. The investor apparently made tons of money with Regeneron over several years and knew the managers on a first-name basis. The investor then proceeded to write $350 on a piece of paper, hold it up next to the Regeneron manager, take a picture (like one of those Powerball winners holding up an oversize check with his or her winnings next to the lottery sponsor), and finish off the jubilation by high fiving the Regeneron executive.

Why do you think the hedge fund investor wrote down $350? If you were to look back at the Regeneron chart, you would see that the biotech stock leaped nearly 10-fold from about $35 in 2011 to more than $350 in 2014. My sense is that the hedge fund investor created an anchor at $350, meaning that she expected to make even more money because her investment thesis suggested that the stock would move up to $400 and beyond. What if the stock went down to $300?

The investor might feel emotions, such as embarrassment, frustration, and regret as she thought back to high-fiving the company when the stock was at $350. These emotions and the link with a specific anchor ($350) might lead to bad investment decisions down the road.

How can we generalize this Regeneron example for our investment process? Essentially any time we become emotionally attached to a historical stock price, an earnings estimate, or company guidance, these emotions may hamstring our ability to predict future outcomes. Anchoring weakens our predictive skills in two ways, *priming* and *adjusting*.

What if I told you that Regeneron was one of the most successful biotech companies ever and then asked you if the stock was a buy or a sell? Alternatively, I could say that Regeneron is running out of money and then ask if the stock is attractive. The statements about success or running low on cash are called *priming* because they are mood altering. The biotech bull run of the early 2010s primed investors to give each other high fives and hope for more upward momentum.

Another aspect of anchoring is called *adjusting*, which injects bias into our quantitative predictions. Imagine that you hear that a house in your neighborhood is going up for sale and you quickly estimate that it's worth $800,000. Later, you hear that the listing agent is selling the house for $900,000. Even if you disagree with the broker, your brain starts adjusting to his estimate, and you think that the house should be worth a little more or a little less than $900,000. The listing agent created an anchor, and now you are adjusting to it.

The same thing can happen in the stock market. Imagine that you bought Regeneron at $350. As you try to predict what the shares will be worth in the future, you may subconsciously reframe the question as, "Will the stock be worth more or less than $350?" What if the stock goes down to $300? You probably would anchor to your starting point ($350) and adjust your prediction from there.

This is where investors get into trouble. Priming, anchoring, and adjusting can lead us to make bad decisions, such as holding onto a loser for too long in the hope of breaking even or ignoring other stocks that could be more attractive. In this particular case, the better investment decision would have been to sell Regeneron in 2014 and own the broader market for the next five years.

Most of this section has focused on anchoring to stock prices, but we can also anchor to other financial metrics, such as earnings estimates, as seen in the GE example at the beginning of this book. GE's management team said that the company would earn $2 per share, and investors kept anchoring to that level of profitability. A better approach would have been to ignore management's guidance and develop independent earnings projections.

BEHAVIORAL COACHING TIP

Emotional attachments to purchase prices or high-water marks can lead to irrational decisions, such as holding onto a stock for too long or underappreciating alternatives. Do your best to ignore (or hide) purchase prices and consider only forward-looking price targets as well as comparisons with other stocks that might be more attractive.

Bad Options and Risk-Seeking

Here's goes nothing.

Emotions can make us do strange things, especially when money and risk are involved. Many people are risk averse if you give them a choice between a sure thing, such as $900 in cash, relative to a 90 percent chance at winning $1,000. The cautious person would take the $900.

But what if you had a choice between losing $900 for sure or taking a 90 percent chance of losing $1,000? The least risky option is to take the $900 loss and avoid the even more painful chance of losing $1,000. However, this is where our emotions take over. When options are all bad, most people become risk-seeking and hope to be in the lucky 10 percent that avoids any loss at all.

Kahneman suggests that people become less sensitive to losses as the potential outcomes get worse and worse. In essence, we feel greater pain by losing $900 right now compared with a tiny chance (10 percent) that we can avoid losing $1,000.[3] You can imagine people saying, "Here goes nothing," as they seek out risky options when all outcomes are bad.

How can we apply this theme of risk-seeking when the chips are down to investing? In general, if we've already lost money on a stock and we see further downside potential, we might take a risk-seeking approach in which we dig in our heels and hope for a turnaround.

Using the preceding example, there might be a 90 percent chance that our stock keeps going down, but we become risk-seeking and hope that we're in the lucky 10 percent, leading us to hold onto the stock rather than calling it quits. A better approach might be to sell the loser and put our efforts into finding a new stock with more upside potential.

Let's look at tech hardware company Cisco as an example of risk-seeking when most outcomes look bad. Cisco shares fell to about $48 (from $58) in late 2019 after the company issued disappointing earnings guidance. Let's say that the company's disappointing outlook led to two possible outcomes for the stock. In the best case, Cisco shares would recover slightly toward $50 but underperform the broader market. In a downside case, the stock would fall further into the low $40s or high $30s on additional guidance cuts. Investors would have three options:

- Sell at the current price ($48) and suffer a loss compared with the $58 high-water mark.

- Hold onto the stock and hope for a recovery to $50, but take a chance at a further decline into the high $30s.

- Buy more of the stock at $48 with the same likely outcomes ($50 best case or high $30s worse case).

Using Kahneman's idea of risk-seeking when options are all bad, investors in this situation might choose the third option and hope that a bigger position in Cisco at $48 can yield a quick profit by selling at $50. However, the best option in this case might be the first one, selling Cisco at $48, taking a loss, and rolling the proceeds into other stocks with more attractive upside/downside scenarios.

BEHAVIORAL COACHING TIP

If your investment thesis is struggling, and it seems like there are few good options for a company or stock you own, be aware that you might be falling into a trap of risk-seeking tendencies. Carefully lay out all your options, and consider cutting your losses and moving on to a different stock with a more attractive risk/reward scenario.

Investors Can Become Risk Averse on the Way Up

In the preceding section, we described how investors can go for broke when options are all bad and make risk-seeking decisions. But what about when options look good? It turns out that many people do the opposite and turn to risk aversion.

Kahneman describes an example with two people, Anthony, who starts out with $1 million, and Betty, whose current wealth is $7 million. Each person has a choice. His or her new wealth is either $2 million for sure, or each has a 50/50 shot at either $1 million or $4 million.

As you might imagine, Anthony has only good options, but he takes the sure thing and grabs the $2 million. Going back to the preceding section, Betty has only bad options, and she becomes risk-seeking, choosing the equal weighted chance of $1 million or $4 million.

However, a rational decision maker knows that the risk-seeking gamble is a better deal. You get a 50 percent chance at $1 million (= $500,000) plus a 50 percent shot at $4 million (= $2 million) for an expected value of $2.5 million. This seems more attractive than the sure thing of $2 million. So why does Anthony become risk averse and choose the less attractive option?

Kahneman believes that *reference points* are critical here. As Anthony sees his wealth going up, he gets a lot of utility (enjoyment or satisfaction) out of his newfound money. Gaining $1 million for sure brings greater happiness than the fear of a risky choice, gaining $3 million or winning nothing.[4]

What does this example have to do with investing and changes in wealth? If a saver has done a good job and has enough money for retirement, perhaps that person will act more like Anthony in the preceding example. If you are investing your own money or are working for a firm that has individual clients, you might also act like Anthony. As your wealth (or your clients' wealth) rises, you might gain more satisfaction by a sure thing, even if there are riskier options with more upside.

Using our Cisco example, you might compare options such as:

- A seemingly low-risk approach of holding a blue-chip tech stock (such as Cisco), or

- A potentially higher-risk strategy of selling Cisco and buying an emerging high-growth tech company.

As your state of wealth increases (Anthony in the example), you might opt to hold Cisco as more of a sure thing. However, a more rational or System 2 approach might consider upside and downside scenarios and go with the more compelling stock. Rising wealth might make us hold onto Cisco longer than we should rather than selling.

BEHAVIORAL COACHING TIP

If your stock has been going up for a while, you might feel rising wealth and then become more risk averse, potentially making you miss out on riskier stocks that have more upside than your current holding. Use caution if you sense a bias for a sure thing such as a blue-chip stock rather than an open-minded approach to up-and-coming stocks that might disrupt the status quo.

The Disposition Effect

While Paul Simon sings that there are "fifty ways to leave your lover," there are only three ways to leave your stock. You can fully exit either a winner, a loser, or a breakeven holding. Rational investors are supposed to avoid falling in love with their stock picks, but many investors face tough decisions with long-held stocks, such as trimming winners or outright sales to make room for potentially better ideas. As you consider selling stocks, does it feel better to sell a winner or a loser? Most people would prefer the enjoyment and satisfaction of locking in a gain rather than taking the short-term pain of selling a loser and confessing that the stock was a bad idea.

Kahneman refers to our preference for disposing of winners over losers as the *disposition effect*,[5] a bias that can eat away at long-term performance. Wait a minute! Investors are supposed to buy low and sell high, right? If we sell a stock that's up, we've made the right investment decision . . . or have we? Let's dig a little deeper.

Back in Chapter 1, we talked about narrow framing, where investors make mental accounts that look at pieces of a portfolio rather than the whole thing. Investors want each little piece, in this case, each stock, to put a smile on their faces as they buy low and sell high. However, we can miss the forest for the trees here.

A System 2 investor would ignore purchase prices and only consider upside and downside scenarios for each stock. Using this broad frame, a better approach is to sell stocks with unattractive risk/reward profiles. So what does this have to do with the disposition effect? Well, what if your winners have a good shot at outperforming your losers? Why would you sell those winners and hold onto losers?

It turns out that selling winners has two problems. First, investors have to pay taxes on gains, and second, stocks with upward momentum often persist in the short term. So selling your winners requires a check to Uncle Sam and lost upside from a modest momentum pattern. In fact, investors give up about 3.4 percent in after-tax annual performance by selling winners rather than losers.[6] Kahneman suggests that we feel pleasure by selling winners that close these mental accounts but that we pay for this enjoyment.[7]

Using our Cisco example, let's say that we made a 50 percent gain on the stock and that another tech stock, Intel (INTC), was down 25 percent from our purchase price. The disposition effect might lead us to sell Cisco because we enjoy the satisfaction of locking in our 50 percent gain. However, if we put aside the historical performance and look at upside potential for both stocks, we might find that Cisco could continue to outperform Intel.

If this is the case, we should rip the Band-Aid off by selling Intel and continuing to hold Cisco. We could get a triple benefit here because (1) the Intel loss offsets other gains for tax purposes, (2) we avoid holding onto an underperforming stock (Intel), and (3) we also hold onto a potential winner (Cisco).

BEHAVIORAL COACHING TIP

If you are thinking about selling two stocks, a winner and a loser, be careful to avoid the disposition effect, where you're more inclined to sell the stock that's up. This bias to sell winners can cost you about 3.4 percent a year in performance. A better approach is to ignore purchase prices, lay out upside and downside scenarios, and sell the stock with the less attractive profile.

Would You Sell This Stock if Someone Gave It to You for Free?

So far in this chapter we've focused on behavioral pitfalls that can lead to bad decisions for stocks we've owned for some time: (1) anchoring can make us hold onto a stock too long, (2) having only bad options can make us risk-seeking, (3) the disposition effect can make us sell winners too early, and (4) rising wealth can make us risk averse and sell too early. No wonder investors struggle with knowing when to sell!

Although these concepts can seem a bit complex, Kahneman offers investors an elegant way of clearing away some of the emotional clutter as we think about pulling the ripcord and selling our stock. Kahneman uses an example of driving through a bad snowstorm to see a big sports game for which we've bought nonrefundable tickets. The tickets are a sunk cost, but we can choose to drive through dangerous weather or cut our losses and watch the game on TV. We can ease the burden of this decision by asking what would we do if we got the tickets for free?[8]

When we own something, our personal history with the object or asset colors our vision and our future decisions. Should we fix up the old house or move? Should we keep the old car or get a better one? Should we hold onto family heirlooms or consider selling or donating the items?

We can try to get a better perspective of our next decision by pretending that someone gave us the object or asset for free. Imagine that you won a prize in a contest or found a rare and valuable object sitting on the sidewalk. Would you treat your newfound wealth the same way as a stock you've owned for 20 years?

The bottom line is to treat our stock like an irreversible sunk cost, but with a twist. Instead of anchoring to the purchase price (a sunk cost), we can simply ask ourselves if we would sell the stock if someone gave it to us for free. If someone gave you Cisco shares at $48, would you treat your portfolio differently than if you bought the stock at $58 and the stock traded down to $48? Getting the stock for free at $48 might take away any feelings of short-term loss or aversion to taxes due after a sale, even if you've owned the stock for years.

In some ways, if someone gives you Cisco shares today, you might treat the asset as the equivalent of finding $48 on the street. This *found-money approach* might give you clearer thinking as you consider your next move with the stock.

BEHAVIORAL COACHING TIP

If you're struggling with a sell decision, pretend that someone gave you the stock for free. This approach can remove some of the emotional baggage with the stock and help you decide to buy, hold, or sell.

Valuation Tools and Selling: Shiller's CAPE

So far in this chapter we've looked at behavioral pitfalls that can lead us to sell at the wrong time, and we've reviewed some ways to avoid these mistakes. As we've discussed throughout this book, a great way to avoid bias in any investment decision (buy, hold, or sell) is to use lots of unemotional data and analysis.

One analytical tool that many investors use when considering a sale is the *price-to-earnings (P/E) ratio*. A high P/E ratio can suggest that it's time to sell an expensive stock. Most P/E ratios are a snapshot in time, looking at a company's earnings this year or next year. However, another way to evaluate whether a stock price is expensive compared with its profits is to look at 10 years' worth of earnings.

Robert Shiller came up with the idea of looking at a decade's worth of trailing profits as a way of smoothing out any boom/bust cycles that might either inflate or underrepresent short-term earnings. Shiller's *cyclically adjusted price-to-earnings ratio (CAPE)* can be a powerful tool for pointing out when markets or stocks are reaching valuation extremes.

Still, as Thaler points out, investors should be careful using Shiller's CAPE as a precise indicator for generating trades. CAPE can be directionally right, but the timing can be way off. For example, in December 1996, Shiller warned Alan Greenspan in a Federal Reserve briefing that stock prices seemed dangerously high. Shiller believed that expensive valuation ratios (such as the CAPE) would revert back to a lower long-term average, implying "a poor long-run stock market outlook."[9] Thaler speculates that Shiller's CAPE warning led Greenspan to his "irrationally exuberant" comment in a later speech.[10]

When the chairman of the Federal Reserve said stocks were expensive, some investors may have listened to Greenspan, observed the rising CAPE, and anticipated a stock market correction. However, those who sold in 1996 missed out on years of above-trend performance. As an alternative, Thaler suggests using the CAPE as a directional tool rather than as a timing signal. As the CAPE rises, long-term stock outperformance becomes more challenging, suggesting a greater focus on potential sales in favor of stocks with lower CAPEs.

Using our Cisco example, we can see that the Shiller CAPE provides mixed results as a buy or sell signal. On an annual basis, the CAPE would suggest selling Cisco during the late 1990s, even though the stock outperformed the market for years.[11] Making matters worse, the CAPE signal flipped and suggested buying Cisco for several years starting in 2000, though unfortunately the stock generally underperformed the market most of those years.

BEHAVIORAL COACHING TIP

Shiller's cyclically adjusted price-to-earnings ratio (CAPE) is a powerful tool for evaluating long-term valuation trends. However, avoid using the CAPE by itself as a buy or sell signal. Consider pairing Shiller's CAPE with other valuation metrics, such as standard P/E ratios, discounted-cash-flow (DCF) models, sum-of-the-parts approaches, and transaction multiples.

Bubbles and Market Timing

Most of this chapter has focused on internal emotions that lead us to sell too early, too late, or not at all. However, let's go back to the external web of bias as we examine a theme that can distract us as we consider a final sale.

One of the concepts we discussed in Chapter 1 was anxiety without accountability, where a market pundit often grabs media attention by claiming that bad news is coming. However, we rarely see the same pundit confess later that he or she was wrong. A related theme is the way investors react emotionally when experts claim a stock or asset class is in a bubble.

According to Thaler, "It is much easier to detect that we may be in a bubble than it is to say when it will pop."[12] Said differently, investors should be careful when hearing experts speculate that a stock or a market is in a bubble. If you believe that your stock or your portfolio is in a bubble, your System 2 skills might shut down as your System 1 thinking enters a mild panic about a potential rush for the exit.

How can investors push back against this external bias when an expert labels a stock or a market as being in a bubble? Using a theme we learned in Chapter 3, we can use cognitive strain to be more suspicious and vigilant when we hear someone say our stock is entering bubble territory. Another option might be to listen more closely to the pundit and see whether he or she clearly lays out a reasonable timeline of catalysts that could pop the asset bubble.

If you are thinking of selling your stock and you see a highly confident speaker on a business news show claim that your stock is in a speculative bubble, you might be more likely to sell right away. However, after fully vetting the case for your stock to be in a bubble, you can take a more rational approach to timing your sale.

BEHAVIORAL COACHING TIP

Market pundits often claim that a stock or sector is becoming an asset bubble. However, these industry experts rarely call the timing of when the bubble will pop. Take a skeptical view if someone speculates that your stock is in a bubble. Look to see if there is a credible story for what will trigger a pop in the asset bubble before selling your stock.

Summary

- Anchoring to a particular stock price can create emotional forces that cloud your judgment and future decisions such as holding a stock too long in the hope of getting back to a purchase price. Consider upside/downside scenarios unrelated to a purchase price or high-water mark.

- When the chips are down and all options are bad, people often become risk-seeking. Take a rational System 2 approach to this situation and consider taking a small loss now to avoid a bigger loss later.

- As wealth rises, many investors feel an invisible pull toward a sure thing, or risk aversion. Push back against this bias and keep an open mind toward owning blue chips (sure things) or less widely known stocks that can seem risker but may offer a more attractive risk/reward profile.

- Many investors tend to dispose of winners because we get a feeling of satisfaction for our smart choices. However, this disposition effect can depress performance through taxes on gains and forgone upside because many winners have short-term upward momentum. Ignore purchase prices and sell the stock with the least attractive risk/reward profile.

- If you are struggling with the pain of losses or the dread of paying taxes on a stock's gains, ask yourself if you would sell the stock if someone gave it to you for free.

- Shiller's cyclically adjusted price-to-earnings ratio (CAPE) can be helpful in evaluating whether a stock is getting cheaper or more expensive, but the CAPE by itself can be a poor timing signal.

- Industry experts often claim that a stock or a market has entered bubble territory, potentially triggering an emotional urge to sell. Hit the pause button and evaluate any possible catalysts that can realistically pop the bubble before selling.

12

Sell and Focus on Continuous Improvement

Congratulations! You've made it to the last stop in our journey, or perhaps roller coaster ride, through the full life cycle of your investment. We've done some initial research, formed an investment thesis, made an initial trade and perhaps a follow-on trade, and now we're ready to sell and start over with a new investment.

Each step in this investment life cycle has its own challenges, but the final action can be the hardest for some people. This is so because many buy-and-hold investors spend most of their time accumulating assets, creating a feeling of discomfort with a final and complete sale.[1] Regret is a key theme in this final chapter, and many investors hold on to their stocks too long as a way of avoiding or delaying regrets they may feel if their stocks underperform the broader market.

This final chapter walks you through suggestions for getting the sale done and then taking a step back to see what you can learn as your stock completes the full investment life cycle. Both parts are critical. If you think that your stock will underperform the market or other stocks, you need to sell while looking for alternatives that can improve future performance for the rest of your portfolio.

However, you also should try to reflect on what went wrong and what went right with your stock in the spirit of continual improvement. As you work toward the final sale and reflection, we start out this final chapter by reviewing emotional challenges that can delay or prevent you from executing the final trade.

Procrastination

Successful investing is not about what you know . . . but what you do.

—Liz Ann Sonders[2]

We've reviewed procrastination three times in this book, and each instance happens when we are about to take action, including the initial purchase, a follow-on trade, and now the final sale. Most of the investment life cycle involves research, analysis, and debating, but trades require taking a risky action, and humans often delay things that are difficult or painful.

Behavioral economist Dan Ariely suggests that "procrastination happens because there is an asymmetry between the costs that you have to pay now and the rewards you expect in the future."[3] In other words, you have to take some short-term pain for a longer-term gain. Although our long-term brain knows that the benefits of a future goal may be huge, unfortunately, we can lose our inspiration "when we have to do something difficult right now"[4] to achieve those goals.

Selling a stock can be emotionally difficult if we've lost money in the investment and have to admit that we were wrong. Many investors find it easier to keep holding the stock and hope that it goes back up as a way of avoiding the feelings of regret that come if we sell a loser. Alternatively, if we've made money in the stock, we may have an immediate cost in the form of taxes on gains.

For this final chapter, we're going back to the beginning and using GE as our example. I struggled with procrastination as I reviewed a full sale of the stock, especially because I suffered meaningful losses in the position right before my debate on a full sale. Fortunately, I applied some behavioral finance concepts, and although the sale was still painful, I avoided further short-term losses.

Be aware that investors often procrastinate before making a final sale because most people prefer to avoid a combination of up-front costs and delayed gratification. There are initial hurdles, such as the painful emotion of selling a loser or the financial pain of paying taxes, whereas the benefits of swapping into a better-performing stock often come gradually.

Fighting Procrastination

Work is a necessary evil to be avoided.

—MARK TWAIN

We've just outlined a problem with investors delaying a final sale, so how can we try to push back against this tendency to procrastinate in the last step of the investment life cycle? Fortunately, psychologists and behavioral economists have come to the rescue and have created recommendations for reversing our urge to delay action.

Let's start with Dan Ariely. As we make a leap between up-front costs and distant rewards, Ariely recommends that we "make the current experience more rewarding and fun."[5] This might be easier for daily work activities that have effort now and rewards later, such as stressful project deadlines or major changes to technology systems. You could imagine pizza parties or happy hours as rewards for engaging in these kinds of up-front costs.

However, when thinking about a final stock sale, it may take some creativity to make the process more enjoyable. Perhaps one way to improve morale ahead of a final sale is to have a group discussion about the benefits of selling your stock and the potential rewards of moving on to another security.

Another approach to beating back procrastination comes from psychologist Carol Dweck, who recommends that we make concrete plans that help us visualize the how, when, and where of an activity as a way of avoiding delays. These concrete mental plans generally "lead to really high levels of follow-through" and raise the odds of success in accomplishing a task.[6]

If you say that you'll sell a stock *later*, you're asking for trouble. However, if you plan to sell the stock on Friday at 2 p.m. right after a team meeting, you are creating mental a cue that might help you fight procrastination. The how, when, and where approach reduces the emotional friction that can delay or prevent your final sale.

Going back to our GE example, I could have benefited from heeding Ariely's advice of trying to make the final sale process more enjoyable as a way of fighting procrastination. Instead of getting bogged down in my recent losses, a better approach would have been to look at upside and downside scenarios.

GE stock might keep going down, but selling GE and swapping into a more stable company might bring relief and a general feeling of satisfaction to my team. I also could have used Carol Dweck's *how, when, and where* approach to have a more structured framework for the final GE sale. Weekly investment meetings can serve as good starting points for time, place, and process for completing a final trade.

BEHAVIORAL COACHING TIP

Try to imagine the pleasurable benefits of the final sale, such as upgrading your overall portfolio, as a way of fighting procrastination. Additionally, force yourself to imagine the how, when, and where of your final trade as a means of reducing the urge to delay.

Win a Few, Lose a Few

I am currently a recovering healthcare investor, having spent 14 years of my career researching diseases as well as companies providing drugs, devices, and services that can treat patients. After years of learning what can go wrong when we have a poor diet and inadequate exercise, I now use prevention as a way to avoid the medical therapies that I used to target for investment.

My wife is a wonderful cook and helps our family stick to a healthy diet, but it's up to me to keep up a personal exercise routine. With a busy family and work life, I try to hit the gym most mornings before the market opens. My hope is that a good diet and exercise can help limit the regret I would feel if I ate terribly and sat on the couch too much.

You might be wondering what this has to do with selling a stock, and I promise we'll get there. One of the benefits of exercising before work is getting the feeling of a small win to start the day. The rest of the day could be a different story. For example, in February 2020, broader markets fell approximately 14 percent in a week as investors worried that the coronavirus would trigger a global recession. During this particular "corona crash" week, I went home every evening feeling the weight of the market losses.

You can imagine that this string of crushing losses might lead down a path of regret or even minor depression, which could trigger bad investment decisions in future periods. However, because I started each day with a win by exercising, the pain of the financial losses abated just a bit. In some ways, this daily routine helped instill a sense that I could win a few and lose a few.

How can we apply this idea of *win some, lose some* to a broader set of economic decisions? Kahneman makes a general recommendation that we put each modest bet in a broader frame of other bets with the expectation that we will win a few and lose a few. This approach helps limit the risk aversion we might feel if we focus on only one outcome at a time and helps limit our emotional reaction when we inevitably lose.

Kahneman gives three guidelines to the win a few, lose a few concept:[7] First, make sure that all of the small gambles you're evaluating are independent of each other. If you are making 10 bets in the housing industry, correlation may get you in trouble. Second, only take on small bets that are unlikely to impact your total wealth. Third, the win some, lose some concept breaks down for highly unlikely or long-shot bets.

If we only think about the money we just lost in the COVID-19 bear market of early 2020, we might become risk averse and sell more stock at a time when we should consider both buying and selling. The win some, lose some concept can help keep us open-minded during emotional and financial ups and downs.

With GE, I felt regret from the financial pain of watching the stock plummet from the $30s to the high teens in less than two years. If I focused on the GE losses and nothing else, I might have made poor investment decisions, such as holding onto the stock and trying to make back my losses. However, I took a win some, lose some view, knowing that I had other stocks that were working. I also knew that I could take the proceeds from selling GE and put them to work in another stock that had a more attractive risk/reward profile.

BEHAVIORAL COACHING TIP

View each investment as a modest bet in a portfolio of other modest bets. Some of these bets will pay off, and others will disappoint, supporting a mantra of win some, lose some. This broader approach to gains and losses may help you complete your final sale and feel better about moving on to your next investment.

Thorough Risk Analysis Can Limit Regret

We just sat there sucking our thumbs.

—CHARLIE MUNGER[8]

Regret can be a powerful emotion, and it can lead investors to make bad decisions. Charlie Munger's opening comment referred to Berkshire Hathaway's regret over watching Google and perhaps missing out on a great time to buy the stock.

While I'm the last person to give Munger and Buffett advice, one observation is that Berkshire's regret from missing Google in the early years might be coloring their views of the stock today. By removing the bias of regret, perhaps a fresh set of eyes could see Google as a stock that can still outperform the broader market.

Investors are risk takers, but taking risk can lead to losses and regret. If we stick with mainstream blue-chip stocks as a way of avoiding regret, there's a good chance we'll underperform the market. So how can investors thread this needle of taking risk while also preparing ourselves for future regrets?

Kahneman suggests being blunt about the potential for regret.[9] If you map out exactly what regret might feel like ahead of time, you might actually experience less of it. Additionally, it helps to get ahead of a toxic combination of regret and hindsight bias. A thorough risk and scenario analysis can help you avoid nasty thoughts such as "[insert expletive] I almost made a better decision!"

Another way of getting comfortable with the possibility of regret is the idea of a psychological immune system, which can provide emotional defenses that make future regrets less painful than you antici-pate.[10] Leaning on this mental immune system can help us gain comfort in big decisions, such as a final sale on our long-held stock.

A final nugget on managing regret comes from Dan Ariely, who suggests that we are more likely to regret action in the short term but regret *inaction* longer term.[11] If we align a long-term investment strat-egy with these regret patterns, we may feel more emboldened to take action now.

Our GE case study fits well here because my team felt some short-term regret right after selling the stock and taking losses. However, with a few years of hindsight, my team and I avoided the deeper regret that comes with inaction. Had we held the stock a few more years, we might have sold later and generated even greater losses.

BEHAVIORAL COACHING TIP

Investing while trying to avoid regret can lead to risk aversion and underperformance. Grab the bull by the horns and get comfortable with the possibility of future regret. This thorough risk analysis can make actual regret less painful than you expect.

Changing the Frame Part 1: Loss Versus Cost

If you pay $5 for a sandwich, do you feel like you just lost $5?
—Richard Thaler, *Misbehaving*[12]

This chapter is all about understanding emotions, such as regret, that can lead us to bad decisions as we consider a final sale for our stock. We generally feel regret because of some kind of loss or missed opportunity. But what if we could change the way we frame the idea of losses and regret? Maybe we could remove some of the emotional baggage around our selling decision and move on to other stocks in our portfolio.

Thaler's opening quote gives us a different way to think about losses. When we buy a sandwich, two things happen. Our wallets get a little lighter, and we get to satisfy our hunger pangs. However, some people only see one side of this equation because they focus on losses.

What if you bought a losing lottery ticket or unsuccessfully played the slots in Las Vegas. Would you feel like you had a complete loss, triggering feelings of regret? Or perhaps is there an offset, where you pay a nominal cost to enjoy the temporary feeling that you could be a winner.

Let's say that you lost $500 in Vegas. One way to avoid regret is to frame this experience as paying $500 to enjoy the excitement of rolling the dice in Vegas. Thaler and Kahneman tend to agree that if you refer to a loss as a cost, it will be less emotional because losses stir up more negative emotions than costs.[13]

Perhaps we can use this logic for investing. If we buy high and sell low, we may regret losing money. However, if we frame the transaction as a cost of doing business, we might limit our feelings of regret.

With GE, I had the chance to sell the stock in 2016 for around $30, but a string of bad news for the company sent the stock down to $18 the following year. If I sold at $18, I might view this transaction as a $12 loss ($30 minus $18). I also might prefer to avoid the feelings of regret that accompany losses, leading me to delay selling GE at $18. However, changing the frame away from losses, I could look at selling GE at $18 as a cost of helping clients plan for retirement. Fortunately for me, I sold at $18, only months before the stock fell to just over $6. In this case, the loss-versus-cost framing paid off.

Putting aside GE and looking at an overall portfolio or asset-allocation decision, if I put all my clients' money in risk-free assets, such as cash or US Treasury bonds, I likely would fail to meet their retirement needs. The price for entering a club where you can beat inflation and save for a comfortable retirement is buying high and selling low *sometimes*. If a stock disappoints, chalk it up as a cost, avoid regrets, and move on to other stocks that may prove more successful.

BEHAVIORAL COACHING TIP

If your stock has fallen below your purchase price, or if you are thinking of selling well below the stock's peak, you may anticipate the regret that often follows losses. Flip the script and remind yourself that disappointing stock sales are a cost of doing business in your investment process. Make the sale, and swap into a new stock with greater upside potential.

Changing the Frame Part 2: Loss Versus Proceeds

In the movie *Caddyshack*, Bill Murray's character, Carl, an eccentric greenkeeper and former caddy, tells a coworker a story with some bad news. Carl caddied for the Dalai Lama, but after the round of golf, the Dalai Lama failed to fully compensate Carl for his service. From one perspective, this is a loss. Carl lost money relative to what he expected to earn.

However, Carl changes the frame and focuses on the good part of his experience, the anticipation of receiving total consciousness on his deathbed, as a gift from the Dalai Lama. While this is a silly anecdote from a slapstick comedy, Murray's story about changing the frame on losses might teach us something that can help us make better investment decisions.

In the preceding last section, we changed the frame of a sell decision to avoid feelings of regret that linger after we lose money. Now let's try another approach to framing a sell decision that also should limit our potential regrets. When selling a stock that's down, you can feel better about what happened if you frame the outcome in terms of how much money you've kept rather than how much you've lost.[14]

Kahneman goes further and suggests that people often become risk-seeking when they frame an outcome in terms of losses. In contrast, when you frame an outcome in terms of how much you've kept, people generally take the less risky path.[15] For investors selling a disappointing stock, look at how much you've kept as a way of avoiding risk-seeking emotions guiding your next move.

Using our GE example, selling the stock at $18 meant I lost about $12 relative to a recent high price. However, one of the reasons I sold at $18 was because I thought the stock was going even lower. A key element of my sell thesis was that investor expectations for GE's future profits, even when the stock fell to $18, were too high. If earnings forecasts fell, say 20 to 30 percent, the stock might follow a similar downward path or worse. If you expect GE shares to fall to approximately $12 and you sell at $18, you can change the frame to focus on what you've kept.

BEHAVIORAL COACHING TIP

Changing the frame to focus more on proceeds of a sale rather than losses can help reduce emotional reactions and risk-seeking choices.

Changing the Frame Part 3:
Focus on Duration Rather than the End

> *Don't do it, you'll regret it.*
> —DANIEL KAHNEMAN, *THINKING FAST AND SLOW*[16]

Our last stop on the regret train is another way to frame losses as a means to reduce emotional investing as you consider a sale. Let's say that your stock is below the purchase price or well below its peak, but you're convinced that it could go even lower. A rational investor would sell immediately. However, some investors can get stuck in quicksand if they hear comments like the opening quote about taking an action that may lead to feelings of regret.

The problem with the emotional recommendation, "Don't do it, you'll regret it," is that the comment overweights the end of a process rather than the duration. We mentally jump to the end of our holding period, anticipate regret, and then look backward to see if we can avoid or minimize feelings of regret. This backward-looking logic focuses on the end of the stock's life cycle rather than the full duration. By holding the underperforming stock, we hope to avoid greater losses and feeling regret later.

Kahneman takes the opposite approach as a way of limiting regret. He prefers focusing on the duration of an experience and looking forward. Let's say that you had a fun vacation, but the trip ended badly because you missed your flight home. Do you feel regret for taking the whole trip? If you focus on the duration rather than the end, you might feel good about most of the trip and just a little disappointed with your travel back home.

Continuing with this vacation example, the phrase, "Don't do it, you'll regret it," has a backward-looking perspective, which may lead to irrational decisions for your next trip. You may remember the bad ending of the last vacation and decide to cancel your next one for fear of regretting your decision.

As I evaluated my experience with GE, it was easy to fall into a trap of focusing on the end and taking a backward-looking perspective. If I sold the stock at $18, I faced losses relative to the stock's $30 price a year earlier. However, using Kahneman's recommendation, I could have focused more on how the stock performed for my clients over many years, along with all the dividends the company paid.

The lazy approach would also be to imagine taking a perceived loss by selling GE at $18 and then trying to avoid regrets. Luckily for me, I generally try to look ahead at the upside I could earn from swapping the $18 proceeds from GE into some other stock with more potential.

Experiment, Test, Evaluate, and Learn

In *Star Wars: The Last Jedi*, Yoda, a small but powerful Jedi warrior, is trying to lift the spirits of a dejected Luke Skywalker. Yoda tells Luke that failure can teach you great things. Do we need to experience failure as a way to learn how to achieve success? Apparently Yoda thinks learning from failure will help other Jedi warriors, but what about the rest of us?

Many people keep making the same decisions and the same mistakes in life and in investing. Why is this? And is there any way to break out of this cycle? You might order the usual at your favorite restaurant rather than trying something new. We have high confidence that comfort food will taste good, but what about that exotic-sounding item on the menu?

What if we experiment with something new, test it out, evaluate it, and learn from it? Thaler recommends this approach for decision making, and I think investors can apply these four steps to investment decisions.

Thaler gives an example of a consulting project he did with General Motors that shows how big organizations often feel overconfident and fail to experiment, test, evaluate, and learn.[17] GM had a pattern of making overly bullish demand estimates every year, prompting the company to make too many cars, which finally led the company to dump the excess end-of-year inventory with rebates and discounted car loans.

GM had a successful rebate and discount program for clearing the excess cars and asked Thaler to help the company understand what drove the consumer behavior behind the discounting. Instead, Thaler pointed out that the real problem was overconfidence in making too many cars. GM ignored Thaler's recommendation that the company's planners learn why they were making too many cars, and unfortunately for GM shareholders, the company kept up the pattern of overproduction and end-of-year discounting.

In this case, Thaler focused primarily on learning, which comes at the end of a decision-making process. GM failed to even learn. Ideally, businesses and investors should learn from their decisions and feed that back into experimenting with the next cycle.

Moving from GM to GE, we can see another example of this cycle of experimenting, testing, evaluating, and learning. In 2017 and 2018, GE paid the price for years of overconfident empire building as expensive and disappointing acquisitions started to bring the company down. GE needed to start the cycle over, learn from its mistakes, and then experiment with a different approach.

During most of GE's collapse, I did a poor job of learning why my GE investment was plummeting. However, I decided to take a "better late than never" approach to learning from my mistakes. In late 2017, I experimented with scenarios for GE's potential 2018 profits. GE failed to pass the test for reaching Wall Street's expected future profits in my evaluation. Using a modified version of Thaler's experiment, test, evaluate, and learn process, I dumped GE shares in November 2017 at $18; the stock then proceeded to crater to nearly $6.

I learned from my GE experience that big, mature blue chips might have too much financial risk despite a reputation built up over decades as companies that can generate shareholder value. I experimented with lesser-known industrial companies, such as Danaher, Fortive, Roper, and Honeywell, and I've been testing and evaluating these alternatives to GE. So far I am learning that non-blue-chip stocks can perform as well as or better than household names.

BEHAVIORAL COACHING TIP

At the end of an investment life cycle, take the time to learn what worked well and what worked poorly. Use these insights to experiment with the next investment. Test out your experiment, evaluate what happened, and keep the cycle going by learning from the process after you sell the stock.

20/20 Hindsight Bias or Misremembering

The world is more uncertain than you think.

—DANIEL KAHNEMAN[18]

Investors often misremember how events played out as they recall their stock-picking choices. A global health crisis in 2020 provides a fresh example of this type of System 1 thinking. In early 2020, a flulike coronavirus emanated from Wuhan, China, and spread globally to become the COVID-19 pandemic, leading policymakers to declare global lockdowns to slow the spread of the virus.

News of the virus emerged in January 2020, even as broader stock markets moved up approximately 5 percent. By late March, the S&P 500 was down nearly 35 percent from late February levels. Looking back, many investors likely misremember how the events played out. With 20/20 hindsight, investors might tell themselves that in January 2020, we all knew that the virus would trigger a recession and a bear market. However, this is false. Why would markets rise 5 percent if everyone knew they were about to plummet 35 percent?

What's going on here? Daniel Kahneman frames this type of situation by connecting overconfidence on the front end of the decision-making process with hindsight bias after an outcome.[19] We often overestimate our chances of success as we plan for decisions such as stock trades. We have a confident feeling that our recent stock purchase will work out.

But then something strange happens. Regardless of the outcome, we look back on our decision with 20/20 hindsight. If the stock goes up, we obviously knew that would happen. And if the stock disappoints, well, we always had a bad feeling about that particular stock.

Thaler describes hindsight bias as "after the fact we feel like we always knew the outcome was likely, if not a foregone conclusion."[20] We misremember after an unlikely outcome. Kahneman adds that "when something happens, you immediately understand how it happens. You immediately have a story and an explanation. You have that sense that you learned something and that you won't make that mistake again."[21]

There are three problems here. We start out with too much confidence in our decision making. Then we make up a linear cause-and-effect relationship between our stock pick and the outcome. Finally, we feel like we learned something from the process.

A better approach is to cool it on the overconfidence leading up to an investing decision, as we describe in creating an investment thesis in Chapter 4. Next, we should avoid rushing to judge why a stock went up or down. By limiting hindsight bias, we can learn that during each investment life cycle we "were surprised again."[22] Kahneman's opening quote, that the world is more uncertain than we think, is a reminder that uncertainty can lead to a vicious cycle of overconfidence, misremembering, and hindsight bias.

Going back to our GE example, we can see hindsight bias in action. After the fact, everyone knew that GE's forecasts were too bullish and that the company's expensive gas turbine acquisition was becoming an albatross. However, this view misremembers the long and painful slide as GE went from a Wall Street darling to a serial underperformer.

BEHAVIORAL COACHING TIP

When we have a good or bad outcome with a stock, we quickly create a story of cause and effect. However, surprises may have turned good stock research into a money loser or a bad trade into a winner. After you've sold a stock, look back on the investment life cycle for surprises that drove performance, and use this knowledge for the next stock pick.

Mindset

I've learned that everyone wants to live on the top of the mountain, but all the happiness and growth occurs [sic] *while you're climbing it.*
    —FORMER NCAA WOMEN'S BASKETBALL COACH PAT SUMMITT[23]

Top-tier athletes can teach investors a thing or two about process and outcomes. The opening quote from Pat Summitt, one of the winningest college basketball coaches, is a reminder that practice and process are just as important as reaching your goals. Tom Brady, former New England Patriot's quarterback, suggests that "if you plan wrong, and then you evaluate what you practice wrong, then when you get to the competition you're already starting out behind."[24]

In the preceding section, we outlined a flaw in the way we judge our investments. Hindsight bias can lead us to the wrong conclusion about our investment process. How can we avoid hindsight bias and learn from both our mistakes and our successes? Stanford University psychologist Carol Dweck has a few ideas.

Dweck established the concept of mindset, where decision makers are either backward looking (fixed mindset) or forward looking (growth mindset). A fixed mindset avoids challenges, gives up, ignores feedback, and feels threatened by others. In contrast, a growth mindset embraces challenges, persists after setbacks, learns from criticism, and finds inspiration in the successes of others.[25]

If your stock is a loser, a fixed mindset might anchor you to the higher purchase price, and you fall into a trap of feeling shame and regret for losing money. After selling a stock, a fixed mindset might ask, "Why did we buy that loser when we had a chance to buy a better stock?" Even worse, a fixed investor mindset can get tied up in knots watching missed opportunities, such as Apple or Amazon, seemingly pass by.

However, a growth mindset might carefully dissect an entire investment life cycle like a miner panning for gold. By extracting the nuggets of what went right and what failed, you can look ahead and try to improve your process for the next stock.

Back in Chapter 4 we recommended doing a pre-mortem before buying your stock. Now it's time for a post-mortem. You might reduce some of the hindsight bias and emotional highs and lows by waiting a few months after each final sale to figure out what went right or wrong.

A growth mindset focuses more on the process, rather than the outcome. During the post-mortem, ask yourself, did you follow all of the initial due diligence steps? Was the investment thesis correct? Did you have a healthy debate on the timing and sizing of each trade? What can you learn for the next investment cycle? If you picked stock A instead of stock B, how did your investment thesis play out for stock B?

Let's apply a growth mindset to a real-world case study and see what we can learn from the GE debacle. The goal here is to focus more on the process, which was mixed, and less on the outcome, which was challenging (but could have been worse).

We fell into a state of cognitive ease as we gave GE's management team a pass and felt that their favorable historical track record increased the chances of achieving future profit targets. This was a flawed approach. A better approach is using cognitive strain, which we discussed in Chapter 3, and remaining suspicious and vigilant when considering a management team's financial goals.

Did anything go right toward the end of the investment life cycle with GE? Probably my best use of behavioral coaching was to quit a risky project when I was overly optimistic about its odds, which I outlined in Chapter 8. GE was a sunk cost for me, and it would have been emotionally easy to anchor to prior highs in the stock and hope for a rebound.

BEHAVIORAL COACHING TIP

Grab a growth mindset and run with it. Focus on your investment process rather than outcomes. Do more of what worked well, and avoid what worked poorly. Steer clear of a fixed mindset that can pump up overconfidence after selling a winner or feed a sense of shame and regret after selling a loser.

Embracing Behavioral Coaching

Name it, claim it, tame it.

—Melanie Farrell[26]

As we near the end of the investment life cycle, we can look back on more than 100 behavioral coaching tips that can improve our investment process and hopefully our results. Does this mean that we're done and that we can go pick stocks with perfection?

Before we pat ourselves on the back too much, and despite our growth mindset and constant improvement, Thaler reminds us that even highly trained professionals are still human and subject to biases. Thaler uses the example of the *behavioral bureaucrat*, where the government tries to protect its citizens, but bureaucrats are human and subject to biases.[27]

If trained professionals, such as full-time investors, remain shackled to bias, does that mean that we should give up because the investment process is doomed to fall into a trap of emotion, bias, shortcuts, and poor performance? To the contrary, Thaler advises that "the knee-jerk claim that it is impossible to help anyone make a better decision is clearly undercut by the research."[28] Essentially, we may need to get comfortable with a middle ground where we acknowledge our biases (name them and claim them) while also accepting behavioral coaching as a way to help minimize errors and mistakes (tame them).

Using our GE case study, we can see successes and failures in our investment process and outcome. We held onto the stock too long, but we used some behavioral coaching techniques and finally sold in the high teens, well above the $6 level that GE would later approach. Our human biases blinded us on the descent from $30 to $18. However, our financial analysis saved clients the pain of owning GE on the final leg down.

What can we learn from our GE experience? The quote at the beginning of this section is a good reminder that investors should name their biases, then accept the fact that we will make mistakes, and finally work toward reducing those errors.

BEHAVIORAL COACHING TIP

Professional investors should get comfortable with the tension between knowing we can help clients and also recognizing that we will make behavioral mistakes.

Frequent Practice and Immediate Feedback

> *It's not supposed to be easy. Anyone who finds it easy is stupid.*
> —CHARLIE MUNGER[29]

You have reached the final section in our journey through the investment life cycle. You're now equipped with a toolbox that can help you identify and avoid behavioral pitfalls as you take on risky investment decisions. This is the good news. However, before you pop the champagne and blow out the candles, I have some bad news.[30]

Perhaps bad news is a little much. The news is more like a coach's pep talk after a final practice and heading into a big game. Coaches want to pump you up, but they also want to keep you on edge as you prepare to face the competition.

So here's my final pep talk. The best way to learn from these 100+ behavioral coaching tips is frequent practice and the opportunity for immediate feedback. It takes a lot of work to pay attention, engage your System 2 thinking to use these concepts, and then get rapid feedback. In some ways, Charlie Munger's quote at the beginning of this section humorously sums up the mental and emotional challenges involved in unlocking the mysteries of the markets. However, the payoff for all this work is the chance to improve portfolio performance through well-reasoned investment decisions.

Before we wrap up this final section, there are two hurdles to the idea of practice and feedback. The first challenge is trying to get immediate feedback, because we often hold our investments for years. The second problem is that because we get irregular feedback, we may struggle to develop investment expertise. If the scoreboard is hard to see, do we know if we played a good game?

Let's start by looking at how investors get feedback. Kahneman argues that gaining expertise requires the ability to effectively test your skills through regular feedback.[31] Some professionals, such as athletes, pilots, and surgeons, develop expertise through frequent practice and immediate feedback, suggesting that these decision makers can learn from experience. But what about the rest of us? Let's look at a broader set of decisions to see how we can learn from practice and immediate feedback.

Thaler suggests that high-frequency and low-stakes decisions, such as choosing lunch in a cafeteria or buying milk and bread at the store, allow for rapid feedback. We get pretty good at making good decisions in these cases. However, as you move up the curve to higher stakes, you get to decisions that are less frequent, such as choosing cars, houses, colleges, careers, or spouses. In these cases Thaler suggests that "we don't get much practice or opportunities to learn."[32]

Let's continue with the idea that investors have the opportunity for some feedback, but it's rarely immediate, other than special cases such as day trading. So, if we get irregular feedback, how can we develop expertise? According to Kahneman, research shows that experience without immediate feedback increases our confidence rather than the accuracy of our ideas.

In fact, Kahneman suggests that some professions, such as finance, have such irregular feedback that many participants fail to learn the rules of the game. Kahneman adds that "[i]t's very difficult to imagine from the psychological analysis of what expertise is that you can develop true expertise in, say, predicting the stock market, You cannot because the world isn't sufficiently regular for people to learn rules."[33]

So how can we try to get more regular feedback and avoid a false sense of confidence? One approach, which we discussed earlier in this chapter, is to do a post-mortem about a year after each investment decision.

I manage a portfolio of 40 to 50 stocks, and my team probably makes 20 to 30 trading decisions each year. Within this framework, we can get fairly regular feedback on our investment decisions. This approach may help for any diversified portfolio with 30+ stocks if you have a three- to five-year holding period.

Another way to learn from experience is to watch for signs of overconfidence. Ask another team member to judge whether your confidence is based on facts and analysis or on emotion and hubris. These two approaches may help you to use these 100+ behavioral coaching tips and develop expertise with frequent practice and regular feedback.

Our GE case study is fitting here because high-quality blue-chip companies rarely implode with the ferocity that ripped into GE in 2017 and 2018. Because investors have few chances to get feedback on investing in these blue-chip blowups, it can be challenging to develop expertise around these situations.

I fell into this trap as I watched the company's fundamentals and investor sentiment slide for months. I finally got my bearings and focused on my process of looking at the ability of companies to meet or exceed future earnings expectations. In this case, I decided that GE would fail to meet investor expectations, and I sold halfway through the blowup. Perhaps next time I see a blue-chip start to blow up, this experience will come in handy as I evaluate my investment decisions.

BEHAVIORAL COACHING TIP

Developing investment expertise requires frequent practice and immediate feedback. Because many investors buy and sell stocks infrequently, consider a post-mortem as a way of getting more feedback. Also, watch for signs of overconfidence that can emerge when you have intuitions but infrequent chances to test out your ideas.

Summary

- Be aware of a tendency to procrastinate ahead of a final sale. Most people like to delay things that have up-front costs (selling a loser or paying taxes) and distant rewards, such as owning a better stock.

- Two ways to fight procrastination on a sale include thinking of something pleasant, such as the benefits you'll get from the sale, and laying out the details of how, when, and where you'll do the final stock sale.

- Take a broader approach to gains and losses with the idea that you win a few and lose a few. This should help you avoid regrets as you complete a sale and move on to other stocks in your portfolio.

- Thorough risk analysis can limit regret. Be honest with yourself that a bad decision could lead to regret. By doing this, the actual regret may be less painful than you expect.

- Periodically buying high and selling low are a cost of doing business if you are taking investment risks. Treat these disappointments as costs rather than losses, and move on to greener pastures with other stocks.

- Avoid feelings of regret if your stock is down when you sell by changing the frame. Focus more on proceeds of a sale rather than losses.

- When considering a sale, push back on any advice that sounds like, "Don't do it . . . or you'll regret it." Look forward and focus on the duration of your investment rather than the end as a way of limiting regret.

- After you sell a stock, learn from your failures and successes. Take this knowledge and experiment with your next stock pick. Test and evaluate your experiment and keep the learning cycle going.

- Expect the unexpected when picking a stock, and be careful drawing conclusions as to why your stock was a winner or loser.

20/20 hindsight bias can make you misremember your decision-making process at the end of the investment life cycle.

- Take on a growth mindset as you evaluate your investment process relative to the outcome. How much System 1 thinking went into your process relative to System 2 thinking? A growth mindset focuses on continuous improvement in your investment process.

- Professional investors can work toward removing bias from their process, but because we are human and far from perfect, we need to be aware that we will make behavioral mistakes. Despite these flaws, our investment advice can more than offset biases if we keep improving our process.

- Investment expertise requires frequent practice and feedback. Consider annual post-mortems for your investment decisions as a way of getting better feedback. Also watch for signs of over-confidence, which may emerge if feedback comes less frequently.

Epilogue

n the 2020 Disney movie, *Soul*, jazz pianist Joe Gardner stumbles into an imaginary world where entertainers are *in the zone*, a place where artists and athletes essentially lose themselves as they are creating music, theater, or sports victories. Gardner describes the spectacular artists and entertainers as having *flow*, a concept developed by psychologist Mihaly Csikszentmihalyi (pronounced "six-cent-mihaly") in which "concentration is so intense that there is no attention left over to think about anything irrelevant or to worry about problems."[1] In a way, flow that removes self-consciousness and distorts time, is at the pinnacle of one of the goals of this book: having fun and getting better at an activity that you passionately enjoy.

In Hollywood, professional entertainers may reach a state of flow after thousands of hours of practice. These professionals have built up a lifetime of experience that can overcome the opposite of flow, in other words, situations that are rare, difficult, risky, and provide little feedback.

For professional investors, getting in the zone or reaching a state of flow is also possible, but it also takes lots of effort, concentration, and experience to prepare for rare, difficult, and risky situations while getting real-time feedback. My hope is that *Stop. Think. Invest.* can help create good habits that get investors closer to this idea of flow. When we stop what we are doing, we can gradually move from System 1 to System 2 thinking and then make better investment decisions. By elevating our awareness of emotions and biases, we can use behavioral finance concepts to constantly refine our skills and make well-informed capital-allocation decisions.

What's next? Now that you've grappled with the 100+ behavioral coaching concepts in this book, do you think that you'll be able to implement some of the themes and suggestions? Don't beat yourself up if you struggle to follow each of the 100+ steps. In a way, this book is a guide to help you avoid as many behavioral pitfalls as possible. If you only follow a few of these steps, take on a growth mindset and pat yourself on the back because you've probably avoided a few costly mistakes.

For investors hoping to implement more of these behavioral coaching tips, remember the planning fallacy and try to make a realistic forecast. There is good news and bad news here. Let's get the bad news out of the way first, which is that time is the enemy of the investor as we wade through a sea of companies, events, data, emotions, and biases.

Why is investing such a time-intensive process that leads many investors to take shortcuts? I would argue that time management is a critical theme for investors who want to implement these behavioral coaching tips and fight back against the urge to take the easy way out through System 1 thinking. Most professional investors are drinking from a fire hose of daily information, making it difficult to switch between thinking fast and slow, to borrow the title of Kahneman's book. To make better investment decisions, you have to shut off the fast-thinking information fire hose and switch on your slow-thinking reflective brain cells.

Of the three parts of *Stop. Think. Invest.*, stopping what we are doing may be the most challenging, because investors have multiple demands, tasks, and responsibilities. But if we can stop and focus, we can become more efficient with the time-intensive front end of the investment life cycle, including data gathering, due diligence, and financial analysis.

Efficiency is crucial for investors because, as my former manager and mentor, Mike Krensavage, used to say, "Work expands to fill time." With this in mind, many investors spend almost all their days analyzing data, leaving little time left over to consider behavioral finance red flags.

In some ways, this book's behavioral coaching suggestions are at the top of the pyramid of workflow in the investment process. At the bottom are the time and effort required to get a basic understanding of financial analysis. Many investors do this through college or MBA classes, the Chartered Financial Analyst course of study, or years of on-the-job training and mentoring from colleagues. Once investors achieve this level of understanding, they generally have to dive into industry analysis. Picking stocks in technology and healthcare can almost feel like picking up French or Spanish. Each industry has its own jargon and financial metrics.

After investors get a handle on basic financial analysis and industry-specific terms and statistics, the next step is the constant flow of news that impacts how investors feel about future company fundamentals and valuation. As you can imagine, most of us can be overwhelmed by these first three levels in the workflow pyramid.

This brings us to the good news, which is that a well-organized body of knowledge from Nobel laureates can help investors become both efficient and highly focused as we work toward a state of flow and expertise. Understanding and adopting many of these behavioral finance concepts may allow investors to Stop what they are doing, Think about the best way forward, and then Invest.

Notes

Preface

1. https://www.ge.com/sites/default/files/ge_webcast_presentation_12162015_0.pdf. Many investors in 2015 likely expected GE shares to closely track the company's earnings. If GE's profits reached $2.00 per share in 2018, up from $1.20 in 2015, investors would be anticipating nearly 70 percent growth over a three-year period, or roughly 18 percent growth in earnings per year. If the stock closely tracked the company's earnings, investors might expect a similar approximately 18 percent rise in their GE stock each year for three years, well above a long-term average return for most stocks in the 8–10 percent range. Historically, many stocks (and stock markets) trade about in line with underlying earnings over long periods, although there can be exceptions. https://www.ge.com/sites/default/files/GE%20Investor%20Update_Presentation_11132017.pdf; https://www.ge.com/sites/default/files/ge_webcast_pressrelease_01312019.pdf. Bloomberg ANR (analyst recommendations) function for GE stock. In 2016 and 2017, about two-thirds of Wall Street analysts had the equivalent of a buy rating on GE, with an expectation that the company's earnings would grow each year through 2018. As the business started falling apart and after the stock lost roughly a third of its value, falling from the low $30s to about $20 in October 2017, about half the analysts still had a buy rating on GE shares. Analyst sentiment bottomed in July 2018, when only about 20 percent of Wall Street analysts had a buy rating on the stock, which was trading around $13. Interestingly, greed overtook fear as GE shares fell even further. When GE shares hit bottom in late 2018 at approximately $7, the bulls started coming back, because nearly 40 percent of analysts had a buy rating on the stock. All references to GE's stock price and earnings per share refer to the period before GE's 1-for-8 reverse split in 2021.
2. Daniel Kahneman, *Thinking, Fast and Slow* (New York: Farrar, Straus and Giroux, 2011), 24.
3. Howard Marks to Oaktree clients, "Uncertainty," May 11, 2020, https://www.oaktreecapital.com/docs/default-source/memos/uncertainty.pdf.
4. Richard Thaler, *Misbehaving: The Making of Behavioral Economics* (New York: W.W. Norton & Company, 2015), 220. Graham's idea with value investing is to use financial metrics to establish an intrinsic value or price target for a stock. If your analysis suggests that a stock is worth $10, but a fearful or pessimistic market price is currently $5, then Graham would suggest buying and holding the stock. Over time, the

irrational market can switch to greed or optimism, driving the stock upward toward the intrinsic value and allowing the investor to sell at a higher price.

5. Thaler, *Misbehaving*, 209, 233.

6. Robert J. Shiller, "Trust Your Gut? Use Your Head," *New York Times*, January 5, 2020, https://www.nytimes.com/2020/01/02/business/gut-feelings-are-driving-the-markets.html.

7. Ibid.

8. Ibid.

9. Richard Thaler and Cass Sunstein, *Nudge: Improving Decisions About Health, Wealth, and Happiness* (New York: Penguin Books, 2009), 9.

10. Ibid.

11. S. Cummings, T. Bridgman, and K. Brown, "Unfreezing Change as Three Steps: Rethinking Kurt Lewin's Legacy for Change Management," *Human Relations* 2016;69(1) 33–60, https://journals.sagepub.com/doi/pdf/10.1177/0018726715577707.

12. Holly Seniuk, Benjamin N. Witts, W. Larry Williams, Patrick M. Ghezzi, et al., "Behavioral Coaching," *The Behavior Analyst* 2013;36(1):167–172, https://doi.org/10.1007/BF03392301.

13. Thaler and Sunstein, *Nudge*, 6.

14. Kahneman, *Thinking, Fast and Slow*. This book inspired me to write a book that builds on the foundation that Kahneman created by channeling many of his broader concepts into a practical, focused, step-by-step checklist for professional investors. I could have called this book *Investing Fast and Slow*, but then I would have fallen into the trap of mental laziness, a form of System 1 thinking that Kahneman warns against!

15. Richard Thaler's comment on the stupidity continuing with NFL draft picks. Interview at https://www.pm-research.com/conversationswiththaler (at approximately 6 minutes and 30 seconds).

16. This book focuses on about 100 behavioral economics concepts, and my sense is that many of these (perhaps 80–90) fall through the cracks and rarely make it into a broader discussion among decision makers and investors. To be fair, academics and experts have identified upwards of 200 behavioral economics theories, as discussed in a Bloomberg News article, "Behavioral Economics' Latest Bias: Seeing Bias Wherever It Looks," January 13, 2020, by Brandon Kochkodin. However, I would argue that many of the 200 themes are less relevant to finance and investing. This book tries to mix theory and practice to establish about 100 behavioral finance tools that can improve an investment process.

17. For interested readers, Michael Lewis's book, *The Undoing Project: A Friendship That Changed Our Minds* (New York: W.W. Norton & Company, 2016), provides a fascinating history of the Tversky and Kahneman partnership that shaped behavioral finance and economics.

18. Roger G. Ibbottson, Thomas M. Idzorek, CF, Paul D. Kaplan, CFA, James X. Xiong, CFA, et al., "Popularity: A Bridge Between Classical and Behavioral Finance," CFA Institute Research Foundation, Charlottesville, VA, 2018, p. 6, https://www.cfainstitute.org/-/media/documents/book/rf-publication/2018/popularity-bridge-between-classical-and-behavioral-finance.ashx.

19. Paul McCaffrey, "Daniel Kahneman: Four Keys to Better Decision Making," Enterprising Investor (blog), CFA Institute, Charlottesville, VA, June 8, 2018, https://blogs.cfainstitute.org/investor/2018/06/08/daniel-kahneman-four-keys-to-better-decision-making/.

20. Thaler and Sunstein, *Nudge*, 9.
21. Malcolm Gladwell, *Outliers: The Story of Success* (New York: Little, Brown, 2008). Chapter 2 discusses Gladwell's idea that you need to spend 10,000 hours doing a particular activity (e.g., music, sports, etc) to build your expertise. On a personal note, my father, Jon Bailey, who's been teaching psychology at Florida State University since 1970, reminded me that Gladwell referred to the idea of 10,000 hours of deliberate practice, which came from my father's colleague, Dr. Anders Ericsson.
22. Carol Dweck, *Mindset: The New Psychology of Success* (New York: Random House, 2006). The paperback version (New York: Ballantine Books, 2007) has a discussion of the growth mindset on page 7.
23. Ibid (paperback), 6.
24. Kahneman, *Thinking, Fast and Slow*, 20–21.
25. Thaler and Sunstein, *Nudge*, 22.
26. Ibid, 19.
27. Hansi Mehrotra, "What Most Active vs. Passive Debates Miss," Enterprising Investor (blog), CFA Institute, Charlottesville, VA, July 1, 2020, https://blogs.cfainstitute.org/investor/2020/07/01/what-most-active-vs-passive-debates-miss/.
28. Vanguard is a global asset-management firm that believes that advisors can add about 3 percent to a client's net performance on an annualized basis over time. Behavioral coaching accounts for about half of this 3 percent benefit. Francis M. Kinniry Jr., et al, "Putting a Value on Your Value: Quantifying Vanguard Advisor's Alpha," Vanguard Research, Malvern, PA, February 2019, https://www.vanguard.com/pdf/ISGQVAA.pdf.

Introduction

1. I followed drug companies at a regional broker-dealer (Raymond James) and later covered medical device companies for Bear Stearns, which JP Morgan acquired during the great financial crisis of 2008–2009.
2. Looking at four of the companies I covered during 2004, Pfizer has dramatically underperformed the broader market, whereas Abbott has performed better. The Standard & Poor's (S&P) 500 Index basically tripled between 2004 and 2020, whereas Pfizer was nearly unchanged, excluding dividends. Abbott, in contrast, was up about fivefold, excluding spinoffs and dividends. These long-term results suggest to me that investment style can help identify winners and losers over long periods of time, even for large-cap companies with complete information transparency.
3. Joe Healy, my former director of research at asset management firm Legg Mason, referred to a fundamentally driven valuation improvement as the best way to find outperforming stocks.
4. Bill Miller managed portfolios at Legg Mason in Baltimore, and his funds beat the S&P 500 for 15 years. I overlapped with Miller during my years at Legg Mason between 2006 and 2014. Miller's approach to behavioral finance grew out of his studies in economics and philosophy and his early career as an overseas military intelligence officer. Miller discusses his views on the behavioral edge in this post: https://millervalue.com/sources-of-edge/. Some investors expand on this concept by proposing a fourth factor called the *organizational edge,* which includes structure, incentives, compensation, and culture. An organizational edge can encourage long-term outperformance through incentives and individual accountability while avoiding groupthink. In a sense, an organizational edge can reinforce some of the behavioral finance best practices within a professional investment firm.

5. Standards of Practice Guidance 2014, Standard II(A) Material Nonpublic Information, CFA Institute, Charlottesville, VA, 2014, https://www.cfainstitute.org/en/ethics-standards/codes/standards-of-practice-guidance/standards-of-practice-II-A#mosaic.

6. Howard Marks to Oaktree clients, "Knowledge of the Future," New York, April 14, 2020, https://www.oaktreecapital.com/docs/default-source/memos/knowledge-of-the-future.pdf.

7. Thaler, *Misbehaving*, 292–293.

Chapter 1

1. Charlie Munger, Berkshire Hathaway Annual General Meeting, Omaha, NE, May 4, 2019.

2. Thaler and Sunstein, *Nudge*, 3, 6.

3. Simone Brands, Stephen J. Brown, David R. Gallagher, et al., "Portfolio Concentration and Investment Manager Performance," SSRN, New York, March 12, 2004, https://papers.ssrn.com/sol3/papers.cfm?abstract_id=846065.

4. Dan Ariely, "Can Too Many Options Make Decisions Impossible?," *Wall Street Journal*, August 9, 2019, https://www.wsj.com/articles/can-too-many-options-make-decisions-impossible-11565370496.

5. "Cyber Heroes Series: Don't Take the Bait," Popcorn Training Pty Ltd., May 2020. The media production company behind the video has a corporate slogan that reads "Human error. Conquered." In a way, this slogan is fitting for some of the broader themes of this book. Human errors stemming from emotions can lead to disappointing investments.

6. Garth Sundem, "This Is Your Brain on Multitasking," Psychology Today (blog), February 24, 2012, https://www.psychologytoday.com/us/blog/brain-trust/201202/is-your-brain-multitasking.

7. Jon Hamilton, "Think You're Multitasking? Think Again," National Public Radio, October 2, 2008, https://www.npr.org/templates/story/story.php?storyId=95256794.

8. Kahneman, *Thinking, Fast and Slow*, 23.

9. Ibid.

10. Bob Browne, remarks at Northern Trust Investment Institute Conference, Chicago, September 12, 2019.

11. Kahneman, *Thinking, Fast and Slow*, 67.

12. Ibid., 66.

13. MSCI All Country World Index (ACWI), published by MSCI, Inc., New York, as of early 2021, https://www.msci.com/acwi.

14. Jeffrey Kleintop, "Your Portfolio May Be Less Diversified Than You Think," Schwab Funds, New York, February 1, 2021, https://www.schwabassetmanagement.com/content/your-portfolio-may-be-less-diversified-than-you-think.

15. J.P. Morgan Asset Management, "Guide to the Markets, U.S. 2Q 2020," New York, as of June 23, 2020.

16. Howard Marks to Oaktree clients, "Uncertainty," May 11, 2020, https://www.oaktreecapital.com/docs/default-source/memos/uncertainty.pdf.

17. Kahneman, *Thinking, Fast and Slow*, 249.

18. Howard Marks to Oaktree clients, "Uncertainty," May 11, 2020, https://www.oaktreecapital.com/docs/default-source/memos/uncertainty.pdf.

19. Kahneman, *Thinking, Fast and Slow*, 248. Kahneman makes a reference to the famous quote from former secretary of defense Donald Rumsfeld, referring to unknown questions or unknown variables. One example could be buying your first

house, when you might not even know what questions to ask. You probably have better questions to ask when buying your second house. Similarly, when browsing for a new stock, you might be unfamiliar with the company, and there are likely unknown unknowns about the business that require more digging.

20. Morgan Housel, "Kahneman on Overconfidence in Investing," The Motley Fool, May 6, 2013, https://www.fool.com/investing/general/2013/05/06/nobel-prize-winning-psychologist-daniel-kahneman-o.aspx.
21. Kahneman, *Thinking, Fast and Slow*, 129.
22. Morgan Housel, "Kahneman on Overconfidence in Investing," The Motley Fool, May 6, 2013, https://www.fool.com/investing/general/2013/05/06/nobel-prize-winning-psychologist-daniel-kahneman-o.aspx.
23. Charlie Munger, Berkshire Hathaway Annual General Meeting, Omaha, NE, May 4, 2019.
24. Kahneman, *Thinking, Fast and Slow*, 273.
25. Thaler, *Misbehaving*, 189.
26. Kahneman, *Thinking, Fast and Slow*, 336.
27. Eric Platt, "The Gospel According to Charlie Munger: Lower Your Expectations," *Financial Times*, February 12, 2020, https://www.ft.com/content/03f977e6-4dde-11ea-95a0-43d18ec715f5.
28. Thaler, *Misbehaving*, 165.
29. Kahneman, *Thinking, Fast and Slow*, 343.
30. Paul McCaffrey, "Daniel Kahneman: Four Keys to Better Decision Making," Enterprising Investor (blog), CFA Institute, June 8, 2018, https://blogs.cfainstitute.org/investor/2018/06/08/daniel-kahneman-four-keys-to-better-decision-making/.
31. Kahneman, *Thinking, Fast and Slow*, 262.
32. Ibid.
33. Ibid.
34. Sell-side analysts have a great understanding of companies and often do a good job of predicting which way profits will go, but I would be skeptical about their stock recommendations. I'm comfortable saying this having been a sell-side analyst for six years. Sell-side analysts work really hard, and they tell great stories, but they have many client and marketing obligations that take time away from focusing on stock recommendations.
35. In full disclosure, I've been on the buy side since 2006, so my writing could be biased toward buy-side speakers!
36. Laurence Siegel is a research director for a financial education and publishing non-profit called the CFA Institute. Jason Zweig, "Why Invest? A 22-Year-Old's Tough Questions About Capitalism," *Wall Street Journal*, January 24, 2020, https://www.wsj.com/articles/why-invest-a-22-year-olds-tough-questions-about-capitalism-11579882164?mod=hp_featst_pos1.
37. Steve Leisman, "Can the Markets Predict Recessions? What We Found Out", CNBC.com, February 4, 2016, https://www.cnbc.com/2016/02/04/can-the-markets-predict-recessions-what-we-found-out.html.
38. Andrew Kaplowitz, "Fortive Corporation: Solid Growth Potential Well Reflected in Stock," Citi Research, July 5, 2016.
39. Thaler, *Misbehaving*, 198.
40. Ibid, 74.
41. John J. McConnell, Steven E. Sibley, Wei Xu, et al., "The Stock Price Performance of Spin-Off Subsidiaries, Their Parents, and the Spin-Off ETF, 2001–2013," *Journal of Portfolio Management* 2015;42(1):143–152, https://www.researchgate.net/

publication/283556164_The_Stock_Price_Performance_of_Spin-Off_
Subsidiaries_Their_Parents_and_the_Spin-Off_ETF_2001-2013.

Chapter 2

1. Kahneman, *Thinking, Fast and Slow*, 85.
2. Ibid.
3. Shahram Heshmat, "What Is Confirmation Bias?" *Psychology Today* (blog), April 23, 2015, https://www.psychologytoday.com/us/blog/science-choice/201504/what-is-confirmation-bias.
4. Michael W. Arone, "Uncommon Sense: What I Learned This Summer: He Who Holds the Data Makes the Rules," State Street Global Advisors, Boston, September 3, 2020, https://www.ssga.com/us/en/institutional/etfs/insights/uncommon-sense/what-i-learned-this-summer-he-who-holds-the-data-makes-the-rules?.
5. Ibid.
6. Atul Gawande, *Complications: A Surgeon's Notes on an Imperfect Science* (New York: Metropolitan Books, 2002), 15.
7. Bernard Shaw, *The Doctor's Dilemma: A Tragedy* (London: Constable and Co., 1922).
8. https://www.goodreads.com/quotes/959873-those-who-have-knowledge-don-t-predict-those-who-predict-don-t .
9. Howard Marks to Oaktree clients, "Uncertainty," May 11, 2020, https://www.oaktreecapital.com/docs/default-source/memos/uncertainty.pdf..
10. Ibid.
11. Ibid.
12. Howard Marks to Oaktree clients, "Uncertainty II," May 28, 2020, https://www.oaktreecapital.com/docs/default-source/memos/uncertainty-ii.pdf.
13. Kahneman, *Thinking, Fast and Slow*, 219.
14. Ibid.
15. "Halo Effect," *Psychology Today* (blog), https://www.psychologytoday.com/us/basics/halo-effect, accessed August 26, 2021.
16. Kahneman, *Thinking, Fast and Slow*, 103.
17. Ibid.

Chapter 3

1. Kahneman describes a concept called *priming*, where a background effect can influence action. In one experiment, volunteers were asked to help others with a task. When images of money were in the experiment room, volunteers acted more selfishly and helped others less often. Pictures of money primed the volunteers to be more selfish. *Thinking, Fast and Slow*, 55.
2. Kahneman, *Thinking, Fast and Slow*, 60.
3. Ibid., 59.
4. SWOT analysis focuses on strengths, weaknesses, opportunities, and threats to a company. Porter's five-forces approach looks at customers, competitors, suppliers, new entrants, and substitutes.
5. Thaler and Sunstein, *Nudge*, 99.
6. At the time, buy-side clients would reward good broker research by doing trades with the sell-side analyst's firm. Additionally, the *Institutional Investor* survey was a way to determine how much value sell-side analysts added. Buy-side analysts would vote for the best sell-side analysts, with the results published in the annual *Institutional Investor* survey.

7. One of my colleagues at Bear was a former orthopedic surgeon named Milton Hsu. Milton kept telling me to "talk to docs!" as the best way to understand medical companies and products. I also test drove the Intuitive Surgical medical robot and performed a discectomy on a cadaver model.

8. Howard Marks to Oaktree clients, "Uncertainty," May 11, 2020, https://www .oaktreecapital.com/docs/default-source/memos/uncertainty.pdf.

9. Kahneman, *Thinking, Fast and Slow*, 205.

10. Ibid., 206.

11. Howard Marks to Oaktree clients, "Uncertainty," May 11, 2020, https://www .oaktreecapital.com/docs/default-source/memos/uncertainty.pdf.

12. Susan Ratcliffe, ed., *Oxford Essential Quotations*, 4th edition (Oxford: Oxford University Press, 2016). https://www.oxfordreference.com/view/10.1093/acref/ 9780191826719.001.0001/q-oro-ed4-00003457.

13. Kahneman, *Thinking, Fast and Slow*, 212, 262.

14. You can also see a link between overconfidence and a coherent story with other high-profile personalities in politics, the media, and sports. Some insiders will say that politics is all about telling stories and influencing people, for example.

15. Paul McCaffrey, "Daniel Kahneman: Four Keys to Better Decision Making," CFA Institute blog, June 8, 2018, https://blogs.cfainstitute.org/investor/2018/06/08/ daniel-kahneman-four-keys-to-better-decision-making/.

16. Ibid.

17. Howard Marks to Oaktree clients, "Uncertainty," May 11, 2020, https://www .oaktreecapital.com/docs/default-source/memos/uncertainty.pdf.

18. Theodore Seuss Geisel (Dr. Seuss), *The Lorax* (New York: Random House, 1971).

19. Peter Clark and Roger Mills, *Masterminding the Deal: Breakthroughs in M&A Strategy and Analysis* (London: Kogan Page, 2013), 148–149.

20. Kahneman, *Thinking, Fast and Slow*, 258.

21. Interview with Dr. Colin Camerer, April 29, 2021.

22. Michael Mauboussin Dan Callahan, and Darius Majd, "Capital Allocation: Evidence, Analytical Methods, and Assessment Guidance," Credit Suisse, Paradeplatz, Switzerland, October 19, 2016.

23. Kahneman, *Thinking, Fast and Slow*, 346. Kahneman also notes a related issue with the agency problem. CEOs are usually agents (managers) rather than principals or owners.

24. Ibid., 345.

25. While Scharf tried to shut down bad sales practices, he also struggled with other challenges amid tight government regulation and penalties for the bad sales practices.

26. Kahneman, *Thinking, Fast and Slow*, 161.

27. Gerry Smith and Katherine Chiglinsky, "Wall Street Has Plans for Newspapers, and They Aren't Pretty," *Bloomberg Businessweek*, February 7, 2020, https://www .bloomberg.com/news/articles/2020-02-07/wall-street-has-no-use-for-newspapers -anymore.

28. Kahneman, *Thinking, Fast and Slow*, 190.

29. Ibid.

30. Ibid., 251.

31. Tim Hartford, "We Need to Be Better at Predicting Bad Outcomes," *Financial Times*, September 20, 2019, https://www.ft.com/content/374fd3fa-dac1-11e9-8f9b -77216ebe1f17.

32. Kahneman, *Thinking, Fast and Slow*, 310.

33. Ibid.

34. Rory Sutherland, "The Art and Science of Business Magic," *The Spectator*, May 7, 2019, https://spectator.us/topic/art-science-business-magic/.

35. Michael Arone, "Uncommon Sense: Three Surprises for 2020 That Deliberately Defy Logic," State Street Global Advisors, Boston, January 29, 2020, https://comms .ssgaglobal.com/rs/451-VAW-614/images/spdr-uncommon-sense-three-surprises -for-2020.pdf?link=Uncommon-Sense-button.

36. Consider discounted cash flow (DCF) modeling or discounting future earnings back and using a price/earnings (PE) multiple.

Chapter 4

1. Howard Marks memo to Oaktree clients, May 11, 2020, https://www.oaktreecapital .com/docs/default-source/memos/uncertainty.pdf.

2. Paul McCaffrey, "Daniel Kahneman: Four Keys to Better Decision Making," CFA Institute blog, June 8, 2018, https://blogs.cfainstitute.org/investor/2018/06/08/ daniel-kahneman-four-keys-to-better-decision-making/.

3. Ibid.

4. Joe Healy was my director of research when I was an equity analyst at asset management firm Legg Mason. Joe was quick to flag team members who hoped that fundamentals or valuation would improve for a stock.

5. Thaler, *Misbehaving*, 186.

6. Ibid.

7. Ibid.

8. Craig Calcaterra, "Opening Day 2019: 'Everybody Has a Plan Until They Get Punched in the Mouth,'" NBC Sports, March 28, 2019, https://mlb.nbcsports.com/2019/ 03/28/opening-day-2019-everybody-has-a-plan-until-they-get-punched-in-the -mouth/.

9. Kahneman, *Thinking, Fast and Slow*, 250.

10. Ibid., 312.

11. Investors may react in an opposite way if there is a small possibility of a reward, becoming risk seeking and overweighting the chance of winning big.

12. Kahneman, *Thinking, Fast and Slow*, 312.

13. The certainty effect also leads people to become risk averse when gains are almost certain because they try to avoid the fear of disappointment. How much would you pay to go from a 99 percent chance of winning the lottery to a 100 percent chance?

14. Kahneman, *Thinking, Fast and Slow*, 328.

15. To be sure, there are plenty of counterexamples, such as successful tech companies (Zoom Video) and consumer products developers (Peloton) that break from a pattern of low growth into much faster growth. Still, these winners are generally rare among the ranks of startup companies trying to make a big splash among investors.

16. Howard Marks memo to Oaktree clients, May 11, 2020, https://www.oaktreecapital. com/docs/default-source/memos/uncertainty.pdf.

17. Tim Hartfold, "We Need to Be Better at Predicting Bad Outcomes," *Financial Times*, September 20, 2019, https://www.ft.com/content/374fd3fa-dac1-11e9-8f9b -77216ebe1f17.

18. Kahneman, *Thinking, Fast and Slow*, 264.

19. Eric Platt, "The Gospel According to Charlie Munger: Lower Your Expectations," *Financial Times*, February 12, 2020, https://www.ft.com/content/03f977e6-4dde -11ea-95a0-43d18ec715f5.

20. In late 2020, Amazon represented about 5 percent of the S&P 500 by market value. By holding more than 5 percent of Amazon in your portfolio, you are making a bet that Amazon will go up more than the overall S&P 500.

21. Thaler, *Misbehaving*, 186.

Chapter 5

1. Some investment firms that use a behavioral edge as part of their process may prefer to avoid investment committees, arguing that group dynamics add unnecessary bias. While there may be some merits to this view, most investment firms have investment committees, and this chapter will try to help investors identify and avoid bias and emotion that can impact decisions.

2. I generally favor a high-conviction diversified portfolio of about 50 stocks, with an average weight of about 2 percent. In this investment process, equity positions below 2 percent of a portfolio are lower-conviction holdings, whereas those above 2 percent represent bold choices or high conviction. In late 2020, CRM had a market weight of just under 1 percent, so in fact a full 1 percent portfolio weighting would be a bold choice. However, for this example, positions greater than 2 percent are more often bold choices.

3. A former colleague David Malmgren, who managed a growth and momentum strategy, used to say, "Buy high and sell higher!"

4. Howard Marks to Oaktree clients, "Uncertainty," May 11, 2020, https://www.oaktreecapital.com/docs/default-source/memos/uncertainty.pdf.

5. Jason Zweig, "Keynes the Investor, in His Own Words" (blog), October 14, 2016, https://jasonzweig.com/keynes-th percentinvestor-in-his-own-words/.

6. Howard Marks to Oaktree clients, "Uncertainty," May 11, 2020, https://www.oaktreecapital.com/docs/default-source/memos/uncertainty.pdf.

7. Kahneman, *Thinking, Fast and Slow*, 44.

8. Ibid., 84–85.

9. Joe Tenebruso, "10 Investing Tips from Peter Lynch That You Shouldn't Ignore," *The Motley Fool*, April 7, 2019, https://www.fool.com/investing/2019/04/07/10-investing-tips-from-peter-lynch-that-you-should.aspx. Also see Peter Lynch and John Rothchild, *One Up on Wall Street: How to Use What You Already Know to Make Money in the Market* (New York: Simon & Schuster, 2000). Many investors think that Peter Lynch viewed good companies as good stocks, but in fact this was just a starting point. Lynch recommended finding companies that offered good (and understandable) products or services, but he then suggested that investors go deeper into financials and valuation analysis.

10. Kahneman, *Thinking, Fast and Slow*, 89.

11. Cass Sunstein,"The Cognitive Bias That Makes Us Panic About Coronavirus," *Bloomberg Opinion*, February 28, 2021, https://www.bloomberg.com/opinion/articles/2020-02-28/coronavirus-panic-caused-by-probability-neglect.

12. Ibid.

13. Kahneman, *Thinking, Fast and Slow*, 144.

14. Ibid., 333.

15. J. B. Maverick, "What Is the Average Annual Return for the S&P 500?," Investopedia (blog), February 19, 2020, https://www.investopedia.com/ask/answers/042415/what-averag percentannual-return-sp-500.asp. The S&P 500 has returned about 8 percent on average each year since 1957, when the index started including 500 stocks. The index has returned ~11 percent annually since 1926, but before 1958, the index only included 90 stocks.

16. Kahneman, *Thinking, Fast and Slow*, 338.
17. Thaler, *Misbehaving*, 190.
18. Ibid., 300–301.
19. Ibid., 357.
20. Ibid.

Chapter 6

1. Martin Lindstrom. "The Truth About Being 'Done' Versus Being 'Perfect,'" *Fast Company*, September 25, 2012, https://www.fastcompany.com/3001533/truth-about-being-done-versus-being-perfect.
2. Procrastination may become more of a problem in later stages of the investment life cycle as investors deal with emotions tied to actual gains and losses, as well as tax implications.
3. Thaler, *Misbehaving*, 17.

Chapter 7

1. Gary Kelly, Twitter post, March 23, 2020, 5:45 p.m., https://twitter.com/gary_kelly/status/1242205868848021508.
2. Howard Marks. Memo to Oaktree clients, "The Anatomy of a Rally," June 18, 2020, https://www.oaktreecapital.com/docs/default-source/memos/the-anatomy-of-a-rally.pdf.
3. Ibid.
4. The idea of an availability cascade captures the interplay between media bias and stock movements.
5. Tom Barkin, "Is a Recession Around the Corner?," speech to Maryland Bankers Association, January 3, 2020, https://www.richmondfed.org/press_room/speeches/thomas_i_barkin/2020/barkin_speech_20200103.
6. Kahneman, *Thinking, Fast and Slow*, 142.
7. Tom Barkin, "Is a Recession Around the Corner?," speech to Maryland Bankers Association, January 3, 2020, https://www.richmondfed.org/press_room/speeches/thomas_i_barkin/2020/barkin_speech_20200103.
8. Kahneman, *Thinking, Fast and Slow*, 339.
9. Ibid., 435. Appendix B in Kahneman's book has a good chart describing the joy versus pain scenarios for gains and losses.
10. Data from Crestmont Research suggest that stocks go up on slightly more than 50 percent of trading days and down on just under 50 percent of trading days.
11. Thaler, *Misbehaving*, 195.
12. Ibid., 197–198.
13. "Book excerpt—'Quotes from the Summitt' by Pat," ESPN, March 7, 2019, https://www.espn.com/espnw/culture/story/_/id/26172217/book-excerpt-quotes-summitt-pat-summitt.
14. Thaler, *Misbehaving*, 195–196.
15. Randy Pausch. "Randy Pausch's Last Lecture: Really Achieving Your Childhood Dreams," speech at Carnegie Mellon University, September 18, 2007.
16. Kahneman, *Thinking, Fast and Slow*, 263.
17. Howard Marks to Oaktree clients, "Uncertainty," May 11, 2020, https://www.oaktreecapital.com/docs/default-source/memos/uncertainty.pdf.
18. Dan Ariely, "What Litterers Tell Themselves," *Wall Street Journal*, September 27. 2019, https://www.wsj.com/articles/what-litterers-tell-themselves-11569590133.
19. Ibid.

Chapter 8

1. Sue Herrera and Bill Griffith, *Nightly Business Report*, PBS, May 1, 2019. https://www.youtube.com/watch?v=K2-IdnqS2_U.

2. Despite my opinion that sell in May and go away is unlikely to make money, I had egg on my face because in May 2019, markets declined 6 percent, suggesting that in the very short term it would have worked!

3. The always remember to buy in November strategy may work a bit better when the Dow Jones has performed poorly during the May to October period.

4. Matthew J. Belvedere, "Warren Buffett's Sobering Advice: 'Reaching for Yield Is Really Stupid' but 'Very Human,'" CNBC.com, February 24, 2020, https://www.cnbc.com/2020/02/24/warren-buffett-reaching-for-yield-is-really-stupid-but-very-human.html.

5. Thaler, *Misbehaving*, 28. In my experience, a high-stakes situation involves any buy, hold, or sell decision on a stock making up 2 percent or more of an equity portfolio.

6. Kahneman, *Thinking, Fast and Slow*, 151.

7. A widely used energy-sector exchange-traded fund (XLE) generated a 34 percent total return from January 20, 2016, to April 27, 2016, surpassing the S&P 500's 13 percent return during the period.

8. Kahneman, *Thinking, Fast and Slow*, 225.

9. John D. Stoll, "'Feel the Force': Gut Instinct, Not Data, Is the Thing," *Wall Street Journal*, October 18, 2019, https://www.wsj.com/articles/the-secret-behind-starbucks-amazon-and-the-patriots-gut-instinct-11571417153?mod=hp_lead_pos9.

10. Kahneman, *Thinking, Fast and Slow*, 253–254.

11. Jason Zweig, "Charlie Munger: 'The Phone Is Not Ringing Off the Hook,'" *Wall Street Journal*, April 17, 2020, https://www.wsj.com/articles/charlie-munger-the-phone-is-not-ringing-off-the-hook-11587132006.

12. Kahneman, *Thinking, Fast and Slow*, 256.

13. Richard Carlson, an expert on happiness and stress reduction, wrote a series of books with the theme of "don't sweat the small stuff."

14. Kahneman, *Thinking, Fast and Slow*, 402.

15. Thaler, *Misbehaving*, 84.

16. Ibid.

17. Jim Suva, "Suva's Weekly Hoot and Call, Digging Deeper into iOS App Store," Citi Research, January 17, 2020.

18. Thaler, *Misbehaving*, 100.

19. Kahneman, *Thinking, Fast and Slow*, 343.

20. Warren Buffett, Berkshire Hathaway Annual Meeting, Omaha, NE, May 4, 2019. Bloomberg transcript.

21. Thaler, *Misbehaving*, 83.

22. I generally recommend a minimum position size of about 1.5 percent of total equity assets. Position sizes less than 1.5 percent generally have little effect on a portfolio, in my experience.

23. Thaler, *Misbehaving*, 217.

24. Melissa Karsh, "Bill Miller's Hedge Fund Rose 120 Percent in 2019 After Fast Finish," Bloomberg News, January 23, 2020, https://www.bloomberg.com/.

25. Ibid.

26. I generally prefer to limit holdings above 4 percent of a portfolio as a way of managing risk.

27. Thaler, *Misbehaving*, 356–357.

28. Ibid.

Chapter 9

1. Procrastinators can rejoice because broker or trading commissions, which historically were another transaction cost, declined to nearly zero in recent years. This means that there is one less reason to procrastinate!
2. Some would argue that losing a battle against procrastination was a good thing in this case because the stock outperformed in 2020 after we debated selling it in 2019.
3. Thaler, *Misbehaving*, 104.
4. Ibid., 335.
5. Ibid., 337.
6. Ibid., 315.
7. Thaler and Sunstein, *Nudge*, 12.
8. Ibid., 7.
9. "Richard H. Thaler: Integrating Economics with Psychology," Royal Swedish Academy of Sciences, October 9, 2017, https://www.nobelprize.org/uploads/2018/06/advanced-economicsciences2017-1.pdf.

Chapter 10

1. The concept of set and forget, or automatic investing, may make sense for some individuals, especially in the early stages of accumulating wealth. However, professional stock pickers should be wary of inertia and the status-quo bias.
2. Adam Lashinsky, "Amazon's Jeff Bezos: The Ultimate Disrupter," *Fortune*, December 3, 2012; also published in the November 16, 2012, online issue of *Fortune*, https://fortune.com/2012/11/16/amazons-jeff-bezos-the-ultimate-disrupter/.
3. Based on a monthly analysis of market correction frequency compiled by the investment firm Northern Trust.
4. Joanna Smialek, "Nobel Economist Thaler Says He's Nervous About Stock Market," Bloomberg News, October 10, 2017, https://www.bloomberg.com/news/articles/2017-10-10/nobel-economist-thaler-says-he-s-nervous-about-stock-market.
5. My colleague Zach Weiss did much of the digging as I reevaluated my investment thesis on AT&T.
6. Kahneman, *Thinking, Fast and Slow*, 348.
7. Ibid., 347.
8. Ibid., 292.
9. Thaler, *Misbehaving*, 154.
10. Kahneman, *Thinking, Fast and Slow*, 292.
11. Dan Ariely, "What Litterers Tell Themselves," *Wall Street Journal*, September 27, 2019, https://www.wsj.com/articles/what-litterers-tell-themselves-11569590133.
12. Jennifer Maloney and Megumi Fujikawa, "Marie Kondo and the Cult of Tidying Up," *Wall Street Journal*, February 26, 2015, https://www.wsj.com/articles/marie-kondo-and-the-tidying-up-trend-1424970535.
13. Thaler, *Misbehaving*, 167.
14. Ibid.
15. James Grant, "'Narrative Economics' Review: Costly Tales We Tell Ourselves," *Wall Street Journal*, October 15, 2019, https://www.wsj.com/articles/narrative-economics-review-costly-tales-we-tell-ourselves-11571180255.
16. Thaler, *Misbehaving*, 167.
17. Idina Menzel, "Let It Go," *Frozen*: Original Motion Picture Soundtrack, Walt Disney Records, 2013, https://www.youtube.com/watch?v=L0MK7qz13bU.
18. Thaler, *Misbehaving*, 149.
19. Kahneman, *Thinking, Fast and Slow*, 297.

20. Ibid., 298.
21. Netflix, Amazon, Disney, Apple, and others produced a torrent of new shows online in the so-called streaming wars.

Chapter 11
1. The BTK Index was up ~300 percent between late 2011 and July 2015 compared with an ~80 percent return in the S&P 500, according to Bloomberg data.
2. A similar warning might be appropriate for technology investors in 2021.
3. Kahneman, *Thinking, Fast and Slow*, 385.
4. Ibid., 275–276.
5. Ibid., 344.
6. Ibid., 345.
7. Ibid., 340.
8. Ibid., 344.
9. John Y. Campbell and Robert Shiller, "Valuation Ratios and the Long-Run Stock Market Outlook: An Update," NBER Working Paper No. 8221, National Bureau of Economic Research, Cambridge, MA, April 2001, https://www.nber.org/system/files/working_papers/w8221/w8221.pdf.
10. Thaler, *Misbehaving*, 234–235.
11. The Shiller CAPE provided a timely signal to sell Cisco (CSCO) in late 1999 because the stock fell nearly 80 percent between early 2000 and September 2001.
12. Thaler, *Misbehaving*, 236.

Chapter 12
1. I discuss investor discomfort with selling stocks in greater depth in this article: Debbie Carlson, "8 reasons to sell a stock or fund," *U.S. News & World Report*, April 25, 2019, https://money.usnews.com/investing/stock-market-news/slideshows/8-reasons-to-sell-a-stock-or-fund.
2. Liz Ann Sonders, "Running on Faith: Are Stocks Discounting too Powerful an Earnings Recovery?," Charles Schwab Asset Management, New York, July 28, 2020, https://www.advisorperspectives.com/commentaries/2020/07/28/running-on-faith-are-stocks-discounting-too-powerful-an-earnings-recovery.
3. Dan Ariely, "An Antidote to Procrastination," *Wall Street Journal*, January 17, 2019, https://www.wsj.com/articles/an-antidote-to-procrastination-11547737784.
4. Ibid.
5. Ibid.
6. Carol S. Dweck. *Mindset: The New Psychology of Success*. New York: Random House, 2006, p. 238.
7. Kahneman, *Thinking, Fast and Slow*, 338–339.
8. Charlie Munger, Berkshire Hathaway Annual General Meeting, Omaha, NE, May 4, 2019, Bloomberg transcript.
9. Kahneman, *Thinking, Fast and Slow*, 352.
10. Ibid.
11. Dan Ariely, "To Buy or Not to Buy," *Wall Street Journal*, November 27, 2019, https://www.wsj.com/articles/to-buy-or-not-to-buy-11574866607?mod=hp_featst_pos1.
12. Thaler, *Misbehaving*, 59.
13. Kahneman, *Thinking, Fast and Slow*, 364.
14. Ibid., 374.
15. Ibid., 365.
16. Ibid., 409.

17. Thaler, *Misbehaving*, 123.
18. Paul McCaffrey, "Daniel Kahneman: Four Keys to Better Decision Making," Enterprising Investor (blog), CFA Institute, June 8, 2018, https://blogs.cfainstitute.org/investor/2018/06/08/daniel-kahneman-four-keys-to-better-decision-making/.
19. Ibid.
20. Thaler, *Misbehaving*, 21.
21. Paul McCaffrey, "Daniel Kahneman: Four Keys to Better Decision Making," Enterprising Investor (blog), CFA Institute, June 8, 2018, https://blogs.cfainstitute.org/investor/2018/06/08/daniel-kahneman-four-keys-to-better-decision-making/.
22. Ibid.
23. "Book Excerpt—'Quotes from the Summitt' by Pat," ESPN. March 7, 2019, https://www.espn.com/espnw/culture/story/_/id/26172217/book-excerpt-quotes-summitt-pat-summitt.
24. *Tom Brady's Playbook: Extended Cut*, video, Adobe Summit 2020: Digital Experience Conference, March 29–April, 2020, https://business.adobe.com/summit/adobe-summit.html?video=4.
25. Dweck, *Mindset*, 263.
26. Melanie Farrell, "Live in the Present" (blog), January 29, 2018, https://melaniefarrell.com/2018/01/29/live-in-the-present/.
27. Thaler, *Misbehaving*, 269.
28. Ibid.
29. Howard Marks memo to Oaktree clients, "Time for Thinking," August 5, 2020, https://www.oaktreecapital.com/docs/default-source/memos/timeforthinking.pdf.
30. Because this book is about behavioral economics, I have to mix in some bad news to fit with the reputation of economics as the dismal science!
31. Paul McCaffrey, "Daniel Kahneman: Four Keys to Better Decision Making," Enterprising Investor (blog), CFA Institute, June 8, 2018, https://blogs.cfainstitute.org/investor/2018/06/08/daniel-kahneman-four-keys-to-better-decision-making/.
32. Thaler, *Misbehaving*, 50.
33. Paul McCaffrey, "Daniel Kahneman: Four Keys to Better Decision Making," Enterprising Investor (blog), CFA Institute, June 8, 2018, https://blogs.cfainstitute.org/investor/2018/06/08/daniel-kahneman-four-keys-to-better-decision-making/.

Epilogue

1. Mihaly Csikszentmihalyi, *Flow: The Psychology of Optimal Experience* (New York: Harper, 1990), 71.

Index

Page numbers followed by *f* refer to figures.

Abbott Labs, xxviii
Accountability, anxiety without, 22–24, 181
Acquisitions, 51–53
Adamczyk, Darius, 54
Adjusting, 173–174
Advisors, roles of, xxi–xxii, xxi*f*
Aetna, 78
Affect heuristic, 35–36
Agent–principal alignment, 99–100
Alternatives, comparing to, 168–169
Altria, 116
Amazon, 63–64, 70–71, 158–159
Analysis (*see* Data and analysis for comprehensive research)
Anchoring:
    definition of, 23
    in evaluation of sales, 171–174
    and predictive skills, 179–180
    and priming/adjusting, 173–174
    procrastination and, 148–149
    for purchase price, 131–132
Animal spirits, in investment decisions, xi–xiii
Anxiety, without accountability, 22–24, 181
AOL, 52
Apple Inc., 148–150
Arch Capital, 49
Ariely, Dan, 121–123, 163, 186, 187
Arone, Michael, 63
Artificial categorization, 138–139

Asset bubbles, xii, 181–182
AT&T, 52–53, 160–161, 166
Availability bias, 10–11
Availability cascade, 115–116

Balanced approach to trading, 154–155
Baldwin, Alec, 101
Barkin, Tom, 115
Barnum, P. T., 40
Base rates, 52, 57, 128–130
Basic assessments, 93–94
Baxter International, xxviii
Bear markets, mistakes in, 127–128
Bear Stearns, 45–46
Beckman Coulter, 48–49
Behavior patterns, expecting changes in, 76–80
Behavioral bureaucrats, 200
Behavioral coaching, xv–xvi
    after stock declines, 112–115
    in investment workflow, 208–209
    and learning from previous trades, 200–201
    to overcome biases, xxxi
    use of term, xiii
Behavioral economics, x, xiv
Behavioral edge, for investing, xxiii, xxx–xxxi
Belichick, Bill, 130
Bentley, Dierks, 26
Berkshire Hathaway, 140
Berra, Yogi, 57

Best-six-months theory, 126
Better Off Dead (film), vii
Bezos, Jeff, 63–64, 158
Bias, 42–44 (*See also* Economic web of
    bias; *specific types*)
The Big Short (film), xii
Binary decision, investing as, 97
Bloom's taxonomy, xvi
Bold forecasts:
    in investment debates, 86–87
    risk associated with, 71–72
    timid choices with, 81–82, 86–87
Brady, Tom, 199
Breakeven effect, 135–137
Broad framing:
    benefits of, 16–17
    for gains and losses, 189–190
    for stock movements, 119–120
Broker commissions, 152
Browne, Bob, 6
Buffett, Warren, 127, 140
Bullish CEOs, 53
Bullish thesis, 71–72

Caddyshack (film), 193
Camerer, Colin, 53
CAPE (cyclically adjusted price-to-
    earnings ratio), 180–181
Caretaker CEOs, 53
Carey, Jim, 96
Carlson, Richard, 134
Case, Steve, 52
Categorization, artificial, 138–139
Caveat emptor, 40
CEOs (*see* Chief executive officers)
Certainty effect, 74–75
CFA Institute, xxx–xxxi
Charles Schwab, 29–33, 36–37
Checklists, investment, 143–144
Chief executive officers (CEOs):
    bullish, 53
    caretaker, 53
    corporate performance and, 48–49
    holdings of, 52–53
    overconfident, 49–52
    sunk costs for new, 54
Choice(s):
    framing, 152–155
    limiting, 2–4
    paradox of, 3

timid, 81–82, 85–86
Choice architecture, 2–4
Choosers, identifying, 43
Clients:
    open dialogues with, 100
    risk frameworks for new, 99
CNBC, 21
Cognitive ease, 40–42
Cognitive strain:
    with big decisions, 41–42
    overconfidence and, 51
    System 2 thinking and, 45–47
Coherent stories, creating, 49–50
Collective blindness, 20–21
Columbia University, 53
Comfort zone, going outside of, 33
Commissions, broker, 152
Committees, investment, 93–94, 151–152
Comparative analysis:
    for broad framing, 16
    limiting endowment effect with,
        168–169
    reducing bias with, 55–56
    (*See also* Head-to-head analysis)
Comparative valuation, 14
Complacency, 158–159
Complete sale evaluation, 171–183
    anchoring in, 171–174
    CAPE tool for, 180–181
    disposition effect in, 177–179
    effect of bubbles on, 181–182
    found money approach to, 179–180
    risk-seeking tendencies in, 174–177
Compliance, group, 150–151
Comprehensive investment research,
    39–66
    beginning process of, 40–47
    cognitive ease in, 40–42
    data and analysis for, 55–66
    identifying company incentives and
        biases in, 42–44
    into management, 47–54
    System 2 approach to, 45–47
Computers, in investing, xvii–xviii
Conclusions, intuition-based, 130–131
Concrete plans, for stock sales, 187–188
Confidence:
    and excessive noise, 70–71
    and telling coherent stories, 49–50
    (*See also* Overconfidence)

Confidence bias, xvi, 20–21
Confirmation bias, 32
Conglomerates, evaluating investments
    in, 25–27
Constructive criticism, 144–145
Consumer behavior patterns, 77–80
Contrarian market timers, 24–25
Corporate performance, CEOs
    influence on, 48–49
Cost(s):
    emotional cost of investing, ix–x xix
    framing losses as, 191–192
    opportunity, 107–108
    sunk, 54, 131–132
COVID-19 pandemic, 58, 121, 189, 197
Covidien, 40, 42–47, 108, 109
Criticism, constructive, 144–145
Crowds, wisdom of, 92
Cruise, Tom, 107
Csikszentmihalyi, Mihaly, 207
Culture of fear, in investment sector, 101
Curated news, 32
CVS Health, 78
Cyclically adjusted price-to-earnings
    ratio (CAPE), 180–181

Danaher, 48–49
Data and analysis for comprehensive
    research, 55–66
    four-step process for prediction,
        57–59
    head-to-head analysis, 55–56
    illogic premium and, 63–64
    reference class forecasting, 59–61
    variable weighting, 61–63
DCF (discounted-cash-flow) models, 181
Debates, over investments (*see*
    Investment debates)
Decision making:
    cognitive strain with, 41–42
    distractions and, 4–6
    emotions and, viii
    hunger and, 101–102
    "keep versus throw-away" decisions,
        163–165
    (*See also* Investment decisions;
        Timing decisions)
Default option, for group trades, 152
Delays, 107–109 (*See also*
    Procrastination)

Depersonalizing holdings, 168
Difficult questions, 89–91
Discomfort, preparing for, 117–118
Discounted-cash-flow (DCF) models,
    181
Disposition effect, 177–179
Distractions, 4–6, 163–165
Diversification:
    adding to concentrated portfolio,
        122
    and principle–agent alignment,
        99–100
Dividend preferences, 17–20
Dr. Seuss, 51
Doomsayers, 22–24
Dow Jones Industrial Average, 126
Dramatic events, 75–76
Due diligence, 45–47, 114–115
Dumb and Dumber (film), 96
Duration of experience, focusing on,
    194–195
Dweck, Carol, xix, 187–188, 199

Econ (type of decision maker), xx
Economic policy, 31
Economic web of bias, xxiii–xxvi, xxiv*f*
    decision makers' influence on, xxv
    interconnected free market in, xxv
    and media, xxv
    and stock declines, 114
Einstein, Albert, 113
Emotional cost of investing, ix–x xix
Emotions:
    decision making based on, viii, 174
    in investment debates, 144–145
    and loss aversion, 117–118
    and prediction, 58
    in selling decision, 191–192
    and stock performance, 112–113
End of process, focusing on, 194–195
Endowment effect, 163–170
    comparative analysis to limit, 168–169
    and holding on too long, 167–168
    and personal stories as distractions,
        163–165
    premium valuation in, 165–167
Enthusiasm, emotional, 58
Equity assets, equal treatment of,
    140–141
Estimates, beating, xxx

"Every Breath You Take" (song), 100
Excess trading, 141–143
Expected returns, 120
Experience:
  focusing on duration of, 194–195
  follow-on trade decisions based on, 132–133
  learning from (*see* Learning from previous trades)
Experimentation, 195–197
Expert opinions:
  in initial research, 33–35
  on market bubbles, 181–182
  in System 2 due diligence, 46
Expertise, practice and, 202–203
External biases, xxvi, 17–26, 28
  anxiety without accountability, 22–24
  in complete sale evaluations, 181–182
  confidence bias, 20–21
  and dividend preferences, 17–20
  mental accounting, 17–20, 25–27
  performance obsession, 24–25
  during stock declines, 113–115
External influences, research to offset, 40–42

Facebook, 79, 106
False narratives, 164–165
Familiarity bias, 6–8
Farrell, Melanie, 200
Fear(s):
  "investing scared," 67–68
  irrational, 19
  of punishment, 101–102
Federal Reserve, 180–181
Feedback, 201–203
Fidelity Investments, 93
Field, Marshall, 99
Final sales, procrastinating about, 187–188
Financial Times, 80
Fixed mindset, xix, 199–200
"Fixer Upper" (song), 85–86
Flow, 207–208
Focusing illusion, 134–135
Following the leader, 93
Follow-on trade execution, 147–155
  framing choices about, 152–155

group compliance in, 150–151
planner vs. doer approaches to, 149–150
procrastinating about, 147–148
trading frictions in, 151–152
Follow-on trade investment decisions, 125–146
  base rates in, 128–130
  breakeven effect in, 135–137
  checklists for, 143–144
  experience-based, 132–133
  focusing illusion in, 134
  formulas for, 130–131
  house-money effect in, 140–141
  mental accounting/narrow framing in, 138–139
  and mistakes in high-risk situations, 127–128
  odds of success in, 131–132
  overconfidence in, 141–143
  sandwich recommendations for, 144–145
  self-control in, 137–138
Forecasting:
  of pattern changes, 79
  of reference classes, 59–61
  (*See also* Bold forecasts)
Formulas, for evaluating follow-on trades, 130–131
Fortive Corp., 19
Found money approach, 179–180
Four question framework, 43–44
401(k) plans, 2
Four-step prediction process, 57–59
Fox Business channel, 21
Framing, 191–195
  after stock declines, 119–120
  broad, 16–17, 119–120, 189–190
  by focusing on duration, 194–195
  of follow-on trades, 152–155
  of losses, 191–195
  narrow, 14–15, 138–139
Franklin, Benjamin, 149
Free markets, xxv
Frozen (film), 85, 167
Fulton, Susan, xiv

Gains:
  broad approach to, 188–190
  as house money, 140–141

and risk aversion, 176–177
   taxes on, 148–149, 152, 178, 186
"The Gambler" (song), 135
Gambles, investments as, 97–98, 189
Gawande, Atul, 33–34
General Electric (GE), vii–ix, viii*f*, 7–10,
   188–189, 196, 203
General Motors (GM), 195–196
Gladwell, Malcolm, xviii
Glengarry Glen Ross (film), 101
Glide path, 50
GM (General Motors), 195–196
Goals, reasonable, 122
Gomez, Selena, xi–xii
Gooding, Cuba, Jr., 107
Google, 5, 79
Graham, Benjamin, x
Great Recession, 24, 128, 129
Greenspan, Alan, 180–181
Group trades:
   compliance in, 150–151
   default option for, 152
Groups, risk aversion in, 100–101
Groupthink, 92–93
Growth markets, 77
Growth mindset, xix, 199–200

Halo effect, 35–37, 92–93
Hamilton (musical), 144
Harford, Tim, 80
"Have fun and get better" concept,
   xviii–xix
Head-to-head analysis, 55–56 (*See also*
   Comparative analysis)
Healy, Joe, 71
Herd mentality, xxv
Heshmat, Shahram, 32
High-risk situations, mistakes in, 127–128
Hindsight bias, 197–198
Holdings, depersonalizing, 168
Home Depot, 56
Home-country bias, 7
Honeywell, 54
Hope, 122, 132–133
Hot hand fallacy, xii
House-money effect, 140–141
Human (type of decision maker), xx
Hunger, decision making and, 91–92

Illogic premium, 63–64

Immelt, Jeff, vii–ix
Inaction, 158–162, 169–170
   checklist to avoid, 161
   and complacency, 158–159
   and regret, 160–161, 191
   and status-quo bias, 161–162
Incentives, 41–44
Indecision bias, 3
Individual stocks, complacency about
   investments in, 159
Individual trades, urgency of, 134–135
Initial investment, 1–28
   expert opinions on, 33–35
   external biases of, 17–26, 28
   halo effect in, 35–37
   hope after decline of, 122
   inside lag with, 30–31
   internal biases for, 1–17, 27–28
   WYSIATI thinking about, 31–33
Initial purchase, 105–110
   opportunity costs with, 107–108
   outside lag and portfolio impact on,
    108–110
   procrastination before, 106–107
Initial research, 29–37
   expert predictions in, 33–35
   halo effect during, 35–37
   inside lag in, 30–31
   WYSIATI thinking during, 31–33
Inside lag, 30–31, 108–109
Inside view, 8–10, 71–72
Insights, from previous trades, 195–196
Institutional Investor, 45
Intel, 60
Intellectual humility, 9
Internal biases, 1–17, 27–28
   availability bias, 10–11
   broad framing to counteract, 16–17
   familiarity bias, 6–8
   and libertarian paternalism, 2–4
   with multitasking/System 1 thinking,
    4–5
   narrow framing due to, 14–15
   outside view to counteract, 8–10
   and risk aversion, 12–14
Intuition, about follow-on trades,
   130–131
Investing:
   checklists for, 143–144
   emotional cost of, ix–x, xix

Investing (*continued*):
  "have fun and get better" concept for,
      xviii–xix
  new ideas about, 1–28
"Investing scared," 67–68
Investment(s):
  duration of, 194–195
  optimism in analysis of, 131–132
  reviewing, 162
Investment committees, 93–94, 151–152
Investment debates, 85–104
  avoiding basic assessments in, 93–94
  and bold forecasts with timid choices,
      85–86
  effect of hunger on, 91–92
  emotional, 144–145
  and halo effect/groupthink, 92–93
  multiple gamble perspective in, 97–98
  outside views in, 86–87
  overweighting rare events in, 96–97
  principal–agent alignment in, 99–100
  probability neglect risk in, 95–96
  removing fear of punishment from,
      101–102
  risk aversion in, 100–101
  System 1 thinking in, 89–91
  uncomfortable recommendations in,
      87–89
Investment decisions:
  animal spirits in, xi–xiii
  binary view of, 97
  irrational, 174, 194
  keep vs. sell, 163–165
  100 steps to better, xiii–xvii
  (*See also* Follow-on trade investment
      decisions)
Investment life cycle, xxiii, xxvi–xxviii
Investment process:
  complacency in, 158–159
  focusing on, 199–200
  framework for, xxiii
  practice and expertise with, 202–203
Investment style, xxviii–xxx
Investment thesis, 67–83
  and bold forecasts with timid choices,
      81–82
  judgment and noise in, 69–71
  long-term, 157–170
  pre-mortem for, 68, 80–81
Investment thesis risks, 71–80

bold forecasts and inside view, 71–72
expecting short-term pattern
    changes, 76–80
planning fallacy, 72–74
possibility and certainty effects,
    74–75
vivid imaging, 75–76
Investor(s):
  behavioral coaching for, xxi–xxii,
      208–209
  rational, 19
  risk-averse, 14–15
  roles of, xxi–xxii, xxi*f*
Investor expectations, goal of meeting/
    exceeding, 68
Irrational decisions, 174, 194
Irrational fears, 19

Japan, 87–88
Jerry Maguire (film), 107
Johnson & Johnson, xxviii
Joyce, Tom, 54
Judgment, influence of noise on, 69–71
Juul Labs, 116

Kahneman, Daniel:
  on availability bias, 10–11
  and availability cascade, 115
  and behavioral economics, x,
      xiii–xviii
  and CEOs' influence, 48
  on cognitive ease and strain, 41
  on disposition effect, 177–178
  and endowment effect, 168
  and excess optimism, 133
  and expert predictions, 34–35
  on focusing illusion, 134
  and four-step prediction process,
      57–59
  and high stakes situations, 127
  and hindsight effect, 197
  on hunches, 20
  on hunger and decision making, 91
  and inaction, 160
  and investing as multiple gambles, 97
  and investor feedback, 202–203
  on loss aversion, 117
  on mental accounting, 18
  and multitasking, 5
  on noise distorting judgment, 69–70

and optimism, 121
and overconfidence, 49–51, 197
on pre-mortem analysis, 80
on probability neglect, 95
on reference points, 176
and regret, 190
on status quo bias, 161–162
and sunk costs, 132
and System 1 and System 2 thinking,
    xx
on WYSIATI thinking, 32
"Keep versus throw-away" decision
    process, 163–165
Kelly, Gary, 112
Keynes, John Maynard, x, xi, 89
Kondo, Marie, 163
Krensavage, Mike, 208

Lag, inside and outside, 30–31, 108–109
Lao Tzu, 34
Larry the Cable Guy, 147
Lazy answers, investment debates
    relying on, 89–91
Learning from previous trades, 185–205
    about growth mindset, 198–200
    about procrastination, 186–188
    with broad approach to gains and
        losses, 188–190
    embracing behavioral coaching,
        200–201
    and hindsight bias, 197–198
    insights from, 195–196
    practice and feedback for, 201–203
    by reframing losses, 191–195
    and risk analysis, 190–191
Learning-by-doing processes, xix
Libertarian paternalism, 2–4
Live quotes, turning off, 137–138
Logic, 63–64
Long-held stocks, 167–168
Long-term investment thesis, 157–170
    and breakeven effect, 135–136
    endowment effect and, 163–170
    inaction and, 158–162
Loser stocks:
    narrow framing for, 139
    selling, 177–178, 187
Loss aversion:
    after stock declines, 117–118
    myopic, 118–120

procrastination and, 148–149
status-quo bias and, 161–162
Losses:
    broad approach to, 188–190
    as costs, 191–192
    and focusing on duration, 194–195
    as proceeds, 193–194
    reframing, 191–195
Lowes, 56
Lynch, Peter, 93

MacArthur, Douglas, xxiv
Magical thinking, 63–64
Management, 47–54
    effect of, on performance, 48–49
    large acquisitions by, 51–52
    overconfidence in, 49–51
    stock ownership by, 52–53
    sunk costs for, 54
    track record of, 48–49
Market(s):
    bear, 127–128
    free, xxv
    growth, 77
    volatility in, 24–25
Market cycle, 113
Market speculation, 182
Market timing, 23–25, 88–89, 181–182
Marks, Howard, x, xxxi, 9, 34, 46, 88,
    113, 121
Massie, Suzanne, 45
Mass-market commentary, from
    experts, 21
Mauboussin, Michael, 53
McKinsey, 52
Media:
    avoiding, 137–138
    commentary from investment experts
        in, 21
    and economic web of bias, xxv
    on free markets, xxv
    headlines and availability cascade,
        115–116
Medtronic (see Covidien)
Mental accounting:
    with conglomerate investments, 25–27
    and dividend preferences, 17–20
    and external biases, 17–20
    in follow-on trade decisions, 138–139
    by gamblers, 140

Microsoft, 5
Mies van der Rohe, Ludwig, 141
Miller, Bill, xxx, 142
Misbehaving (Thaler), xiv, 191
Misremembering, 197–198
Mistakes, in high-risk situations, 127–128
Mosaic theory, xxx–xxxi
Multiple gambles perspective, 97–98
Multitasking, 4–6
Munger, Charlie, 1, 12, 17, 57, 81, 132, 190, 201
Murray, Bill, 193
Musk, Elon, 32
Mussio, Michael, x
"My Shot" (song), 144
Myopic loss aversion, 118–120
MySpace, 106

Narrative economics, 164–165
Narrow framing, 14–15, 138–139
New clients, risk framework for, 99
New England Patriots, 199
News, curated, 32
Nobel Prize in Economics, xiv, 23
Noise, judgment based on, 69–71
Nonconsensus stocks, 89
November, buying in, 126–127
Nudge (Thaler), xiv, 2

Oaktree Capital, x
Odds of success, for follow-on trades, 131–132
Open debates, encouraging, 101–102
Opinions:
    expert, 33–35, 46, 181–182
    writing down, to prevent groupthink, 93
Opportunity costs, 107–108
Optimism:
    after stock declines, 121–123
    in investment analysis, 131–132
    pessimism vs., 121
    societal value of, 20–21
Outliers (Gladwell), xviii
Outside lag, 31, 108–109
Outside view:
    for bullish thesis, 71–72
    to counteract internal biases, 8–10
    in investment debates, 86–87
    reference class forecasting for, 60

Overconfidence:
    of CEOs, 49–52
    excess trading due to, 141–143
    and WYSIATI thinking, 32
Overweighting:
    due to vivid experiences, 76
    of end of process, 194
    in investment debates, 96–97
    in investment thesis, 74–75
    with probability neglect, 95
    of small risks, 22
    of stocks, in portfolio, 24–25
    of variables with likely outcomes, 62

Painful sensations, preparing for, 117–118
Palo Alto Networks, xxvii–xxviii, 3, 9
Paradox of choice, 3
Pausch, Randy, 121
Payers, identifying, 43–44
PBS *Nightly Business Report,* 126
P/E ratio (price-to-earnings ratio), 13, 180–181
Performance obsession, 24–25
Personal stories, as distraction, 163–165
Pessimism, 22–24, 121
Pfizer, xxviii
Pharmaceutical sector, halo effect for, 36
Planner approach to follow-on trades, 149–150
Planning fallacy, 59, 72–74, 208
The Police (band), 100
Poor Richard's Almanack (Franklin), 149
Porter's five forces, 43, 44, 64
Portfolio performance:
    outside lag and, 108–110
    reviewing, after setbacks, 122
Possibility effect, 74
Practice, learning from, 201–203
Predictions, 31–33, 57–59
Premium valuation, 165–167
Pre-mortems, 68, 80–81
Prep sessions, for committee meetings, 101
Preparing for painful sensations, 117–118
Price-to-earnings ratio (P/E ratio), 13, 180–181
Priming, 173–174
Principal–agent alignment, 99–100

Probability neglect, 95–96
Problem finding, 113
Problem solving, 113
Proceeds, framing losses as, 193–194
Process-based focus, 199–200
Procrastination:
    about follow-on trades, 147–148
    fighting, 187–188
    before initial purchase, 106–107
    learning from, 186–187
Procter & Gamble, 6
Profit-seekers, identifying, 44
Punishment, fear of, 101–102

Rare events, overweighting, 96–97
Reagan, Ronald, 45
Recency bias, xv, xxvii, 26
Recommendations:
    sandwich, 144–145
    uncomfortable, 87–89
Reference class forecasting, 59–61
Reference classes, identifying, 60
Reference points, in evaluations,
    176–177
Reframing losses (see Framing)
Regeneron, 172–173
Regret:
    framing losses to prevent, 191–195
    inaction and, 160–161, 191
    risk analysis to prevent, 190–191
    risk aversion to avoid, 13–14, 160
Retirement savings plan, 2, 152–153
Risk(s):
    defining, 12
    framework for, 99
    gauging, 16–17
    investment thesis, 71–80
    overweighting, 22
    policy to avoid selling, 118–119
    possibility effect for, 74
    taking on, 88–89
Risk analysis, 190–191
Risk aversion:
    to avoid regret, 13–14, 160
    and complete sale evaluation,
        176–177
    in group settings, 100–101
    internal biases related to, 12–14
    and multiple gambles perspective, 98
    narrow framing with, 14–15

Risk seeking:
    after gains, 140–141
    choosing among bad options, 174–
        176
    and framing outcomes as losses, 193
    playing catch-up via, 136
Rockefeller Center, 87
Rogers, Kenny, 135
Rumsfeld, Donald, 8

Salesforce.com, 85, 88, 90
Samuelson, Paul, 23
Sandwich recommendations, 144–145
Savers:
    individual, xxii
    roles of, xxi–xxii, xxif
Scharf, Charlie, 54
Secular change, xxix
Self-control, 17–20, 137–138
Selfridge, Harry Gordon, 99
Sellers, incentives for, 41–42
Selling stock:
    concrete plans for, 187–188
    with emotional attachment, 191–192
    and "keep versus throw-away"
        decision process, 163–165
    loser stocks, 177–178, 187
    tools for, 180–181
Sell-side analysts, 21
Setbacks, optimism after, 121–123
Shaw, Georg Bernard, 34
Shiller, Robert, xi, 11, 164, 180–181
Short-term pattern changes, 76–80
Short-term performance, for stocks,
    118–119, 136
Siegel, Laurence, 22
Simon, Paul, 177
Situational awareness, 41–42
Sizing of trades (see Investment debates)
Son, Masayoshi, 130
Sonders, Liz Ann, 186
Soul (film), 207
Southwest Airlines, 112
Speaking up, 143–144
Spinoffs, 26
Standard and Poor's (S&P) 500 Index,
    88, 159, 197
Star Wars: The Last Jedi (film), 195
Star Wars: A New Hope (film), 130
Starbucks, 5

"Status quo or back to zero" framing, 152–155
Status-quo bias, 154, 161–162
Steinbeck, John, 91
Stephenson, Randall, 52–53
Stereotypes, 52, 128–130
Sting, 100
Stock(s):
    complacency about investments in individual, 159
    disposition effect for, 177–178
    long-held, 167–168
    loser, 139, 177–178, 187
    nonconsensus, 89
    winner, 177–178
Stock bubbles, 181–182
Stock declines, 111–123
    availability cascade and, 115–116
    due diligence in, 114–115
    economic web of bias and, 114
    investor emotions and, 112–113
    loss aversion and, 117–120
    optimism in, 121–123
    problem-finding mindset for, 113
Stock movements, broad framing beyond daily, 119–120
Stock ownership, by management, 52–53
Stock performance:
    and investor emotions, 112–113
    myopic loss aversion with, 118–119
    obsession with, 24–25
    short-term, 118–119, 136
Strategic risks, CEO's underestimation of, 50–51
Stress tests, pre-mortem for, 80–81
Success, probability of, for follow-on trades, 131–132
Summitt, Pat, 119, 198
Sum-of-the-parts approaches, 181
Sunk costs, 54, 131–132
Sunstein, Cass, 95
Sutherland, Rory, 63
Suva, Jim, 137
Swenson, David, 89
SWOT analysis, 42, 44, 64
System 1 thinking, 32
    defining, xx
    internal biases related to, 4–6
    in investment debates, 89–91
    and time management, 208

System 2 thinking, 202
    about sunk costs, 131–132
    after stock declines, 114–115
    defining, xx
    due diligence with, 45–47, 116
    by investment committees, 93–94
    in investment debates, 89–90
    multitasking and, 5
Systemic approach to research, 42–44

T. Rowe Price, 158
Taxes, on gains, 148–149, 152, 178, 186
TD Ameritrade, 29–33, 36–37
Tesla, 32
Testing, 195–197
Thaler, Richard:
    on achieving compliance, 151
    in *The Big Short*, xi–xii
    on desirable business culture, 101–102
    on endowment effect, 164–168
    on extreme forecasts, 71
    four basic questions of, 43
    on hindsight bias, 197
    on humans and econs, xx
    on market speculation, 182
    on mental accounting, 25–26
    on narrow framing, 15
    on overconfidence, xiv–xv, 195–196
    on overweighting stocks, 24
    on self-control, 137
    on setting and following rules, 143
    "status quo or back to zero" concept of, 153
Thinking, Fast and Slow (Kahneman), xiii–xiv, 194
Thoreau, Henry David, 55
Time arbitrage, xxix–xxx, xxxf, 26, 30
Time management, 208
Time Warner, 52–53
Timid choices:
    after bold forecasts, 81–82
    in investment debates, 85–86
Timing decisions:
    inside lag and, 30–31, 108–109
    outside lag and, 108–109
    procrastination in, 106–107
    and WYSIATI thinking, 31–33
    (*See also* Investment debates)
Trading frictions, 151–152